PARK LEARNING CENTRE

The Park Cheltenham
Gloucestershire GL50 2RH
Telephone: 01242 714333

UNIVERSITY OF
GLOUCESTERSHIRE
at Cheltenham and Gloucester

WEEK LOAN

Visit the *Managing Interactive Media, fourth edition* Companion
Website at www.pearsoned.co.uk/england and to find valuable
student support material including:

- Audio and text files of interviews with key industry players
- Links to relevant websites, including a link to the authors'
  website which contains additional information and resources

- 4 MAR 2009

2 5 NOV 2009

3 0 NOV 2010

2 1 FEB 2011

1 4 MAY 2013

49766 08/06

PEARSON
Education

We work with leading authors to develop the
strongest educational materials in computer
science, bringing cutting-edge thinking and best
learning practice to a global market.

Under a range of well-known imprints, including
Addison-Wesley, we craft high-quality print and
electronic publications which help readers to
understand and apply their content, whether
studying or at work.

To find out more about the complete range of our
publishing, please visit us on the World Wide Web at:
www.pearsoned.co.uk

Managing
Interactive Media

Project Management for Web and Digital Media

ELAINE ENGLAND
ANDY FINNEY

Fourth edition

 ADDISON-WESLEY

Harlow, England • London • New York • Boston • San Francisco • Toronto • Sydney • Singapore • Hong Kong
Tokyo • Seoul • Taipei • New Delhi • Cape Town • Madrid • Mexico City • Amsterdam • Munich • Paris • Milan

Pearson Education Limited
Edinburgh Gate
Harlow
Essex CM20 2JE
England

and Associated Companies throughout the world

Visit us on the World Wide Web at:
www.pearsoned.co.uk

First published 1996
Second edition 1999
Third edition 2002
Fourth edition 2007

© Elaine England and Andy Finney 1996, 2007

ISBN: 978–0–321–43693–1

British Library Cataloguing-in-Publication Data
A catalogue record for this book is available from the British Library

Library of Congress Cataloging-in-Publication Data
England, Elaine.
    Managing interactive media : project management for Web and digital media / Elaine England, Andy Finney. -- 4th ed.
        p. cm.
    Rev. ed. of: Managing multimedia. 2002.
    Includes bibliographical references and index.
    ISBN-13: 978-0-321-43693-1
    ISBN-10: 0-321-43693-8
    1. Multimedia systems. 2. Multimedia systems. 3. Interactive multimedia--Authorship. 4. Project management. 5. Web site development. I. Finney, Andy. II. England, Elaine. Managing multimedia. III. Title.

QA76.575.E56 2002
006.7--dc22
                                                                    2006052613

10 9 8 7 6 5 4 3 2 1
11 10 09 08 07

Typeset in 9.75/12pt Galliard by 30
Printed in Great Britain by Henry Ling Ltd, at the Dorset Press, Dorchester, Dorset

The publisher's policy is to use paper manufactured from sustainable forests.

Contents

Preface   xi
Acknowledgements   xiii

1 **The IMP (Interactive Media Project) context**   **1**
  Industry Insight   1
  Overview of the interactive project process   1
  The interactive context and project management   3
  What is a project?   6
  What is a project manager?   12
  Overview of the project management role and interactive projects   14
  Summary   14
  Top Tips   15
  Application Task   16
  References/Resources   16

2 **Initiating interactive projects 1**   **17**
  Industry Insight   17
  Overview   17
  Why is this stage important?   18
  Other types of project initiation   25
  Summary   29
  Top Tips   29
  Application Task   30
  References/Resources   31

3 **Initiating interactive projects 2 – scoping the project**   **34**
  Industry Insight   34
  Overview   34
  The project scoping dilemma   35
  The project scoping questionnaire   40

Managing smaller projects 66
Work Breakdown Structure (WBS) 66
Summary 69
Top Tips 70
Application Task 71
References/Resources 71
Appendix: Scoping questionnaire 72

4 **Stakeholders and their influence** 81
Industry Insight 81
Overview 81
Stakeholders and interactive projects 82
Who are the key stakeholders in the project? 84
Authority and responsibility 85
RACI responsibility chart 86
What form of communication is best? 88
Industry Insight 2 91
Summary 91
Top Tips 92
Application Task 92
References/Resources 93

5 **The client/developer partnership approach to projects** 94
Industry Insight 94
Overview 94
The project's 'business case' 95
How to talk in business terms 98
Industry Insight 2 98
Development process controls 102
Summary 110
Top Tips 111
Application Task 112
References/Resources 112

6 **Troubleshooting common development problems of interactive projects: developer perspective** 114
Industry Insight 114
Overview 114
Developer perspective 115
Risk exposition: developers 115
Summary 125
Top Tips 125
Application Task 126
References/Resources 127

7 **Troubleshooting common development problems of interactive projects: commissioner perspective** 128
Industry Insight 128
Overview 128

Commissioner perspective 129
Risk exposition: commissioners 129
Summary 137
Top Tips 138
Application Task 139
References/Resources 140

8 The users' contribution; usability and accessibility 141
Industry Insight 141
Overview 141
Who brings what to the party? 142
Usability: its history and pre-disposition 143
What is interactive usability? 143
Accessing the site/ease of search 148
Usability: return on investment 149
Where does accessibility come into this? 150
Where does testing fit into this? 151
Summary 152
Top Tips 153
Application Task 154
References/Resources 154

9 Interactive media testing and archiving 157
Industry Insight 157
Overview 157
General concepts of digital media testing 158
The software approach debate 160
Types of test (technology/functional) 163
Quality assurance 163
Archiving 163
Summary 169
Top Tips 170
Archiving 171
Application Task 171
References/Resources 172

10 Legal issues 1 174
Industry Insight 174
Overview 174
What is a contract? 175
Clearances 180
Ownership of code and other assets generated in the project 181
Freelancer and contractor contracts 182
Selling at a distance 182
Data protection 183
Cookies, mailing lists and marketing messages 184
Accessibility 185

Libel 185
Jurisdiction 186
Summary 187
Top Tips 187
Application Task 188
References 188

11 Legal Issues 2 – intellectual property 189
Industry Insight 189
Overview 189
What is copyright? 190
In the beginning 190
Getting a copyright 191
Moral rights 192
Exceptions 193
The World Wide Web 194
Databases 197
Music 198
The public domain and clip media 200
Patents 202
Summary 204
Top Tips 204
Application Task 205
References/Resources 205

12 The e-marketing revolution and its impact 206
Industry Insight 206
Overview 206
Why are these concepts important? 207
Marketing principles and new media 209
Summary 223
Top Tips 225
Application Task 225
References/Resources 226

13 Team management and interactive projects 228
Industry Insight 228
Overview 228
Interactive media teams – who? 229
Interactive media teams – are they different? 229
Characteristics of successful teams 235
Summary 237
Top Tips 237
Application Task 238
References/Resources 238

Glossary 240
Index 280

Supporting resources

Visit **www.pearsoned.co.uk/england** to find valuable online resources

Companion Website for students
- Audio and text files of interviews with key industry players
- Links to other useful websites, including a link to the authors' website, which contains additional information and resources

For instructors
- PowerPoint slides that can be downloaded and used for presentations

For more information please contact your local Pearson Education sales representative or visit **www.pearsoned.co.uk/england**

Preface

This book builds on the previous three editions of *Managing Multimedia*, but the emphasis, and so the title, has changed in line with the developing interactive media industry. Previously we have concentrated on 'how to' develop interactive media projects at the middle management level. This was often a hybrid role of part manager and part specialist in charge of the project development team who still had a hands-on responsibility for some of the development. This can still be the case, but increasingly, the role of the project manager has matured to encompass more of the upper management aspects of the role at the expense of the hands-on specialist role.

With this in mind, we have introduced many new aspects that relate to setting the project up in a way that aids smoother development, soothes the communication between the clients (stakeholders) and developers, advises on optimizing the business context that affects projects, and takes more account of the user's role in design. Project management methodology has been shifting over the last few years too and the implications of this are addressed. Technology has moved on apace, as expected, so innovation in this is one of the areas that interactive media professionals naturally take into account. However, the software approach underlying the utilization of the technology has been undergoing a quiet revolution and implications from this are drawn out. Finally the law has been catching up with the innovative uses of communication, advertising, searching and storage mechanisms that online media offers. The legal chapters give a good basis for you to take stock of the way you handle the issues in your projects.

This 4th edition follows in the footsteps of the previous editions, but the substance is different. Each chapter begins with an Industry Insight that sets a context for the chapter. The stronger emphasis on industry opinion is matched with the extra resources you can find at the companion websites for the book. Here you'll find industry sector-related interviews and podcasts, and PowerPoint presentations for each chapter. These will be particularly useful for lecturers and students of Interactive Media but because these are industry focused, they are equally relevant for continuing professional development for people working in the field. See www.pearsoned.co.uk/england and www.atsf.co.uk/mim.

Each chapter also contains Top Tips. These focus on key actions (strategy) to put in place and indicate the benefits of doing these (the pay-off). This reinforces the business perspective that should drive decisions on projects for a company dependent on producing multiple interactive media projects. Finally there is an Application Task to encourage the reader to apply the learning to their ways of working.

If you are familiar with the 3rd edition of *Managing Multimedia* you will also notice that this edition is slimmed down from two books to one. In this way we are concentrating on the people and processes of interactive media. The technology aspects will be more of a feature on the accompanying websites instead.

Acknowledgements

 People

Ailsa Barry, Head of Interactive Media, Natural History Museum, London, UK

Peter Bennett, CEO, London Translations Ltd, London, UK

Scott Berkun, Project Management and Product Design Consultant, http://www.scottberkun.com/

Federico Biancuzzi, Freelance writer, Security Focus, Calgary, Canada

James Bielefeldt, Web Consultant, MO, USA

David Cameron, Head of Interactive Programme Management, BSkyB Isleworth, Middlesex, UK

Dr. Leonardo Chiariglione, CEO, CEDEO, Turin, Italy

Paul Doleman, Former Chief Sales and Marketing Officer, Latitude, London, UK

Matt Farrow, Head of Information and Knowledge Sharing, WWF, Godalming, Surrey, UK

Barry Goldberg, Vice President Project Management, Agency.com, NY, USA

Asad Habib, Head of Quality Assurance, Kuju Entertainment, Sheffield, UK

Jac Holzman, Chairman, Cordless Recordings, NY, USA

Nigel Hudson, Group Manager, ADASIS, ADAS, Wolverhampton, UK

Shannon Kalkstein, Head of Project Management, Tribal DDB, London, UK

Bob Little, Managing Director, Bob Little Press and Public Relations, Herts, UK

Pat McCellan, Vice President, Managing Director, Jack Morton Worldwide, San Francisco, USA

Jagoda Perich-Anderson, Associate Director, Shared Strategy for Puget Sound, Seattle, WA, USA

Aleksandra Puxley, Head of Project Management, CIMEX, London UK

Keith Robinson, Blue Flavor, Seattle, USA

Hal Robinson, Joint Managing Director, Librios, London, UK

Matt Sharpe, Senior Project Manager, Tribal DDB, London, UK

Mike Sisco, President, MDE Enterprises, Columbia, TN, USA

Barret Stanboulian, Managing Director, Hasmodia, Dorking, Surrey, UK

Russell Stannard, Senior Lecturer Interactive Media, University of Westminster, Harrow, UK

Henry Steele, Associated Professor of Marketing & International Business, School of Business, The Open Polytechnic of New Zealand

Alison Webster, Head of Online Content and Partnership Development, National Archives, Kew, UK

Troy Wilson, Vice President, Marketing and Business Strategy, Geosoft Inc. Toronto, Canada

● Institutions/companies

BIMA (British Interactive Media Association), London, UK

MIT Open Courseware, Cambridge MA, USA

The Design Council, London, UK

NESTA (the National Endowment for Science, Technology and the Arts), London, UK

New Media Age, London, UK

Latitude, London, UK

We both recognise that many of our past and present colleagues, clients and associates, and those that have attended our training courses, have contributed to the span of experience here, and we thank you all – too numerous to name individually. We'd also like to recognise our debt to all those that have persevered through some problematic years to what is now emerging as a successful interactive media industry.

Elaine England
Andy Finney
November 2006

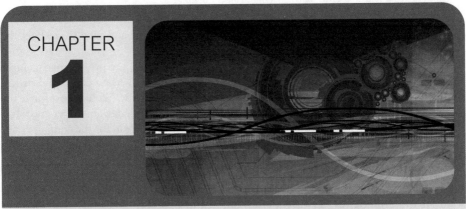

CHAPTER 1

The IMP (Interactive Media Project) context

Industry Insight

A growing international market is there to be won by creative ... businesses that are able to innovate and do not see any inherent conflict between creative excellence and commercial success.

NESTA Report (the National Endowment for Science, Technology and the Arts, UK), Creating growth, page 4, April 2006 http://www.nesta.org.uk/assets/pdf/creating_growth_full_report.pdf

● Overview of the interactive project process

Interactive media is extremely diverse. Some see it in terms of horizontal technologies like web and mobile; others view it as vertical markets such as e-marketing and e-learning. Then there are always the activities like search engine optimization and web analytics that cut across everything. This is an 'industry' that spreads and diversifies like few others. The only constant is that nothing stands still. There is seemingly no limit to the creativity that can be applied, and this is what entices people to work in it.

The problem is that, although the industry is intangible by nature, the business world needs to manage it, track it and guide it to produce meaningful results. This is where project management comes into the process; but this is affected by the working practices that are emerging in the industry sectors.

Some of those sectors – such as web development, e-learning and e-marketing – have grown strongly. They have defined working processes tailored to their requirements. Some things – and podcasting comes to mind here in its similarity to radio – are traditional media in a new skin with new freedoms and opportunities. Other sectors – iTV advertising, mobile and PDA – are emerging quickly and have less well-defined working practices. Despite these diversities, there are still common elements and it is these that we will focus on while explaining where the differences occur and why they affect the management and production processes.

While all these interactive media sectors have been emerging, the project management industry sector has grown rapidly as well. It has expanded its own processes and procedures, adapting to new demands from business and management. We'll try to forge the best fit between the interactive sector, project management knowledge and experience. It is this blend that will stand the professionals of tomorrow in good stead for the coming years.

And finally . . . there have been underlying changes in design and programming within the last few years too. Software has adapted to meet the challenges of the fast-changing requirements of users and clients. Design and build practices have altered as a consequence. Both sets of professionals are now faced with new decisions. In fact, some of the boundaries between design and build have become blurred to such an extent that hybrid skills encompassing both activities are in demand. In IT itself, new competency sets are emerging that recognize the need for business and management skills as well as 'pure' IT skills. In this way, several aspects that touch on project management of interactive media are shifting towards the vision that we have always held: the skill sets for interactive media project management combine core professional skills with business and management expertise.

Every project has a life cycle. In broad terms it is conceived, carried out and completed. A client has a requirement and someone – in this case an interactive media developer – works to fulfil that requirement. Everything else is just detail: but, as they say, the devil is in that detail and this is why this is a book and not a single piece of paper. We'll begin by looking at a variety of project types.

The diagram below shows the main stages in the life cycle of an interactive media project:

- the start phase (the approach to this phase can vary depending on the sector);
- content definition, selection and structuring;
- layout, look and feel of the content;
- functionality or the navigation between pieces of the content;
- tracking and monitoring of the user.

Information from this last phase, as it applies to various users and their requirements, is collated and fed back into the loop to drive a revision cycle and so can be the initiating intelligence for requirements. (See Chapter 12 for more on how marketing intelligence can establish clear business requirements.)

As we'll see, although this cycle here is outlined as a linear progression from start to conclusion of a project, there is much dissension about how to define stages of a project. Does marketing intelligence drive the requirements and so in turn the initiation? What stages overlap or happen simultaneously? How do iterations across stages occur? At what stage should the users be involved? How should client-generated changes be handled? What software approach should be taken? How much testing should be employed and when? The devil really is in the detail.

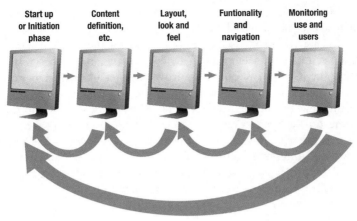

The project high-level life cycle

The interactive context and project management

A successful project is defined as one that is completed on time and within budget while meeting its business objectives. Working from this definition, the project life cycle can be seen as a circle where the projected time and cost for defined tasks is completed, the objectives for the interactive product are met and the clients are satisfied.

Any costs incurred by the developer need to be understood across all activities undertaken in the company. Even those activities that seem small enough to be insignificant, such as so-called 'quick fixes', can amount to a lot of costs over a period of time. A business cannot absorb costs to its detriment indefinitely. So cost is an absolute that has to be monitored through a company for all its employees from directors down. The idea of capturing costs for activities, perhaps through timesheets, is anchored here within the life cycle because it is an absolutely fundamental part of the approach to project management that will be developed throughout the book. This monitoring of time and costs can be an issue in companies; but it is essential for financial health.

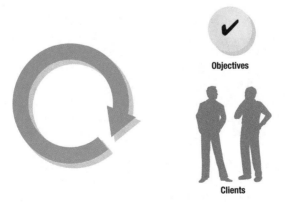

Project model 1 – circle

The interactive context can place some extra pressures on the developers because the clients may appear to change their minds about what they want during the course of the project. There are usually two types of reasons for this – internal and external – either of which can make it seem that the client is moving the goal posts. Pressures internal to the client company can come from changes in management personnel, strategy, or both. External pressures come from the fast-changing market that in turn feeds through to new or redefined requirements which the company and therefore the project then have to achieve. The neat circle that represented a successful project changes under the pressure of such circumstances and is bent into a U shape. Here the objectives at the beginning are different from those at the end, and a gap opens up that will affect the projected time and cost unless the developers recognize what is happening and take measures to avoid or accommodate this.

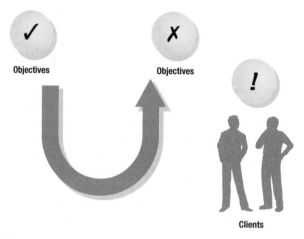

Project model 2 – U shape

The developers themselves and the processes used by the developer company can exacerbate any mismatch. However, if the developer's processes are designed to expect changes and react quickly to them, this may ameliorate some of the problems. The software development might embrace rapid application development (RAD) or Agile processes, and these offer faster responses to a changing IT environment which includes interactive product development. If the developer cannot respond quickly to changes, time can become an issue with the result that a project takes longer to reach its objectives than was expected. We can represent the type of project that runs out of time as a letter J and notice the gap between the beginning objectives and the end objectives. There is an imbalance between the changes the client wanted and the response of the developer. The costs projected at the beginning of the project will also be affected.

In interactive projects, development time is often an issue because the unexpected happens; the client's objectives change and so they want changes in the project. All this will affect the budget but, when the budget has been estimated around one set of criteria which has now changed, it can be hard to get the client to realize that extra budget is likely to be needed as a result. If at the end of a project the client complains

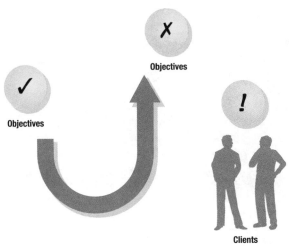

Project model 3 – J shape

that the project does not meet the business needs, the developer company should seek to understand whether this is because the business objectives or the market changed around them without them monitoring the situation, or because the development time was just too long to deliver the objectives before the market changed. Whatever the analysis, the developer company should take stock of how it is working with the clients and with its development processes in order to fit the market conditions better for the future. (See Chapter 12 on Marketing to see how you can take control of this by helping to gather market intelligence that sets business directions/requirements.)

There is another scenario where the developers know more about the state of the interactive market and its general trends and requirements than the clients do. The clients may stipulate what they think they need in terms of their perception, their internal politics or their previous understanding of both non-interactive and interactive products. They may not fully understand the behaviour of their customers/users in an interactive environment. This is going to cause problems for the developers unless the clients are prepared to listen to them and follow advice. You can represent this as a Z shape project where the clients and their objectives are pulling in one direction and the customer/user's wishes or expectations are pulling in another. The developers find themselves trapped in the middle trying to fulfil objectives that they know will not be appropriate for the users.

If the developers see that there is a mismatch between the clients and the market, they may try educating their clients, or they may build more user involvement into the development process so that their feedback helps the clients refocus their objectives. This is a delicate balance, and why the so-called 'stakeholders' in a project, with their business concerns and their influence on the client side, are increasingly recognized as a significant influence. This is a trend in general project management where developer companies have learned to their cost that if they do not constantly monitor their clients, their business and its changing needs in relation to the project development, they will end up with a market mismatch and a dissatisfied client. If clients are not satisfied, they may take their future business elsewhere, and many interactive companies will attest that most of their revenue comes from return business. It is in your interest to satisfy your clients. However, if this involves a significant amount of change, then

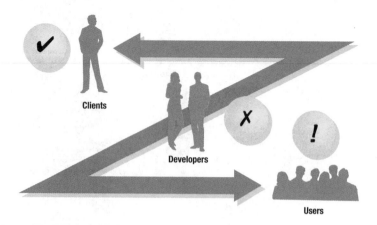

Project model 4 – Z shape

the company cannot fulfil a contract where the agreement for payment was based on a completely different set of criteria from those that conclude the project. Here lies the dilemma. If you help set the business requirements that you know you can fulfil, this can help in this type of situation. (See Chapter 12 on Marketing for more on this.) If you set up change management procedures at the beginning of a project, this will ensure cost adjustments to match changes. (See Chapter 5 on Client/developer partnership and Chapter 6 on Troubleshooting: developer perspective for more on this.)

● What is a project?

It has become apparent through talking with various development companies that a lot of extra work done by their production people is interwoven with the core work commissioned directly by clients. Often this extra work has not been designated as 'project' in the strict sense and so a lot of expended time and effort over the course of a few months is not recorded in timesheets or analysed. Even if time and cost tracking is in place, some things will be hidden under 'admin' or some other catch-all category. This is dangerous. You need to know exactly what resources/staff you have available at any one time and where their time and effort has been placed, or the company cannot reach a true understanding of how it is operating and what return it is getting. Because of this vagueness we have decided to explain what a project actually is, the various types of projects you might do and why it is important to gather information about the varieties for the business.

Your people need to talk the same language about the different types of project that your company takes on, and it is important that any new staff are inducted into how projects are designated, how they are monitored, what records they need to keep and what information they need to convey. This can vary considerably between companies.

Client projects

Generally companies know that they win pieces of work (projects) from clients or sponsors and they work on them. This is what we would usually think of as projects, and there is not, in general, any vagueness about the definition. However, sometimes the one client is large and active and there may be several projects on the go for them at any one time. Some of these may be very small and fast turn-around, almost as adjuncts to a main project. Some others might be spin-off projects where an extra section or department of the client has been introduced to you through the main project and then commissioned their own piece of work. Yet others are almost extensions of the main project where extra phases with refinements are approved almost as a rolling project. Perhaps now you are beginning to realize that what is designated 'a project', even for a single client, may not be as straightforward as first imagined.

It becomes very important from a business point of view to know exactly what is happening with your staff. Just imagine that there is one main project that you are handling from a client that (for the sake of argument) is a fictional company who produce hand-made chocolates. We'll call this company, and project, Chocolace. You are developing a website to enable their outlets to order stock online and get it dispatched more efficiently. The main project of gathering the stock requests and dispatching them begins to expand as the outlets become more vocal about other information they'd like to have, such as the companies' health and safety inspection visits roster and their results. So extra information and features are being fed back into the project by the users – sound familiar?

This is a business to business site but, in the course of specifying this site, the marketing department decide they want to have a public online site serving different purposes that features very different information – a business to consumer site. Meanwhile, Chocolace starts asking if it will be possible to track the stock to the delivery points. The outlets say it will not be enough for them to know the stock has been dispatched from the warehouse and they want better information about when the stock will arrive at their location. You mention the possibility of tracking where their delivery vans are by tracking the drivers' mobile (cell) phones and keeping in contact with them via SMS mobile messaging, among other options. During discussion you are told that the delivery company is actually a subsidiary company of your main client, the chocolate company. Should you treat them as a separate client? Is this a separate project?

Next, the accounting section at head office realize that the outlets will be equipped with a laptop and Internet connection. They start to see the opportunity to get the outlets to submit daily and weekly returns online, and they have asked for a meeting. Will their needs be encapsulated into the initial project or will they be a separate project? You can see how quickly the one main client and a project can spiral.

This is how one project can split into several or just get bigger and bigger so that no one knows where the beginning and end are, what the agreed costs for which bit are and so on. Tight control is needed, and a view needs to be taken by both parties on whether these are changes, additions or new projects. A lot comes down to how an interactive development company designates a project against an agreed cost and time, and if the extra is a start of a new phase of the main project or a new project. Some companies give all projects names or numbers and denote extras by adding characters or more numbers.

So, in our hypothetical example we can imagine that 'Chocolace 1' might be the main project, 'Chocolace 1a' and 'Chocolace 1b' might be extensions and additions to the main project, 'Chocolace 2' could be the new project addressing the public site and so on. Other companies prefer to be more explicit in their names as it makes it easier for the staff to identify which project they are working on and what time to log to which project. So 'Chocolace Outlets' and 'Chocolace Public' might be plausible. Some companies just have project numbers that are allocated on the next number given by the accounts department, for example. Whatever is chosen, there needs to be some system that is central and consistent. Someone has to know the project name, the length of time it is meant to take, the staff/resources it needs when and the cost agreed to date. During the project the name or number is used to make sure costs are allocated appropriately.

You may be part of a large company and work with 'internal' clients. These are other parts or departments of the company that give you projects to complete for them. Essentially, these projects need to operate as if the clients are external clients. You need to know how much time and effort you will be expending for them and cost this. If changes to the project occur, then you'll need to adjust your estimates accordingly. This should happen even if there is no real transfer of money between the client department and yours or you will have no control mechanisms. However, this is growing increasingly unlikely since cross-department budget transfer is the norm. When used in the chapters, for 'client' transpose 'internal client' if this fits your way of working.

Bread and butter projects

The beginning of a large new project is always exciting. This is when staff are challenged to come up with creative but workable ideas that will suit the brief. The excitement begins to wane as the project cranks through to implementation and the ideas are fleshed out. It is hard to sustain focus to the end of a project. The staff want to keep abreast of new ideas and opportunities. Motivation can become difficult in the team. They want to move on to something new and exciting.

But, from the business point of view, several large projects that take a fair amount of development time and have stages of payment at quite long intervals will make cash flow through the company haphazard. The company has to pay a lot of ongoing costs such as staff salaries, rent or mortgages for premises, technical infrastructure and so on. So it might be worth considering that several ongoing projects with well-established clients can alleviate this by smoothing out the payments and cash flow. You may have got to the stage with some clients that they are making frequent payments for rolling extras as agreed with them for refining new pieces of functionality for their applications.

These can be seen as 'bread and butter' projects. They are not the challenge they once were at the beginning of the relationship with the client, but that relationship is solid and the work is constant. From the business perspective, these are good stable projects that improve the cash flow. They may not be the most profitable projects at this stage of their life cycle, but steady money through the door is as valuable as the larger more profitable but spasmodic projects; so you mustn't see 'bread and butter' as a pejorative term. The company may be best served by having a balance of both of these types. However, the company may have to devise a strategy to address the problem of maintaining the motivation of staff required to work on these more steady projects for long periods.

Investment projects

Sometimes your company may decide that it will be prepared to do a project for a client for a lot less than the true cost. This can happen when the company wants to get into a new market segment or work with a new technology platform, surmising that the experience in the area will bring in new clients or allow them to offer new expertise and opportunities to existing clients. This then becomes an investment project where the difference between the true cost of doing the project and the cost charged out equals the investment that the company is making on the return of future work won on the back of the original project.

A project manager needs to know that this is an investment project and that it is not expected to be brought in on the budget quoted to the client. He or she will need to try and bring the project in within budget, but that budget is the investment figure plus the cost quoted. So the timesheet analysis will still need to show the actual costs, what is charged out and what is accepted as investment costs.

Over a year, the company should have estimated how much investment time and effort (and therefore cost) it can afford, and it should be watching the development of such investment projects to contain them within their projected investment budget. Then, it should be reviewing the projects won on the back of the investment to understand if the investment was warranted. This should also help to make better investment decisions for the future.

Maintenance projects

These can be easy to spot – ongoing work to update and support the result of a previous project – but are often not given project numbers or names. They are regularly felt to be too small to count as a real project. There is almost an embarrassment about them. However, they are like 'bread and butter' projects and can be essential for the company in several ways: they allow a good cash flow; they can engender trust with the client that the company will keep assuring the quality of the product; they keep staff expertise topped up. These are real projects and should be treated as such. They have time, cost, resource and quality elements that should be monitored and recorded. The company needs to recognize how many staff and how much time are used on maintenance projects over a year against the profit generated from these projects. If they are not tracked, a company cannot accurately measure which types of work and which balance of work and staff might suit them best.

Quick fix projects

Although companies try to ensure that the project is completed to a robust standard as agreed with the client, there may be many reasons why the result of a previous project fails in certain aspects once it is in use. Often the company's account manager (or equivalent) has been contacted by the client with a specific 'small' requirement and deems that a fast response is needed to stabilize the client relationship. The account manager may have the authority to have promised the client a response for no charge, or be in a position to realize that the defect is the responsibility of the developer and should be done at no cost to the client. But, there is a cost to the company and this should be recorded so that over a year these 'quick fix' projects can be assessed and action taken if necessary.

Such analysis might show that there are a lot of these projects and that collectively they drain the company of a quantifiable amount of money in terms of time and resources. This might indicate that quality assurance of the projects before they leave the company has not been sufficiently robust and that perhaps the technical section needs more resource in this area, that more time for this should be accorded in the body of development work than previously, the content has not been firmed up enough or that a change in the software development approach might prove useful. Unless the company begins from knowing what an annual figure for such projects amounts to, how can they assure themselves that they have implemented a strategy and that it has had a positive impact? Other factors like the experience level of the staff, the stability of a platform and its related software and so on also need to be taken into account, but the basic knowledge of how much these projects cost the company is important.

R&D projects

Research and development projects are similar to investment projects, but there are important differences. Investment projects have some money paid by the client and another sum contributed by the company in terms of time and resource expended. Pure research and development projects will be internal projects that are completely funded by the company itself. In some cases, funding may have been won from outside sources that contribute towards the company's research project.

Several people in the company might have personal research projects. The lead graphics designer might be tasked with searching out the most creative work displayed on the web, for example, and then, say once every two months, giving a lunchtime seminar to anyone interested in the findings. If the company has agreed that hours of a person's time should be put towards such work that will serve to update or increase the company's expertise, then these are research projects. They can be small, as in the example given, or they might be large, as in the company allowing a team to put together a sample project involving a new platform or use of technology in order to raise the company's profile, increase their brand standing, increase their expertise, enter a competition or other reasons.

Again, unless these are identified as projects and tracked as such, how will the company know how much research and development has taken place and if it was worth it?

Good will projects

It might surprise people to learn how many projects are done for nothing, or for very little money. A company might decide that a small project to serve the community in some way might help raise their profile locally, for example. Sometimes, a company will adopt a charity on a year by year basis and decide how it can use its expertise to its advantage without detracting from its main workload.

Other 'good will' projects can sometimes be levered into the workload by top people in the company because they are put in a difficult position. Take for example the primary school that wants a strong website – the managing director has three children in it and so is approached for help. Or, the head of design is asked to help out with the college play by producing the programmes, posters, tickets and the play's website. Or, the local university TV production department wants a mentor company for their students completing an iTV module. These things happen. But, a company needs to know how many 'good will' projects are undertaken to understand how many and what type it can endorse and sustain and when they might tip the company out of balance. It is a director's responsibility to know these sorts of things and a project manager's to understand precisely what to call a project of the varying sorts that he or she might be asked to run.

Despite their 'free' or 'promotional' nature, it is still important to manage such projects as if they were being paid for. They take time and resources just like any other project.

Pitches/tenders/winning projects

Many companies forget that costs are incurred when staff expend effort in winning new business and that such time and resource costs need to be tracked as projects in their own right. It is important to note how much this costs a company because these are investment projects – with the great majority done for free in the hope of winning the budget for the real job. If too many are done at too high a cost and not enough are won to more than compensate for the expended effort, a company can get into serious financial problems quite quickly. Or, if too much cost is expended upfront for a relatively small return from the actual project won, then the company has to ask if it was worth the effort.

These can be deemed investment projects, but they are better kept as a sub-group so that expenditure on them can be clear. When you are involved in the top pitches or equivalent, they are worth serious money and so serious time and effort is expended – which means of course that high speculative costs are incurred. These projects and the considerations around them are covered more extensively in Chapter 2 on Initiating interactive projects; however, they feature here so that their true status as projects in their own right is established. Companies may designate them Project Name/Number P or T for 'pitch' or 'tender', or whatever convention they like, to identify this activity prior to winning the real project, but their cost to the company must be recognized in order to aid strategic decisions about the direction the company should take.

If this phase of the project is fully paid for – and in a few cases it is – then it can be treated as the first phase of an ordinary project. If this phase is subsidized to a certain extent by your own company, then it may be designated an investment project until the pitch is won and the client begins to pay. iTV production companies may work more in this fashion where they may have to come up with an idea, pitch it to management, win approval and budget and then produce the project. It is also likely that an iTV component will have been included in the planning and funding for a television programme, since more and more programmes have enhancements of this nature.

Perhaps now you'll appreciate why we are concerned about defining project types: there are many varieties and interactive companies have no set way of defining them. This raises the question that if they can't define them, how are they tracking them? If they are not tracking them for the time and costs involved, how does a company know where its profits or losses are coming from? How does it make decisions about future business potential and so on?

● What is a project manager?

Once we start to query what a project is, it follows logically that we need to understand the role of the project manager who is responsible for these projects. This has become quite a complicated topic because, as the interactive sector matures, the range of responsibilities and skills of the project manager has expanded. The structures of companies they work for vary quite considerably and so their own place within the structure varies as well. In some senses there has been a move towards the more traditional view of project management where the project managers are administrators with a more strategic role compared to the hands-on production project manager that was the previous model for the interactive sector.

You need to decide where your job fits along this range from 'hands-on' to 'strategic' since your focus and responsibilities will change accordingly. Your approach to the projects will change too. The following paragraphs outline several types of project management, so which one or ones are closest to your role?

The programme manager/project manager

A programme manager is responsible for over-seeing a group of large-scale projects. Traditionally these have been different projects for different clients (even if the clients are internal clients). In the interactive sector, we have seen that a large client may have several projects of various types on the go at any one time – see the Chocolace example above. One person may be the main contact or manager over-seeing the day-to-day contact with this client. This person may be called a variety of titles from director, account manager to project manager, but the key aspect of the work is that there are several large discrete projects to look after.

The overhead for managing and co-ordinating the people involved with these projects, within the client company or companies and within the production cycle inside the interactive company, is high. The onus of the work for the project manager may be sorting out the high-level specifications and agreements for the projects, sorting the lines of communication and the frequency and type of communication and checking that the assets that are needed are provided at the right time. They may work with the equivalent of a production project manager and a team for each of the large projects.

Traditionally, a programme manager has held a strategic position inside a large company where the shaping of the type and number of the projects that will be developed, the winning of the go-ahead approval within the company and firming the budget lines might be the main responsibilities. Or, a company might have already decided these and will appoint a person to over-see the programme of work to sub-contract, over-see the tender process or whatever. An example of this in the interactive sector might be the government deciding to offer some specialized funding for certain interactive projects as seed funding to help innovation in a particular direction that it sees as important for the economy. A person who sits in the position of implementing this strategy may have a programme manager role without that specific title. Another example of an interactive programme manager might be someone inside a TV company who is responsible for outsourcing some interactive work and for co-ordinating some internally produced interactive projects.

The high-level or administrative project manager

Again, this has been a more traditional project manager role outside the interactive sector where the level of documentation needed to represent a project and the number of influential people affecting the progress of the project have warranted a member of staff who was dedicated to these aspects of managing a project. This person may sit either within the commissioning company or the developer company or there may be a person in each company. It depends on the companies and the nature of the project. Many small and medium-sized developer companies cannot financially support a separate administrative project manager and these companies collapse the project manager role into a hybrid of the administrative project manager and the production project manager as outlined below.

Whether a separate role exists for one of these style project managers will depend on how formally documented and administered a project is. Much of this may depend on the system of project management adopted by each of the companies – the clients and their suppliers. Sometimes the client may dictate that the developer use a particular method of project management – such as the Prince2 methodology. This is covered in detail on the website (www.atsf.co.uk/mim) because it is growing strongly in popularity, particularly in Europe. This method is an open approach to project management where the guidelines can be adapted to suit the project. It was started by the UK government to help in their own control of all projects that they administer, and they have encouraged their suppliers to conform to its premises. Sometimes winning an interactive project for them, or other advocates of the system, might be dependent on your company having a Prince2 project manager in the team.

The Prince2 guidelines employ a formula that ensures that certain stages of a project are thoroughly analysed and documented and that the plan is revisited at regular intervals over the course of the project. The system tries to ensure that the product developed meets the business needs and the needs of its users, while involving all the relevant stakeholders and keeping them appraised of the project's progress.

As the interactive sector matures, the role of the formal administrative project manager is becoming more widely accepted and implemented. There is still a tendency for this project manger to be more hands-on than a completely traditional administrative project manager since interactive project development experience is considered a strong part of the skill set and one that gives credibility to the role for all those involved. This is primarily because, although interactive projects and the sector are maturing, they are still sufficiently different from traditional projects to be seen as higher risk and therefore needing stronger personal experience of the area.

The pull towards the role of a project manager being more administrative – either from the client's or the developer's own management – may well be completely at odds with the programmers in the development team if they are trying to follow a modern approach to software development such as Agile. The more modern approaches react against the use of heavy documentation and administration. This is an area where tension can be inadvertently caused inside the developer's company because of conflicting processes. (See more on this in later chapters.)

The production project manager

This is the most common implementation of the project management role in the development/supplier side of interactive projects. Most often the project manager has been part of the core interactive development team earlier in their career and is then elevated to the team leader or project manager position. Quite often they are asked to retain some aspects of the hands-on development while managing the team, working with the clients and doing aspects of the administration that the company expects.

● Overview of the project management role and interactive projects

The interactive sector is still maturing, so the separate roles covered in the last few pages have not become established in the same way that they have in other sectors. There is recognition given to them here as emerging roles. However, it remains true that if traditional project managers from other sectors are utilized in the interactive sector, they lack insights into how the role needs to adapt to the nuances of the interactive sector, how they may need to vary the role to suit the more fluid ways of working, how they may need to operate and relate to the various people in the project in different ways from those they are used to, how they may need to adapt the documentation requirements to suit the way of working and how to assess risks in such an innovative and creative sector. Lack of involvement in creativity of ideas and innovation may, even on its own, be enough to differentiate a traditional project manager and their experience from the interactive sector and its project management needs. It can be quite a shock for a conventional engineering project manager to be confronted for the first time with a creative project.

The opposite is also true. The traditional project managers and their working methods now have more relevance to, and synchronicity with, the interactive sector and they will continue to become closer as it matures. As more people from both parts of project management grapple with and define the emerging needs of the interactive sector, a better fit of experience and skills will emerge and more definite roles for each of the types of project management mentioned here will firm up.

Summary

Over the last few years a good deal has happened to change the working context for those in the interactive sector. It has split into sub-sectors that have their own ways of working. It has integrated with the mainstream of business so that there are more project types, with extensions and adjuncts to main projects. This means that there is more for management to track and appraise. Because of these circumstances, the role of the project manager has widened to accommodate the responsibilities of a programme manager and an administrative project manager as well as those of a production project manager.

Top Tips

Strategy	Potential pay-off
Construct a high-level project life cycle diagram appropriate for your company to educate your new clients in how you work.	Make them aware of the processes so there are no surprises for them along development.
Changes and the time it takes to implement changes are both danger points that will work against successful project completion, with effects on both time and budget. How does your company off-set these risks? Find out and devise a plan if there isn't one.	If you can deal with these using strategies from both sides of the client and developer mix, you are more likely to achieve a successful project.
Encourage your client to involve the users of the product early in the life cycle if you feel that they are pushing their own agenda and one that won't suit their market.	The feedback from the users will drive the product development in the right direction rather than the project having the 'Z' characteristics mentioned in the chapter.
What types of project are your company involved with? How are projects designated in the company? How are they tracked?	If you find gaps after reading the chapter, work with the right people to define the situation and decide what to do about it. Get your company to understand itself and its business potential better.
Assess the role of the project manager or equivalent in your company. Are there different needs for different types of project? Do responsibilities change along the range as outlined here?	Perhaps more has been expected of your role than is feasible. Where should your focus lie for the projects you are involved with now? Strategic, administrative or production? Get a clearer understanding of your role. You will be able to perform better and perhaps make the case for extra resources.

Application Task

1. Think through the projects you have worked on in your present company – over the last year if possible. List them and define them according to the project categories given in the chapter, or formulate your own names to suit the types of project. Add up the money coming in from the budgets for your projects and the cost that the company expended on the goodwill, quick fix, R&D or investment projects. See the rough calculation of money in and money out through your responsibilities. Does it surprise you?

Project no./ name	Type e.g. pitch, quick-fix etc.	Budget projected	Cost at finish	Costs covered by your client	Costs covered by your company

2. Get your colleagues with the same role as you to do this exercise and compare what you find. Have you looked at your company from this point of view before? Does it affect the way you see your role and responsibilities?

3. If you can't do this because you don't know the costs of the projects, why is that? How is the company keeping project cost information . . . or isn't it? If it isn't and you are meant to be a project manager, you can't do your job effectively without it, so raise the issue.

● References/Resources

This chapter was based on experience and there are no other recommended references at this time.

Web link

Interactive media and Prince2 project management methodology
http://www.atsf.co.uk/mim

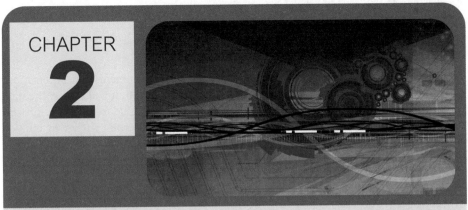

CHAPTER 2

Initiating interactive projects 1

Industry Insight

Another key challenge for both the design profession and its business partners is to accept the fact that it's worth taking the time to prepare a proper design brief prior to commencing design concept development. This process will actually save time and ensure more effective design results.

Peter L. Phillips from the Design Management Institute, written online for the Design Council, Briefing section, 'Challenges' http://www.designcouncil.org.uk/briefing

● Overview

Just as the definition of a project can vary, as we saw in the last chapter, the initiation of a project can vary depending on the interactive sector, the types of project your company develops and the types of client your company serves. Winning projects drives the turnover and success of your company and so it is vital to get this part of the process right.

Your own company may have dedicated people whose responsibilities include finding new business: business manager, marketing manager, account director are some of the job titles that do this. Finding new business or developing new business from existing clients produces the new projects that keep the company going. The project manager's role is closely linked to this work and so he or she may to some extent be involved in finding and winning new business depending on the company. In small and medium-sized companies, it is more likely to form a part of the role and responsibilities of the team leader or equivalent, but it still has to happen.

Your clients may have their own project managers or equivalent. You may need to work together to match the processes expected in the client company to the processes you work with in the development company. These can be set from the beginning of the project. In fact your counterpart may have done a lot of work that could help you prior to the tender process.

● Why is this stage important?

The initiation of a project, from whatever source, sets up agreements and expectations which then influence the whole of the project development. So, if you can be there, at least you'll know what you are inheriting and you might be able to affect the process to suit you and the development team better. Or, if this is someone else's role and you are fed up with inheriting projects that have too many development traps, you need to understand the process to be able to influence those people involved in project initiation and get them to implement changes to help you and the team.

The concept of 'initiation of a project' needs some explanation because what is initiation to you may be rather different for other people. Take, for example, a large commissioning company that issues a tender for some interactive work. They may have followed several pre-defined stages of a project (in their terms) to arrive at the tender process, including getting the financial backing, assigning a project champion, making the business case and so on. They will have initiated the project inside their organization according to their conventions. If you win the work, then you may initiate the development of the project inside your own company. So for you, the initiation may begin here, but it could also be the end stage of initiation as far as the client is concerned. (See the section on p. 27 later in this chapter which looks at Prince2 project management methodology. If this applies to you, that section will put the process of project initiation in context.)

If the commissioning company is not large, or for some other reason has not had its own formal internal process to initiate a project, then you may have to work harder to extract the information you need to propose your preferred solution for their concerns. You may have to do a lot of groundwork that in other circumstances would be seen as the client's responsibility.

It is important to realize how the start point of a project can vary depending on the circumstances and the people involved. It is up to the project manager to even this uneven playing field; to make sure that as much of the right information as possible is provided at this initial stage to serve the developer company best. It is far better if the commissioning company has taken its responsibilities seriously and has the information ready to provide.

On-going and return business

This is the key driver for business in the interactive sector and many projects are offered to a developer company as the result of previous projects for the same client. It is in the company's best interests to win return business as long as the relationship is sound and the new projects generate money in a way that is appropriate for your company and the direction it wishes to pursue.

The use of interactivity in all forms of communications is expanding and new technology platforms are continuing to come on stream and even become profitable; both of these trends promise expanded communication channels. Businesses are trying to tap into the best each trend can offer. This is true irrespective of whether a new communication channel is being used for business to business, business to consumer or even consumer to consumer. Communication means the ability to influence people, and the possible returns from this communication include generating sales, generating business/brand recognition and loyalty. With this expanding interactive market, clients are interested in trying out possibilities and are receptive to ideas. They are willing to listen to proposals for pieces of work and so this makes it easier to sow the seeds of return or on-going business as you are implementing a current project.

If you build up trust between yourself and your clients, they will be more prepared to listen to you and favour you with new projects. So whoever is the key contact for the client is in a strong position to influence them from the 'inside' on where they might want to place their money in future. It is important to keep your key people up to date with the trends in the interactive sector so that they can inform the clients and work with them to identify how these trends may suit their own customer needs.

While these key people can influence the clients, they also set the parameters for the new projects. They need to be briefed in what your company is capable of, what it would like to get involved with, what it might invest in through some joint work with the clients, and which bits of the new trends cost more and why. These key people need the rounded view of what the clients might need and what your company would like to do, together with an understanding of the projected costs. Then these key business-winning people can act responsibly in informing the clients and educating them as to what is possible, what the trends are and what the likely costs could be. This will set up the new projects in a way that should serve the development team better.

If your key people sow the ideas of new business, they should work effectively with their commissioner contact to ensure that these ideas are well received inside the organization and that they are formulated as new projects and officially backed in line with the practices of the commissioning company. If the new ideas are accepted as new projects, they need to be designated as such, have budgets allocated to them, have the backing of the right people and so on.

Your key people should take note of the advice given below explaining the range and type of information that makes for good project initiation inside the commissioning company. If the client's company adheres to these practices already, your people can help them follow them. If they don't have these practices, your people may help to educate them into using them since getting this part right makes for a smoother, easier development path that will serve both of you well.

Considerations

If a person has worked well with a client and has established a good relationship with them, there may come a point when the client has influenced the staff member more than he or she has influenced them. The staff members may act more in the client's interest than in the company's interest. They are said to have 'gone native': this is hard to spot and control. They continue to win business from the client, but it may become more difficult for the company to achieve a result commensurate with the time and cost invested. In this case perhaps another person needs to take part in the new business negotiation to advise the key person on how to progress this from your own company's perspective.

Tenders

The process of pitch and tender is a controversial area and one that is generating a great deal of debate. We'll outline what these processes are and then look at the issues.

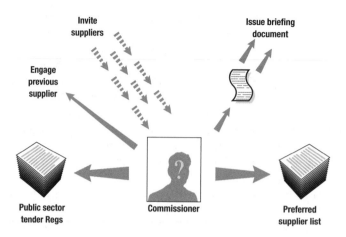

Tender options

If commissioning companies decide they want to have a piece of interactive work done for them and they need to find a supplier, they have several options. They can go to previous suppliers with the extra work, they can indicate that they would like suppliers to tender for a particular piece of work, they can describe the work needed in a briefing document and invite suppliers to tender, or they can look at their company's preferred supplier list and ask one or a few selected companies to tender. They may go to a tender broker company who will select and vet some potential suppliers to pitch for the work.

Public sector tenders

In many countries, including the USA, the UK and Europe, there are legal requirements that affect the tendering procedure – particularly if the work is to be carried out for publicly funded bodies. This can supersede any tender requirements that an individual company, county or state might have introduced themselves.

For example, in the European Union (EU), publicly funded companies seeking to carry out new projects may well find themselves constrained by legal considerations. Their procedures require work to be advertised in a way which is transparent and encourages unrestricted trade. This refers to the EU Procurement Directives which are revised every two years. They dictate tender thresholds (the proposed total value of the work) above which the work must be tendered following the guidelines and directives.

We don't intend to go into this in detail here, but use it only as an example of a statutory tendering process. If you wish to follow this up for comprehensive information, please follow the referenced website link for the Office of Government Commerce at the end of the chapter. At the time of writing, the threshold for smaller projects lies at €80 000, for example. Otherwise, if you are a reader outside the EU, you should look up the requirements relating to your own country through your government websites.

The principle of free trade and open, transparent competition drives this and other such tender processes. It has been instituted to counter nepotism, corruption of officials and non-transparent awards of work contracts and to achieve open and fair competition for work between companies.

Some of the tender processes in the interactive sector follow these procedures. They affect the advertising of the piece of work, the amount of time for suppliers to respond, the type of brief the commissioner provides, the information the supplier has to provide, the contractual ways of working if you win the tender and so on. Your company may be involved with some of these. You can see that the amount of time and effort that is needed just to take part in the process can be large. It may be important that some of your staff are skilled in this in order to ease the process if you are involved with this type of project.

Private company tenders: commissioner perspective

Most of the tenders for interactive work operate through private businesses and are not subject to these legal processes. But often the larger companies have devised their own requirements because they have found the tender process to be fraught with difficulties. From their point of view, they may put out an invitation to tender or a request for a proposal and get swamped with many indications of interest. This means that they would have to take a long time to sift through these applications in order to move to the next stage where some companies are invited to pitch for the work. You can see that in such a fast-moving environment as the interactive sector, elongating the initiation stage of a project works against the commissioning company and has consequences for a supplier too.

To counter this, some commissioning companies prefer to approach a few suppliers and ask them to pitch for the work. This gets them to the pitch stage faster. Another screening mechanism that is used is the 'preferred supplier' list or roster where the company maintains a list of companies it might work with according to past experience. This list might itself be the result of a competitive process with occasional updates. The commissioners then approach a select few of these to pitch for new work.

Considerations

By restricting the tender process in some way the commissioners may miss out on new companies that could have the potential and the skills to address their needs better than the existing relationships. Preferred supplier lists might have been drafted according to traditional work done for the company rather than interactive work. We have listened to commissioners who are forced to select from lists where the supplier companies may have some limited interactive experience but are not really proficient in the finer aspects needed for the job. Commissioners need to be confident that their suppliers are up to the job.

Private company tenders: developer/supplier perspective

The developers find themselves in difficulties whatever system is employed for the tender process, and there are extra considerations because of the nature of the interactive work involved on top of these. If the commissioner selects a few companies and asks them to pitch for the work, other companies can feel aggrieved, wondering why they were excluded. They want to know if they were even considered and on what grounds they were discounted so that they can try to remedy any deficiencies for the future. They may well feel that their trade has been restricted by the practice.

If the commissioner has used a 'preferred supplier list', the developer can feel at a disadvantage because they are not on the list already. They may feel resentment that they cannot hope to get on the list. This might be because the list is seldom revised or because of the conditions the company imposes on suppliers to get on their list in the first place.

Often the conditions have been made very general to address all 'suppliers' of goods and services from building maintenance to stationery supply. The prospective interactive supplier has to jump through bureaucratic hoops and answer pages of inappropriate questions such as what their health and safety policy is, and they may tacitly assume that the developer will have 'operatives' on site carrying out the work, as if they were cleaning the windows. Many are put off by the process itself since they feel they should be judged by their work and what it can offer. Small interactive companies find the bureaucracy too onerous and time consuming and they haven't got the resources to address it. The feeling of restriction of trade can also be an issue.

Considerations

You need to consider the ratio of tenders and the amount of work and therefore cost to your company of completing the tender process. This can be expensive and you may not have realized it. Some tender processes are more onerous than others. Look also at the pitch process outlined below to have a rounded view of whether you really want to pitch and if you should feel aggrieved at being excluded from a pitch.

Pitches: commissioner perspective

Selecting a developer is not easy. You may realize that you need to improve your existing interactive offerings and perhaps try out some new ones. But understanding why your company has this need and what the business case is in measurable terms can take time and effort on your part. The important part of the pitch process for you is providing a good brief for the prospective supplier.

Essentially, once you have short-listed the companies to pitch to you, either through open tender or closed tender to selected companies, those companies enter a competition to present you with ideas that convince you to give the project to them. They have to address the issues you have presented in the brief, demonstrate how they will achieve these and describe the processes they will follow. They will also need to convince you of the credibility of their company. To do this, they have to put in quite a considerable amount of work so that their examples are telling and their arguments convincing.

You listen to the responses, watch the presentation of their ideas, assess if these meet the brief effectively and look at their projected costs, before making decisions. Some companies use evaluation templates to assess each pitch against given business criteria. These are used to make awarding the pitch more objective and allow the commissioner to give constructive feedback to the pitch companies that lost the project.

Because there is general unease in the industry about the tender and pitch processes, there is a move by some trade bodies to have an accreditation procedure for developers. They suggest validating different levels of proficiency for a developer to attain. Then commissioning companies could select the level of complexity of their proposed project and send the tender request to companies of that level of accreditation. This accreditation practice is seen as addressing the difficulty of the commissioning company receiving too many tenders so that the pitch selection becomes onerous. It is also seen to address the issue of pre-selecting developers/suppliers through closed lists.

Another alternative to these problems is the 'matchmaker' or 'broker' company. These companies vet prospective developers and act on behalf of commissioners to request companies to pitch. They perform the pre-selection process in fact by trying to match the commissioner with supplier.

Considerations

The developer companies are often expected to pitch for free. They incur quite considerable costs, but only one company wins the pitch and may then recoup some of their costs. Could you as a commissioning company imagine working this way?

How good are your project briefs? The pitch is only as good as the clarity of the brief. It is less subjective when the brief makes a clear business case and highlights the user needs. Otherwise, the developers will be working from vague criteria and may suggest that the first paid stage is an analysis of the business case and user needs. Guidelines are emerging now for commissioners to help them formulate better briefs. (See the references at the end of this chapter and encourage your company to analyse them and use them to their advantage.) Working from a marketing perspective of knowing your customers and markets helps to formulate clear business cases. (See Chapter 12 on Marketing for more on this.)

Developer companies are becoming more selective in deciding where and when they will pitch, even if invited to pitch as part of a closed process. They are recognizing that it does not make economic sense to expend such time, energy and cost unless they are better assured of winning. Look at the figures that these companies are using to make these decisions in the following section. Can you blame them?

Pitches: developer perspective

Once the developer gets to the pitching part of a tender process, this generates a great deal of activity for them in a short space of time because the pitch presentation is often held quickly after the shortlist has been released.

Pitches need several people from the company to work on the brief. This pitch team might span the whole company from director through account manager or equivalent, team leader/project manager, to design and back-end production. They need to come up with suitable ideas, to look at the commissioning company's existing positioning, take stock of their business case (if they have one), pool what they know of the users and market segment, flesh out some design examples, work together to arrive at some cost estimates and a plan of work, decide how to present their own expertise, prepare and rehearse the pitch presentation; finally, several key people need to go and present the pitch on the given day and time.

Some companies have dedicated pitch teams because they pitch regularly enough that, if they didn't have such a team, they'd keep disrupting their on-going projects by pulling staff members off these to work on the pitch. A dedicated team may be an unaffordable luxury for small companies, however. Other companies rotate who might be involved with pitches at any one time, because there is the perception that these short bursts of pressurized activity and creativity for pitches are the pinnacle of people's expertise. Everyone likes the creative ideas-driven part of the interactive process even if it is undertaken at high stress.

So, the company has completed all this work and it makes the pitch, but only one company wins the pitch. The commissioners have listened to many ideas from the short-listed companies and often like some ideas from one company but others from another. They might relate well to the cost plan of one but not another and so on. The commissioners sit in a privileged position as the budget holders. It is at this stage of the pitch process that things can and do get sensitive for all the companies involved for many different reasons.

Developers who analyse in real terms how much they are investing in pitches in a year and compare this with the number of pitches made which lead to real business will find some genuine surprises.

Some disturbing figures have emerged from a report in late 2005 indicating that on average over a year interactive agencies in the UK spend the equivalent of £38 000 on pitches where they are not successful. On top of that, even if they win, about a quarter of the contracts never start because the commissioner company withdraws, citing such reasons as the CEO has had a change of mind about rebranding and so on. Faced with figures such as these, companies are rethinking where, when and even if they can afford to take part in pitches. Some companies are refusing to take part even if invited to do so.

Considerations: The pitch process under the spotlight

There is confusion between developers about the premise of the pitch process. Some are against the closed pitch and preferred supplier lists because they say this screens them out of trade so they cannot take part. Others point to the costs of taking part but losing or never getting to contract even if they win. Conversely, commissioners can find the open pitch process overwhelming when too many companies want to take part.

There are moves to address some of these issues because it is recognized that both sides can be disadvantaged. These include guidelines to try and limit the number of potential suppliers that pitch, but allow a cycle of introducing new companies to the selection process. This contains the process for the commissioners while offering the chance to companies that may have been excluded in the past.

Considerations: Why pitches can turn sour

Developer companies believe that if they have done of lot of ground work for free and in good faith for the commissioner, it is unethical if the commissioner takes ideas from one company and uses them with another. Commissioners have been known to bargain with a company, for example offering to award the project but asking them to implement another company's ideas for less than the quoted cost. Some developers are now taking out 'Pitch Protection' policies that they ask commissioners to sign prior to pitching, so that there is a written and more transparent agreement about non-disclosure and non-use of any ideas or material offered in the pitch unless it is successful. This is because ideas *per se* are not protected by intellectual property laws. (See Chapter 11 on Intellectual property for more on this.)

On other occasions, the companies that pitch have to agree to conform to conditions from the commissioner company. These have been known to include granting the rights to any intellectual property generated at the pitch stage. You may need to read any tender or pitch conditions very carefully to understand what you may be giving away even if you do not win the pitch. Some developer companies walk away from pitches and tenders that appear unfairly biased against them.

Developers in the pitch process are vulnerable. They all want to win and so, if the commissioners try to squeeze deals from them, the developers may agree to do extras or cut the budget or whatever it takes for the sake of winning the business. This is a lose/lose scenario because the developers will still have to make a profit to survive in the long term and will have to take short cuts on what they have promised if they are to fulfil the agreement. Internally, the team that have to pick up the project, including the project manager, may well grumble about the account manager or equivalent who was at the pitch and brokered a deal by promising too much or by over-selling. This is quite a common complaint.

From the commissioners' point of view, if they have forced the developer to promise too much and negotiated them down, the quality of the product or the timescale for production may well be sacrificed for the cost. Commissioners often complain of over-selling by developers at a pitch giving rise to expectations which are not in fact fulfilled in the project. This may be a natural tendency by the sales people from the developers, but it can be aggravated by the negotiation stance as outlined above and, in this case, the commissioners may need to take some of the responsibility for such a situation.

Sometimes commissioners do not relate well to the idea of a dedicated pitch team since they feel that the people who scope the project should work on it or else the quality might suffer. Sometimes also they feel that they have been 'sold to' by a strong team chosen for its pitch skills and then abandoned to other people in the company who are less skilled. In such cases, the client could even insist that the project contract mentions specific people in the development team by name – but this might affect the costs.

● Other types of project initiation

'**Through-the-door business**' is where clients contact the developer directly because they have seen their work, they have been recommended, they are responding to marketing or they have some connection with the company. This is all good news for the developer as there is a neutral, or even slightly favourable, position to start the relationship and it is less formal than the tender and pitch situation. However, even if the prospective clients have approached the developer, and the relationship appears laid back, the developer needs to have a clear idea of exactly what is needed, why, and where and how the product is expected to perform. In this case, the developer should institute a thorough scoping exercise with the new client to understand what is to be achieved, in what timescale and for what cost. This is addressed in Chapter 3.

Overall then, the tender and pitch processes engender a great deal of dissension between commissioners and developers/suppliers, and perhaps now you can see why. It will be important to keep an eye on developments so that any resolution through the use of guidelines, written evaluation criteria that are used to screen companies tendering, accreditation procedures and so on can be taken on board if they prove suitable.

Marketing lead project initiation

It's interesting that developer companies that are marketing-driven begin the project initiation process with an appraisal of the competitors (market) and the customers (users). This is particularly true if the client does not provide a business case based on these needs. It makes a lot of business sense to derive your business case from knowing the market, your users' needs and where you stand in relation to these, because this gives strong clear directions – often measurable – about what you need to achieve. In many cases, marketing-oriented developer companies will explain to the client that they will start the process by doing a paid market assessment and user needs assessment to produce the business case that will allow measurable returns.

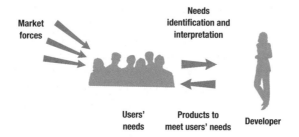

Paid market assessment stage

Once the market analysis and user needs are clear, the design and build process can be worked out accordingly to suit these needs. Testing to ensure robustness and fitness for purpose is part of the process. This gives clarity and purpose to the development process, and the project is less likely to go off track in business objective terms.

This approach can be difficult if your clients are not used to paying for initial stages of projects, are not used to a marketing perspective or believe they have already got a clear business case to offer you at the brief. The approach can succeed if you build up good intelligence on several parts of the interactive market and have a sound client base in these areas. It may be your unique selling point. It can help off-set some of the changes that pervade projects because clients keep changing their minds about their requirements. A market, competitor and user appraisal should provide a more stable base for business needs. (See Chapter 12 for more on marketing and its impact.)

Interactive games (initiation)

The interactive games sector has evolved differently to the rest of interactive media. Their projects follow more of the music industry's, and perhaps the TV and film industry's, model of initiation. They are producing consumer titles of games that compete for sales. The games are regularly ranked in sales charts, just like music. If the game sells well, the profits can be used to invest in new titles. Otherwise, the games company needs to come up with an idea and sell the idea to a sponsor, and producers with a track record of hit games will find it easiest to do this. In many games cases, the sponsors are the games publishers. Many of the publishers are also games hardware suppliers, such as Sony PlayStation or Microsoft X-Box, and one factor in the business model for games involves exclusivity on particular platforms: the complete opposite of the philosophy of web design.

The interactive games industry operates differently from the rest of the interactive sector at the beginning of projects, and we will not be covering their approaches here. Once the project is firmed up, many of the project management processes in this book can be applied to this sector.

Prince2 project management and project initiation

Just in case some of you have become Prince2 accredited, or for those that have heard of this methodology and wonder where it fits with interactive projects, we'll highlight some main points.

This methodology is growing in Europe. It is an open project management approach that can be adapted for any project. This system addresses project initiation and it has a formal document called the PID (Project Initiation Document). However, the perspective taken is for a project originating inside a company. It guides people on how to move the idea of the project through the stages to acceptance within the company. This involves getting the right people with budget authorization on board, showing that the project principles serve the business case and involving the users or their representatives in the process. Once the project has been approved internally, the company may well need a supplier or suppliers. Then the company might move to the tender process or refer to their supplier list, etc. In this way, the project in Prince2 terms may actually span processes in both the commissioner and supplier (developer) companies.

If the commissioning company has a Prince2 project manager then the briefing document should be straightforward, because he or she will have carried out much of the groundwork that we have seen is necessary to make your job as the developer/supplier that much easier. The PID will outline the people involved, the budget, the business case, the authorization path, the stakeholders, the project board responsibilities, the standards that the company operates, the standards expected of the supplier and so on. This document should have informed the brief. If you recognize that your counterpart is a Prince2 manager, then you might ask for a copy to inform you more.

The Prince2 methodology can work to your advantage because it means that the commissioners take their part of the partnership seriously. You, as suppliers, will need to understand the extras that they ask for as a matter of course within this methodology, but the clarity of the processes should mean that, overall, you'll be saved time and effort.

If you are a Prince2 project manager on the supplier side, then you might find the task of generating a PID problematic for a project since the commissioner or client and their users need to be involved. If you try to apply the PID within your own developer company, it may make more sense as a tool for educating the client and educating your colleagues to grasp the high-level information and processes that can be applied to aid the partnership approach between commissioner and developer. (See more on the Prince2 processes and interactive media projects on our website, www.atsf.co.uk/min.)

Prince 2 is a systematic and heavily administrative approach to project management. It evolved to manage large projects, but it can be scaled down for smaller projects. Its approach, however, would seem to be at odds with the emerging Agile software development approach to interactive projects. Agile rejects documentation, heavy administration and systematic linear progress. (See more on Agile and its premises in Chapter 9.) The two approaches may clash so the developer project manager should be aware of this as a possibility.

iTV project initiation

Interactivity is a fast-growing addition to television broadcasting. Often there are websites attached to TV programmes or iTV applications transmitted in the digital TV signal which are linked to the programme then being broadcast. This is often referred to as 'enhanced' TV. Sometimes content is viewed entirely by using the interactive stream, giving viewers access-on-demand to things like news, sport and weather; or the possibility to enjoy self-contained 'adventures' played with characters from the TV shows. This kind of application is often referred to as interactive television: iTV. Television advertising can also be enhanced in this way and, if the viewer's receiver has a return path, such as via cable or a telephone line, quite sophisticated interaction, such as purchasing, is possible.

Historically, TV projects have had rather different initiation processes, compared to websites for example, and even these have varied depending on the TV company. Essentially though, heads of various departments (such as drama and sport) have pitched and lobbied whoever controls the channel or station for production budgets which are then, in turn, pitched for by producers with ideas for individual programmes or series. They might put forward ideas that include interactive components of web and mobile, as well as a core TV programme. Producers compete against other producers and other departments for a share out of the total budget pot. The producers can be in-house or, increasingly, they can be independent production companies.

Interactive television advertising will be put forward by brands and their agencies specing out a campaign that includes an interactive advert. This will be one part of the overall advertising spend, and the necessary air time and data-channel space will be bought to run it. Sometimes clients want experience of interactive adverts as part of their research and development and market analysis, and they'll want to try out any prospective new channel.

Initiation of projects can be affected by the sector of the interactive industry, as this illustrates. You'll need to fine-tune the concepts in this chapter to match your project initiation methods accordingly. Initiation can affect development because it sets parameters for the project that developers then inherit.

Summary

The pre-project development is not straightforward, but it affects all the rest of the project. Many of the difficulties that arise during development can be traced back to lack of clarity at this stage. So it is in your interests to get this right as early as possible.

If the clients have addressed some of the key issues so that their authorization and budget control, their lines of communication, their understanding of their users, market and business case and so on are clear, then your job becomes easier.

If the clients have not addressed these issues, then you have to try and fill in the blanks to reach agreement on what you are trying to produce and who will influence the process. Until you know enough about what you are trying to achieve you will find it difficult to formulate a cost or quality level.

This information exchange is often couched in the tender and pitch process that forms a large part of winning new business for many of the interactive sectors. These processes have their own limitations and considerations as explained. If you can sow the seeds of new business as on-going or return business, you need to get your client's contact to act responsibly within their company and set the right parameters for a successful new project as outlined here.

Whatever way new business is won, the development cycle will be affected by the process, the people and the information exchange. Success or failure starts here.

Top Tips

Strategy	Potential pay-off
On-going and return business seeding – engender this by giving clear guidelines to your key people. Cover what your company would like, how to match your clients' business needs and what information to harness to help them with their internal seeding process.	Return business, more projects, smoother development paths.
Research and understand the tender processes and assess how your company relates to these processes. Share this knowledge with your colleagues. Decide if and how to move forward with tenders and under what conditions.	Less wasted effort. Faster decision-making about this form of new business and its value to the company.
Assess how much pitches cost your company (see the task below). Decide how to improve your pitches to win more business. Decide how to target your effort to more viable pitches.	Less wasted effort. Saving on costs. Improved pitches to wins ratio. Better targeted effort.

▶

Talk to your clients about the pitch process and get their perspective. Work together to understand how to improve this process generally for mutual benefit.

Improves the relationship and trust. Cements the 'partnership' ideal for successful projects. Improves the pitch process for both sides.

For smaller quicker projects where the clients may make the approach to you directly, build the relationship first and move to use clear, consistent, targeted questions to help you extract a good brief from them. Resist moving forward until you understand the parameters of the project.

Any education of the clients by whatever means at the initiation of the project will make the development stages smoother. Sound relationships and trust provide good building blocks for successful projects.

Application Task

Developers

1. Consider the pitches for work you/your company have done in the last 12 months. Estimate the amount of cost in terms of time and effort you and your team have put in for them. What was the projected win worth? How many did you win? How many did you lose? How much money will you recoup on the wins against the costs incurred? What have you learnt from this exercise and how will it affect the way you operate?

Pitch name	Pitches won	Pitches lost	Cost of pitch	Budget won	Budget lost	Ratio of budget to pitch cost
Totals						

2. Do you know why you lost the pitches? Are there any prevalent reasons given? How can you work to address these? Devise a strategy to counter the top two and see if this makes a difference to the number of wins you get.

3. If your company does not work in the pitch and tender way, analyse where the time and effort of the employees have gone into winning new business. Work out how much it costs to win X amount of business and who is involved.

Commissioners

1. Does your company operate the tender and pitch process? If so, how? Do you gather the information that will serve you best, as outlined below, and include it in the briefing document? Do you follow Prince2 project initiation processes? Would they help?

Information for Interactive briefing document	Gathered always: Yes or No	Comments
Business case with measurable objectives		
Timescale		
Interactive target audience		
Interactive market analysis		
User perspective/needs		
Interactive sites/products you like and why		
Budget holder + projected budget		
Communication lines		
Roles and responsibilities		
Quality + standards expectations		
Present interactive technical circumstances		
Legal and usability considerations		

● References/Resources

Books

Caplin, S., Banks, A. and Holmes, N. (2003), *The Complete Guide to Digital Illustration*, New York, USA: Watson-Guptill.

Crawford, T. (2006), *The Graphics Design Business Book*, New York, USA: Allworth Press.

Phillips, P.L. (2004), *Creating the Perfect Design Brief*, New York, USA: Allworth Press.

Sebastian, L. (2001), *Digital Design Business Practices*, 3rd edn, New York, USA: Allworth Press.

Waters, J.F. (2004), *The Real Business of Web Design*, New York, USA: Allworth Press.

Web links

UK Office of Government Commerce (Policy section)
http://www.ogc.gov.uk/index.asp?docid=397

Xplane collects blogs and sorts them into categories for you. The following is useful
Xplane Publications Design Blog – category Design for Business
http://xplane.com/xblog/?cat=66

Design Council – Business section, range of useful information
http://www.designcouncil.org.uk/briefing

Public sector tenders

Is accreditation the way forward? – article on public sector tenders and the client/
supplier debate, British Design Innovation, 2006
http://www.britishdesign.co.uk/index.php?page=newsservice/view&news_id=4508

Guidelines for commissioners for tenders and pitches

The Design Council
www.webdesignforbusiness.org.

Scottish Enterprise
http://www.scottish-enterprise.com/sedotcom_home/services-to-business/
going-online/choosing-ebusiness-suppliers.htm
http://www.scottish-enterprise.com/publications/guidance_notes_for_the_
tendering_process.pdf

Advertiser–Agency Relationships: A 'Best Practice' Toolkit – ISBA (the Incorporated
Society of British Advertisers) – look under their Publications section for Industry Best
Practice
http://www.isba.org.uk/isba/_documents/Best-practice-toolkit.pdf

How to write the perfect brief, no date given
http://www.harmony.co.uk/writing_brief.asp

Guidelines on writing a brief for museums, MDA, no date given
http://www.mda.org.uk/design.htm

Guidelines for developers for tenders and pitches

Pitch protection information, MCCA, no date given
http://www.mcca.org.uk/home.aspx?pid=22,55,0

Report – Statistics about the costs of pitching and more, Dec. 2005
http://www.firedog-design.co.uk/blog/2005/12/08/£38000-is-the-
average-annual-cost-to-pitch-if-you're-a-uk-design-agency/

What clients look for when choosing a new media agency, Juliet Blackburn, no date given
http://www.bima.co.uk/content_resources/presentations/What-clients-look-for.ppt

10 tips to a prosperous client/designer relationship, Ray Noland, heartfelt advice from an experienced freelancer, Aug. 2004
http://theblacklistmag.com/blacklist02/?Editorial_-_10_Tips

Creating the perfect design brief, Peter L. Phillips, adapted from his book of the same name, 14 June 2005
http://www.graphics.com/modules.php?name=Sections&op=viewarticle&artid=235

Call and response: handling RFP tension, Nick Gould, 29 Aug. 2005
http://www.digital-web.com/articles/call_and_response_handling_rfp_tension/

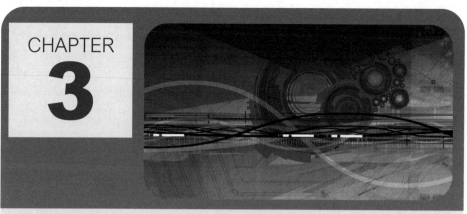

Initiating interactive projects 2 – scoping the project

Industry Insight

My advice is to be very careful about doing any project that hasn't been thoroughly scoped out in advance. Even if you're starving for work. By 'thoroughly' I mean that you, the client, your mom and your dog all know in fairly granular detail what's expected and when.

Scoping projects, D. Keith Robinson, of Blue Flavor in the '7nights' blog, 16 Nov. 2005
http://www.7nights.com/asterisk/archives05/2005/11/scoping-projects

Overview

You can see from the title that we have linked project initiation and scoping together. It was difficult to decide how to split them because sometimes they are separate, sometimes they are linked and sometimes they are intermingled: it depends on the level of detail that is established on the project and the stage at which this happens.

As you will have seen in the last chapter, the more formal project management methods talk about project planning and initiation because, with larger client companies especially, project ideas may have to be sold into the company through an internal process before they reach the attention of the developers. The client companies may then issue a call for tender or use some other appropriate method to outsource projects to potential suppliers. At this point, part of the initiation often includes getting to know more about the project before you present your reply to the call, prepare a pitch presentation or whatever. It's the attention to the level of detail that moves initiation into scoping the project. Sometimes, however, the client will not allow further contact before a written response to the brief on pain of disqualification, to avoid disruptive lobbying or calls on their time. The client may also wish all involved to work from a level playing field as they might have devised evaluation criteria to mark the responses against. So if they give extra information to one potential developer they will skew their evaluation criteria. (See Chapter 2 on the pitch and tender processes.)

● The project scoping dilemma

The conundrum for developers is how can they quote for a project if they don't know exactly what they are being asked to produce? If they under-estimate they will have to try to capture more budget or risk pulling their company down. If they work backwards from the potential budget and they scope out what they think they can do for the money and the given brief, what happens when the client asks for more or asks for changes? If the developers are given a solid timescale, they will scope out what they can do in the time for the brief and put a cost on it. What happens then if the client asks for more or asks for changes?

The scoping of a project is all about negotiation of what can be produced to suit the client's needs at a level of detail that helps the developer define the resources and skills they will need, the amount of time to produce, the assets they will need to create or obtain, the testing and deployment of the product into a known technical environment and the costs associated with all these.

In project management terms this would be what is known as the Work Breakdown Structure (WBS) of tasks and sub-tasks, the projected hours these would take, staff/assets associated with the production and the costs attached to the project across a timeline of development. Most project management software programs offer a WBS tool, and it can be useful for estimations even on smaller projects. It is important if you are linking budget information to tasks and staff timesheets and, perhaps, generating automatic invoices from the information. There needs to be some interlinking of these to allow an instant progress and financial impression of the project for management. Some companies give their clients access to summaries of such information online during the project. Some clients will insist on this level of information and access to it.

We do not go into detail about these packages here because, first and foremost, defining the scope of the project aims at getting the best detail about the project to enable you to estimate costs and timescales, and this has to be done no matter how you move forwards. However, this analysis will also be invaluable for the next stage of work breakdown if you do take that route.

Your project cost estimate is linked to understanding what the project is about at quite a detailed level. This is why D. Keith Robinson issues the warning in the industry quote above. Scoping can go very wrong and you can be drawn into working for nothing, creating debts.

Don't under-estimate the project management or admin

The more people are involved in the scoping exercise the more onerous it can become. You may have to deal with several managers of different sections in the client organization to get the right answers to your questions so that you can take a stab at a cost estimate. When the projects are smaller, you may find that the people you are dealing with can answer the questions and take full responsibility for them. One person may combine the roles of the managing director, the marketing manager and the technical manager of the client's small company, for example.

You should have a standard set of questions to help you define what the project is all about before you scope out the timescale for delivery, the costs involved, the stages the project will follow, the quality and standards the client expects. This will help you to define the true nature of the project. Consider setting a minimum amount of information your company needs before you can start an accurate assessment of time and costs. You need to build some leeway into your negotiations to reflect the uncertainties of the scope, and to quantify any extras in terms of time and cost as they firm up. You will also have to consider how much of your time will be needed to get the answers to your set of questions. Larger clients tend to take a lot longer, but small and medium-sized businesses may answer them in full in the first couple of meetings.

It's a good idea to educate your client about the way that you will work. You may start by saying things like, 'Given X, we will be able to do Y in this time and for Z cost, but if X changes or has additions, Y and Z will change.' Leeway over time and cost can be expressed as 'tolerances' in your verbal negotiations if you find it necessary. This is a positive term covering uncertainties in costs which is acceptable to both parties. It is used in the Prince2 Project Management methodology. You are perfectly right to cover yourself with contingency in time, cost and features of the product, although the term contingency, or its derogatory equivalents like 'slush fund' are often viewed negatively. You should not abuse this or you will damage the relationship with the client. If the 'slack' is found to be unnecessary – although, despite best endeavours, this is usually unlikely – then you should use the excess to polish up the quality of the project towards the end when you are confident it can be achieved on time and within cost.

What is the minimum information you need to scope?

To arrive at an interactive project estimate you need:

- the business problem(s) the client wants to address (the business case);
- what they hope to achieve for the business by solving these (business objectives);
- what they hope to achieve for the users by solving these (user objectives);
- the target audience, their present profile and behaviour with the relevant technology;
- the proposed timescale;
- the name of the budget holder;
- the likely budget;
- the present technology infrastructure the client has available;
- any preferences for features they have seen used by competitors;
- any known constraints (e.g. approval by a compliance department or guardians of corporate style);
- the communication paths with named people to consult and work with;
- the sign-off authority and turn-around time for sign-off;
- the change management process to be used.

These can be reorganized to show the primary implications for the developer in terms of the basics of project management – the time, cost and quality of a project:

Time	
Client-driven	The proposed timescale
Control factors you need	The sign-off authority and turn-around time for sign-off
	Any known constraints (e.g. compliance or style approval)
	The communication paths with named people to consult and work with
	The present technology infrastructure the client has available
Cost	
Client-driven	The budget holder
	The likely budget
Control factors you need	The sign-off authority and turn-around time for sign-off
	The change management process to be used
	The present technology infrastructure the client has available
Quality	
Client-driven	The business problem(s) the client wants to address (the business case)
	What they hope to achieve for the business by solving these (business objectives)
	What they hope to achieve for the users by solving these (user objectives)
	The target audience, their present profile and behaviour with technology
	Any preferences for features they have seen used by competitors
Control factors you need	The change management process to be used
	The present technology infrastructure the client has available

The questions you ask about the quality of the project are there to give you enough information to decide on the general features you will offer in terms of look and feel (what will work with the users and fit in with the client's image), navigation (what content structure the users will relate to and what fits with the client's need to position themselves in the market) and how much content of what media type will be covered under the structure headings. (See Chapter 8 for more on how to define precise usability and accessibility levels of quality.)

So you will show that you are the right company for the job by:

- collecting the right information;
- translating this information into appropriate solutions;
- showing that these solutions will fit the client's needs.

You can see from the table above that the control factors or processes that you need to help you during the project are often the same across time, cost and quality. This is because they are linked and any change to one has an impact on the others. If you establish the sign-off person(s) and the time for the sign-off period linked to milestones of development, you are establishing points of time in the project that can lead to staged payments linked to these milestones – provided you have produced the amount and quality of this part of the project as agreed. If there are particular constraints that have been identified because you asked about them, they can be factored into the development and accounted for in the timescale.

The same is true of the communication paths. If the project is large, you may need to keep several people in the client's company in the loop in different ways. This can affect how much time it will take to have successful sign-off or to off-set interference from people who try to change aspects that have already been agreed. More around these issues will be covered in Chapter 4 on Stakeholders but, if the communication takes a relatively long time, it will demand more of you and/or some of your team and so the increased cost of your time and resources will need to be factored in. The more people are involved at each stage, the more likely it is that someone will ask for changes in the quality in some way, so there may be an impact on quality from this process.

The change management process needs to be established by you as a priority at this point because changes in the project are inevitable. Neither you nor the client can make a definitive answer on unstable factors. You'll both try hard to establish the present position and an end point but, if the market shifts, the users change their behaviour, the company changes any of its parameters – such as restructuring, different staff to deal with, or the amount of information to be covered – your project will be affected and you need to control the impact. The change management process means explaining and putting into the formal agreement with the client the way that any changes they need to make to anything relating to the project will be handled by you. This usually means that the client will have to identify what they want, put it in writing to you, that you will assess what impact this will have on the time, cost or quality of the project and get back to them with this assessment. Then they can make a decision on whether to proceed with the changes, agree to the change in the development time these may cause, and pay for the additions. Because the change management process works across all the parameters of time, cost and quality, you can see that it is a fundamental process.

The client's current technology infrastructure can affect the project in several ways. You need to have a sound technical analysis to understand exactly what they have, the conditions that affect any new deployment and any variations that your company will take on board to fit into their infrastructure. If they will be introducing a new platform capability or new infrastructure, these will have separate considerations affecting time and costs. So, some technology considerations might be as basic as the kind of server their website will live on, their intranet and their security needs, or they might involve the adaptation of their content across various platforms such as iTV, mobile, podcast and so on. All the answers affect the costs and the time needed to achieve the desired fit and may affect the level of quality that can be achieved. If you do not understand all the implications of the technology solutions you offer against the present position of the client, you will run into difficult times on the project.

How much detail?

Too little detail is dangerous and too much detail can make the management over-complicated. This can only happen if you fail to analyse the detailed information successfully in relation to the project. But the most important focus for you is the relevance of this information in relation to the client, the users, the project and your company. All of these can affect the details you'll need. The client and users may have specific market sector, usability and accessibility needs. The project will have its own boundaries and objectives. Your company will have quantifiable experience and potential that will serve the project differently from others.

Because these factors are fluid for each project, you have to take the responsibility for defining the detail in ways that suit your company and the project. The following detailed questionnaire (The Project Scoping Questionnaire) offers guidelines only. Each company should tap into the experience of its employees across all the specialisms to draw out the questions that each section would like in order to determine their fine solutions and use this to tailor-make a questionnaire. This will change from company to company, depending on the sectors they represent and the pool of experience they have at their disposal. The questions also need to respond to changes in technologies from the programming, the platforms, the design trends, the content trends, the standards in place and so on, so the questionnaire will have to evolve.

It is a good idea to plan regular meetings across a year with the relevant people, specifically to ask them to update the questionnaire. This includes the equivalent of the team leaders/project managers as well as functional heads for the specialisms. Each section needs to ask their people for input to upgrade the questionnaire to keep it current. The project managers should build in any changes that their experience with projects has uncovered. They will benefit a great deal from swapping experience with other project managers and using this as part of their self development.

● **The project scoping questionnaire**
(refer to the chapter appendix for a complete copy)

Project internal and external contacts

Project name/no:

Contact details

Client/Organization name:

Address:

Tel: Mobile: Fax: Email:

Website:

Project contacts:

Name(s): Position(s):

Direct line Mobile Email:

Project management tools

It is still surprising how many interactive companies do not operate a specific project-based process within their organizations. This would include giving the project a unique identifying name or number so that the team can keep timesheets according to the specific project and the management can call up an overview of progress on screen at will. A number is potentially less ambiguous, but a name would be easier to remember: if you choose a nomenclature you should stick with it.

Using a project-based process system, the client can have access to specific elements of the project in progress such as graphics to approve, the project Gantt chart to see progress against timescale, and they can receive automated invoice sheets linked to the timesheets and tasks carried out, and so on. There are many more project tools available now to serve even specific sectors of interactive projects. Some companies have built or tailored their own systems to suit their working practices. Client expectations are being raised to include having online access to a project development web space and test site. The ways of working are evolving, and interactive companies should make an effort to keep up to date.

The software tools to help track and maintain progress have become more sophisticated. Some of our own earlier concerns about the amount of administration to operate these systems against the potential pay-off have been addressed. The tools have become more flexible: the collapsed role of the project manager/team leader with that of the specialist and hands-on worker has shifted to some extent depending on the project, the client and the market sector. It is becoming more common now to find interactive project managers who have increased administrative responsibilities. It is a sign of a maturing role. The Prince2 project manager specialists are, however, far more administrative than their usual interactive role equivalent, and they find difficulties applying the Prince2 principles when moving into the interactive environment from other sectors because of the hands-on expectations and creative aspects in the sector.

Just defining the project name and number here in the questionnaire, then, presupposes that the company has an established system for working with projects. Look up the trends in the interactive sector and project-based tools for enterprise project management, cross-project management, creative project management and online project management in the links given in the resources section at the end of the chapter if you need to. Use of these in a way that suits you is an increasingly important indicator of credibility for clients.

Project contacts

Just because this appears to be an easy section of the questionnaire, it can get overlooked. It will save a good deal of time and effort if all the people can tap into this as an online resource and keep the details up to date. It is quite common for people and their contact details to change over the period of the project and frustrating if you can't reach the right person for a number of days when you need a quick answer to a vital detail, so don't forget to include a contact for someone who might know where other people are, like a receptionist or PA.

The whole context of contacts and communication paths in the project, and the relative influence that these contacts have on the project, is covered in Chapter 4 on Stakeholders. This will demonstrate the importance of the people involved and their bearing on the project. It will explain how they can inadvertently interfere with or hold up the project, unless you take control of this process from the beginning. Just knowing their contact details is not enough. You need to probe deeper and get specific intelligence on their responsibility to the project and the amount of influence they can bring to bear. Because interactive projects are now more often part of core business for clients, the type and number of people involved in taking decisions during the project has increased. Interactive projects are becoming more like other projects in this respect and often require more admin as a result. Read Chapter 4 with this questionnaire in the back of your mind.

Previous interactive media experience

Previous interactive media experience

Online

None ☐   A little ☐   Fair ☐   Good ☐   Experienced ☐

Mobile

None ☐   A little ☐   Fair ☐   Good ☐   Experienced ☐

iTV

None ☐   A little ☐   Fair ☐   Good ☐   Experienced ☐

Offline

None ☐   A little ☐   Fair ☐   Good ☐   Experienced ☐

Experience description

Online

Products: Producer:

Mobile

Products: Producer:

iTV

Products: Producer:

Offline

Products: Producer:

Prior experience affects everyone, and clients are no exception. It sets up expectations, which you need to understand. They may have had good or bad experiences. You can learn what they like and don't like in terms of ways of working as well as any preferences they may have for interactive features. If they are return customers, you need to find out as much as you can from the people who worked with them before. In fact, you should have done this prior to the first meeting if it was recognized that they had been clients previously. Even if they are previous clients, it is still good practice to find out what they particularly liked and disliked the last time. At the very least it will help you address any issues they raise.

You need to cover their experience with any kind of project, and the draft questionnaire includes online, mobile, interactive TV and offline as examples which may or may not apply in each case. Whatever sort of project you are working on, experience in one kind has both positive and negative impact when moving to another, and affects expectations. For example, a client may have a large text-based website which the user navigates by using a search facility, because the company deals primarily in information. Marketing consultancies would fall into this category, where they offer summaries of their respective reports to tempt people to buy the whole report. The text-driven nature of the website may well be the most appropriate way to convey the information. However, if the company decides to develop a marketing DVD or CD to give away at conferences, the interactivity of the website will not necessarily be the best model for the new purpose and delivery medium, even if they believe it will be. Some of the content may be useful, but it'll need a new treatment to achieve the impact they want.

Statement of what the client wants

Client's initial statement of what they want

It helps to formulate what the client says they want at the beginning of the interview. They may be very focused and know their needs precisely. In this case the rest of the questions confirm their needs and develop the detail. The more precise they are, the easier your job will be – unless they have misjudged what can be achieved or how to make best use of the medium. The more vague they are, the harder you will have to work to get a good specification. An example of what you might enter here for a relatively small and straightforward project would be:

> *This is a specialist small firm producing garden furniture and ornaments. They want to set up a website to evaluate the potential for sales of their products over the web.*

Notice that they have not said that they want to sell their products on the web. At the moment a database of products and payment structure for selling online would not be a confirmed need, although you might help to indicate this potential to them. Alternatively, you might have put:

> *This is a specialist small firm producing garden furniture and ornaments. They think they want a website, but first they want advice as to what information to place there, some costings based on different types of site, and the type of benefits they could expect from their investment.*

This should trigger you to shelve the questionnaire, show them examples of your work and demonstrate the features of some equivalent small specialist retail sites to help define the component parts of a site that would suit them. Once they have an understanding of what is possible, they should be allowed to discuss the possibilities and probably return for a more productive meeting. It might help them to take the questionnaire away in this case so that they can prepare the answers to the queries.

In the case of a corporate client, there might be several section managers involved. Then a more gentle lead-in where you try to understand their expectations of the processes involved, demonstrate some of your company's capabilities, listen to their reactions and explain your way of working might lay the ground better for the stronger analysis via questionnaire. The processes do not have to be rigid and can be tailored to suit the type of project and client.

For larger projects, the clients may well have followed guidelines for developing a good brief (see Chapter 2) and have a wealth of information about their interactive users, their profiles, their business needs, their brand strategy and so on. But if they don't have these and they are a large company, you may have to take a view on how you proceed to gather the details that are important in coming up with some solutions, the time and cost to yourselves to do this and whether you are prepared to do it at your own cost or not. Some market-driven developer companies suggest an initial paid stage for competitor, market and user analysis. (See Chapter 2 for more discussion around the present trends for the industry as well as Chapter 12 on Marketing and its impact.)

Type of project

The delivery medium affects the specific type of project that will be produced. Online projects have proliferated and expanded to serve platforms other than the web with extensions for mobile communication (phones, G3, iPod, PDAs) and iTV among others. Classification of project types in this fast-moving marketplace has not yet become codified. So the following is offered as the starting point and should be tailored accordingly.

Online project type

Internet site (new) ☐ Hybrid (Web/DVD/CD/Mobile/iTV) ☐

Intranet ☐ Mobile ☐

Website make-over ☐ Other (stipulate) ☐

Set up new facility

(If yes, domain name suggestions?)

Add/change existing facility

Internet/intranet/make-over

It is important to clarify the differences between these categories. The Internet offers general public access to electronic information. An intranet provides closed access to electronic information and is usually company-specific. There's a variation called an extranet that allows nominated companies or individuals access to all or part of an intranet. If the site is going to be new then the company needs to put forward suggestions for its domain name. This is not always straightforward, as others may have already taken the most obvious choice. The sooner this is confirmed the better and, if the company cannot come up with suggestions, ask them to give you three approved alternatives as soon as possible. Remember that it may be appropriate for them to take variations of a name in different top-level domains in order to protect their 'turf'.

The general scope of the project will be linked to the type of delivery and the access to the online facilities. Setting up a secure international corporate intranet and providing the design templates for each division to insert their own content while retaining the common 'corporate' approach is very different from designing a small company profile website to be published on the Internet.

In the intranet example the technical specification aspects can be complex, with several servers spread around the world and the security implications involved in linking them through the Internet. Such data links may already be in place, but it is not uncommon for a large organization's IT structure to have grown spasmodically, and it may be difficult to find out exactly what is in place and who is in charge of the various parts. On the content side, the number and type of templates will take a long time to establish, with the potential for cultural or linguistic differences and even office politics conspiring to confuse the issue. It may well emerge that a database might be the most efficient way of dealing with varying amounts of the data, and this might have to be built from scratch. Training people to input the data is likely to be necessary as well.

The small company website profile, on the other hand, may mean no more than several sets of pages linked by a straightforward structure with the option for the client to come back with material to update the pages as and when they wish. The technical and design aspects are much more straightforward in this case. The company will either have its own server or will be renting space from an Internet Service Provider (ISP), but in either case setting the website up on the server will be relatively straightforward. Hopefully the only awkward issue will be getting the right domain name. (There's some background on legal implications of domain names in Chapter 11 on Intellectual property.)

Hybrid Web/CD/mobile/iTV

The term 'hybrid' can have many meanings. A hybrid project can be a mixture of online and offline components for a single project, for example a DVD that links to a website to add dynamic content. We can refer to this as an Internet/DVD hybrid or a Web/DVD hybrid. This could be a disc that can take updates from the Internet or it could be a website that picks its larger assets, such as movies, from a disc on the local machine. The term hybrid, for example, is also used to describe a component that mixes different formats – usually a CD-ROM that is designed to look 'native' on more than one computer platform, such as Windows and Mac. There are tricks that can be played with the DVD format that allow the production of a disc that can be read as a CD in a CD drive and as a DVD in a DVD drive, and this may be extended with the new high-definition video versions of DVD.

Ideally, any hybrid project should aim to separate its content from the display format, to avoid having to duplicate content. This might be difficult for a DVD with a website but, in the case of a news site that feeds stories to a website, really simple syndication (RSS), interactive TV and mobiles (using WAP), it is vitally important that a common pool of content can be displayed in a variety of ways. This is the basis of content management. It is even possible for end-users to choose their own format, and this is at the root of accessibility, since the kind of web technologies used by people who, for example, prefer to have a web page read to them by their computer work best when the material is properly formatted.

A hybrid project involving online and offline components needs to combine elements of this questionnaire and an offline questionnaire. You should devise an offline questionnaire for your own company requirements if you need one. In your negotiations they should be treated like two separate projects and costed as such, taking into account any overlap of assets and data. Often the client does not understand the term 'hybrid', and it raises the idea for them to consider. In this case, you should take the opportunity to explain the issues and indicate that if they want a DVD it needs separate specification and costing.

In this way, there are no hidden expectations, and they will expect separate costs to be associated with a DVD from the beginning of the relationship. If they originally reject the notion but suddenly change their mind in the middle of the project and want one, you will be able to remind them of the discussion and indicate that they originally wanted a website only. Accordingly, the assets and information have been oriented to that delivery platform only, and a DVD will mean more work for you and therefore cost more now than if they had decided on a hybrid in the first place. As long as you have covered this earlier, it makes extra payments more palatable to the client, even though they are usually annoyed – more with themselves, it should be said.

Mobile

Because of the success of cellular mobile phones – in Europe particularly – many new media companies have been asked to develop projects for WAP, i-mode or mobile web browsing. These projects count as online because the interaction takes place over the network and, with the advent of what are known as 3G phones, the bandwidth available and the functionality of the handsets have increased. The phone is likely to have a web browser built in and text and images can be displayed on the mobile phone's screen. Older types had to use the slimmed down WAP code, but later phones, often morphing into hand-held computers and organizers, could display real web pages. With its roots in Japan, the i-mode system also aimed to improve the capabilities of mobiles as a viable alternative to web browsing desktops. Although the amount and type of information are limited by the size of this screen, the telcos have been keen to understand what the public will access in this way.

The gradual switchover from analogue to digital television will free up some of the radio spectrum currently used for TV, and there are claims on this space being made by the mobile phone industry for new services, as well as new mobile digital TV technology and high-definition television broadcasts. So mobile applications can only become more popular, and you may find it useful to think of mobile as a term meaning any system that the user carries around with them and can interact with.

One important element of mobile technology is that the phone network knows who the user is on an individual basis, including their location, to a much greater level of detail than is possible on the Internet. There is also a built-in mechanism for charging, often by using the facilities of the SMS texting system. The user will usually download an application on demand. These are important factors influencing the kinds of applications that can be delivered to mobile users.

iTV

The communication with a mobile user is usually done on an individual basis, but an interactive TV viewer is usually part of a more amorphous and largely anonymous mass. An iTV receiver will download its interactive applications from a continuous loop transmitted alongside the main programmes (known as a carousel). In the UK this is often referred to as 'red-button' programming because the viewer calls it up by pressing a red button on the remote control. There has been some criticism of 'red button' interactivity because of the limitations imposed by both the functionality of the set-top box or integrated digital TV in which the application has to run and the available bandwidth. However, the link with television programming provides an opportunity to enhance the TV experience with things like extra information on the subject of a programme or follow-ups to advertisements. These will be specially-written applications, but iTV can also carry news and other information which can be drawn from the same sources as other formats and specially formatted.

Interactive television delivered over a cable TV or Internet protocol (IPTV) network has a good reverse path and it is possible to provide on-demand or 'pushed' programming and billing as with mobiles. Satellite broadcasting of itself offers no practical return path, but many satellite receivers include a telephone connection so that, although full two-way interactivity is limited, there is enough capability to handle low-bandwidth transactions by the viewer, such as voting, competition entry, requesting a mail-shot or phone call after an advertisement or even buying items on a shopping channel.

With all interactive TV, one almost omnipresent application is the electronic pro-gramme guide or EPG, which can be used to program a recorder for time-shifting. In an environment of hundreds of channels, the EPG is the only real path to visibility: no EPG slot means no viewers! Usually a digital TV supplier will have its own EPG but it is possible for an alternative to be deployed. Although iTV functionality is limited, there is an opportunity to include high-quality audio and video streams, which offer opportunities for an ingenious developer.

Market sector of the client

Market sector			
Commercial ☐	Corporate ☐	Government ☐	Education/Training ☐
Advertising ☐	Marketing ☐	Entertainment ☐	Games ☐

The major categories of commercial, corporate, government, education/training, adver-tising, marketing, entertainment and games are included as an indicator of your potential administrative overhead. As a rule, small general commercial sites allow you more free-dom and versatility when compared with the others. Decisions can be given to you faster, and your work can progress more smoothly. With the other sectors, and with large commercial clients, it is often much harder to get clear statements and directions. You may be held up for long periods waiting for confirmation of how to proceed, even if you follow our advice given elsewhere about establishing authority and sign-off. The internal cultural and political nuances associated with large commercial sites or the other specialist sectors cannot be ignored in your attempt to size up the scope of the project.

Project content bias

Project content bias		Importance ranking	Size of section (large, medium, small)
Company profile	☐		
Information gathering	☐		
Information dissemination	☐		

Retail (products or services description) ☐

Database access/development ☐

Marketing/advertising ☐

Redesign site front end ☐

Online transactions ☐

Branding ☐

Redesign site ☐

Others (specify)

The projects will often span several of the components under this heading, and it helps to understand this as soon as possible. The bias on the type of data will help to determine the type of interactivity needed, which will in turn have an effect on the programming and design. A recruitment agency website, for example, may need part company profile, part information gathering (prospective job candidates posting their CVs), and part information dissemination (searches of the database of current jobs on offer). These begin to give a good indication for the scope of the project, as you may then try to refine exactly what is needed under each component. You should be beginning to recognize the need for co-ordinating and agreeing the essential aspects of content for the company profile, layout of online forms, several layers of search facility and so on.

If the site is to have a retail bias then an online database of products and services with online and offline payment options may be necessary, probably with links to credit card handling. There will be regulations on distance selling to consider as well as the implications of sales taxes, which can sometimes depend on the customer's location as well as your client's. The company may already have a digital database and may link this to product availability and dispatch. On the other hand, none of these may be in place and all may need to be developed from scratch. Commercial online database development may be part of your skill base or you might have a partnership or alliance with a software company to develop this part of the project while you develop the front end. The important thing is to realize that this needs precise definition by a competent person.

If a sizeable database is part of the brief, whether the project is e-commerce or a volatile information site, a separate questionnaire would need to be completed with the client's software representative and your senior database member of staff to ensure that the scope of that pure software development is thoroughly understood. Other aspects are related to this definition. The security of online transactions is an issue that necessitates clarification and firm agreement. The type of encryption and secure servers would also need to be defined although, for most purposes, the standard web security verification, based on electronic certificates, would be adequate: but someone has to obtain the certificates. Don't forget that any website that allows input by its users is at risk from accidental or deliberate 'out-of-scope' input and must be able to ignore or deal with this gracefully. If end-users (such as members of the public) are carrying out electronic transactions, the database system needs to be able to cope with them backing out of a transaction without completing it, and this influences the database design. The specialist questionnaire needs to check on the company's policy for exchange of data across its systems and across the firewalls it might have as security. All these can have implications on the size and true scope of the project and need to be understood by the right people.

If the brief shows any marketing and advertising bias, this indicates the need for a clear understanding of the image the company wants to convey and who they are trying to reach. These components have a particular bearing on the look and feel of the site, and have to have careful treatment. The same is true if you are asked to redesign a site. In this case, your client will be expecting to improve their image and may have identified necessary new components. Because the medium is so volatile, the breakthroughs in programming suddenly allow new features of interactivity or design. Redesigning sites is often connected with introducing these new features. As they occur frequently, it is not uncommon for high-profile sites to be redesigned every six months or so. This creates a drive to keep up with the fashion, and it causes a ripple effect across other sites. However, while new web browsers bring new technologies and techniques to the web designer, not all web users keep up with the trends and some may deliberately disable them, and so any use of new features has to be made knowing that not all potential viewers will see them. The amount and type of log analysis on user behaviour that would be collected and the use of pre-release user trials would also need consideration for these types of projects.

Advertising and marketing interactivity have grown quickly to become strong subsectors. As the number of Internet users has increased and the capacity for broadband has allowed easier access to rich media assets, these disciplines have begun to find their niche in interactivity to the extent that they can make clear business cases for interactive use against traditional advertising and marketing uses. In some ways, the interactive sectors can provide better information about the use and uptake of these services through log tracking methods than was possible with traditional uses. The ability to form communities of use around a product or brand that are willing to receive news about other similar products, generates business. That the communities are tempted by online offers to increase their loyalty to the brand is a strong incentive to push these sectors into trying out new interactive technologies. Because search engines have become a popular way to search for items that a user wants, search engine optimization (SEO) has become big business in its own right. It promises to place the client closer to users who have already indicated through their search terms that they might be interested in the client's offerings. (See more about marketing as an interactive sector in Chapter 12.)

Importance ranking

If the clients have identified several components, use the ranking column. Because the amount and type of information can be infinite, you need to get the client to recognize their priorities. This is to encourage them to be realistic and to help you to apportion your effort. If, later, the client does not like your quote, it will help you make edit decisions to prune the material that is least important to them. They may well say that each component has the same importance, so you might enter equal ranking numbers for them. The aim here is for you to understand if and where there might be leeway.

An alternative way of approaching this quick form of ranking with clients is called MoSCoW. This gets the client to define what they must have (M), should have (S), could have (C) and want (W) but will wait for next time. The principle is the same – clarifying the most important needs for the client. You may find that you need to do the more extensive scoping analysis at this point because the clients are not able to define their needs. The MoSCoW principle comes from Rapid software Application Development (RAD) processes and is part of a complete methodology for handling fast production of more traditional projects. RAD has evolved now to be seen as part of Agile software development techniques. We have just borrowed the high-level idea here not the whole process, so recognize that people from software backgrounds may think that using this MoSCoW acronym indicates that you will use the complete methodology. It is important that you make it clear whether you are using it all or not. (See Chapter 9 for more on Agile software development approaches.)

Other companies have employed 'use cases' or 'use scenarios' with their clients. These get the client to focus on exactly what they want the application to do in user terms. The developer can then interpret these into functionalities that are needed from a development perspective. (See more on use cases in Chapter 8.)

Size of section

The amount of information you are given to structure for the site affects the time needed to complete the project and therefore the cost. Although it is all relative, you have to try and understand the amount of material within each section to get a feel for how to apportion time and resources as well as cost. One company's expectations of a company profile might be succinct and neatly contained in a single page; another might see the profile as a major component, with several sub-sections and lots of media. They might both have ranked the profile as the most important to them, but their expectations of how you will deliver it can be very different. These queries might tease out several aspects that are important for you to note, so have some blank sheets ready. They often prompt healthy discussion between the client's representatives themselves, and they may want to consider their options before they answer. That's fine. Get them to note down the queries they want to discuss 'off line', but continue with the questionnaire, as other questions might prompt similar responses and they will need to go away to consider their answers to all of them.

If you are getting the impression that the clients have a lot to think through, or recognize they have limited time in which to make their decisions and would be receptive to help, it is at this stage that you could remind them that an analyst or consultant from your company could facilitate their discussions. These people could help them align their decisions to their business strategy while firming up their directions ready for this project. This service would be offered with a price tag, but once the client's awareness of the issues has been raised through the questioning process they should have more confidence in you and recognize the value of the offer.

Functionality requested

Functionality requested

Site personalization ☐

Registration ☐

Site search engine ☐

Profiling ☐

Content management system ☐

   Total ☐

   Partial ☐

Catalogue ☐

Survey/Quiz facilities ☐

Mapping/location identifier ☐

Newsletter/Online journal distribution ☐

RSS feeds ☐

Advertisement spaces ☐

E-commerce transactions ☐

■ Home country only ☐

■ International ☐

■ Including paid-for downloads ☐

Others (specify)

[_____]

[_____]

You may well have a company bias for the type of interactive project you do, and you may be winning new projects on the back of this experience because your clients know you have been successful in the sector. Your list of the types of functionality that are the most relevant for your client pool may well vary from, or expand, those listed here. The listing is useful because it can act as a checklist of the things your clients expect, the things they didn't know about but you can explain and the things that you see as trends for their competitors. This can be very useful client education since they may well be attracted to some of the functionality once you explain the benefits, but they may not have the budget for all at this time. However, you may sow the ideas for follow-up business later by indicating the possibilities of other interactive functionality.

Client database

Client's database			
None ☐	SQL flavour ☐	Access ☐	Other ☐

Server-side technology

PHP ☐	ASP ☐	Perl/CGI ☐	Java ☐

Other (specify)

Some of the functionality that is defined may well depend on the technology that the client uses already. Your people need to check what their infrastructure is to understand precisely what they will need to do and which skill sets they will need in order to match the existing technology base. Again, your specialist may well have a long separate set of queries that need to be answered, so this could be the tip of the iceberg. One thing you will know from this high-level query is if your specialist foresees difficulties and if he/she wants to probe deeper. Your reaction to this should be to hold off quoting a price for this part of the work until you are confident about what it really means to your people.

Browser/platform expectations

Browser/platform expectations

Either:

Developer policy accepted i.e.

Development only for X browser and X versions on X platform   yes ☐   no ☐

Or:

Client wants:

Browser(s).

Versions supported:

Plug-ins.

Platform(s).

Allow Flash?   Yes ☐   No ☐

Allow Java?   Yes ☐   No ☐

Allow JavaScript?	Yes ☐	No ☐	
Allow ActiveX?	Yes ☐	No ☐	

Or:

Client does not know ☐

Client contact name for answers	
Tel:	
Email:	

This is the section where you are trying to understand how much extra programming will be involved to make the application work for particular browsers and their various versions and whether the application needs to work cross-platform. A web page may appear differently on some browsers due to subtle (and sometimes not-so-subtle) quirks in the way the style sheets for the pages are rendered. How important is an exact look from browser to browser? Do they want to make use of browser programming with Java, JavaScript or ActiveX (noting that this choice has implications for cross-platform compatibility)? Will they use plug-ins even though some users may have to download them to view the pages?

You may have the opportunity to influence the decisions here if you have access to data indicating the most used browsers and platform. However, your client may have better data on the specific target users from their own research and understand the target audience better, particularly if you are developing an in-house application for a large company. The significance of the browser and platform was much less of an issue a few years ago but, as the capabilities and functionalities have increased, the workload for getting an application to work across versions and types has increased as well. Many new media companies have been caught out by this and, as a result, are now stipulating which browsers and versions they will support as a matter of company policy. This means that if the client has different needs or won't accept company policy, they will have to pay extra for the work involved for their specific requirements.

Site maintenance

Site maintenance

Client to maintain:	
You to maintain:	

Search engine optimization

Client to organize:	
You to organize:	

Log analysis

Is this needed?

On server?

Client to do

You to do

If yes: How much is wanted? Subcontract to specialist company?

It is important to raise site maintenance early in the discussion. If the client is going to update the content, a program to manage the website's content – a content management system – might be appropriate and they may already have one that you'll need to take into account. You have to know the competence level of those who will be involved so that you can design templates for the content management accordingly; and include the content management system in the budget. You may have to provide training as part of the deal, and this has to be costed. If you are going to maintain the site, a whole set of agreements on how often, how much and what to do about introducing new elements will be needed. Maintenance is often forgotten, but is crucial for all companies to consider. Many still under-estimate the on-going involvement in updating content on a site after its launch – and the on-going costs. The responsibilities should be sorted out early on to avoid difficulties later. Remember that a website is more like a magazine than a book – it needs to be updated regularly to stay alive. In fact, some websites are more like newspapers and update very regularly – even continuously.

Even if your client is going to take responsibility for updating the content, you may be asked to host the website or co-locate a server or rent space on the client's behalf. You need to get an understanding about what this means in terms of on-going effort and costs from your technical advisor. Also, the client may want you to provide log analysis reports on the site daily, weekly or monthly. How much effort and cost this will generate depends on the information they want and in what form, so more precise detail is needed before you add this in.

The analysis of the website logs (more properly called access logs) has become increasingly important as the market data and usability data they can provide indicate trends of use. The work involved means setting up the logging and perhaps configuring or even writing analysis programs to interpret this in meaningful ways for the client. If the client holds their own servers, their own people should handle this aspect for them, but if you are hosting their site, or if another company hosts the site for your client, you may need to take care of these aspects on your client's behalf. Defining whose responsibility and how much work is involved will affect your company's time and costs. Many of the larger companies now have a log analysis system that you'll have to work with.

Getting a website up at the top of a listing on search engines such as Google has increased dramatically in importance recently. The technique is called SEO and some companies specialize in it. You may find that your client already has agreements with one of these and that you'll also have to liaise with them as part of the extended project team. If this is the case, the admin aspect of the project increases as the number of people to inform about the state of development or to seek approval from increases. This will add to your time and cost.

Benefits/achievements wanted

Benefits/achievements wanted

Not applicable [   ] (Reason)

Through this application the organization wants to achieve:

1.
2.
3.
4.
5.
6.
7.
8.

The users of the site will benefit from or fulfil needs by:

1.
2.
3.
4.
5.
6.
7.
8.

If you were a user what search words/phrases might you use to locate the site?

If the client has been able to define their initial statement earlier, this set of questions will probe their understanding in order to clarify their thinking. It is not easy to define objectives for the company or for the users, but if the client does not attempt this, the specification will lack direction and will tend to meander. You will be given mountains of information to structure for no real reason unless you get the client to focus on these core issues. It is their responsibility to provide the answers to these questions. You shouldn't have to surmise why they want the site and what they expect from it in terms of their company and their own customers. By asking the client to imagine a potential customer deciding on search terms to use with a search engine, you help them focus on their customers' requirements. Ask the client to prioritize the terms they put forward and this will demonstrate what they consider the most important parts of the site to be. The importance of the client knowing their potential customers and the interactive business objectives for their company has increased over the years as general business and interactive business processes have merged into a common business strategy.

However, if you recognize that the client has not done a market, competitor and user analysis to arrive at their search/metatag terms, you may offer to research this for them through market analysis as a paid stage. (See Chapter 12 for more on marketing and its impact.)

Interactive media companies are realizing that if clients have not thought through their complete online business strategy they will not achieve what they need from the project. In this case they may turn round and blame the developer for the lack of achievement. It is important to be diplomatic at this stage but, if it appears that the client is entering into the unknown, you, as developer, have to choose whether you are able and willing to help them through. This is not development so much as consultancy, and it needs a different way of costing. You will probably have a stop/start progression where you develop lots of prototype concepts that are thrown away as your client refines their thinking. Finally a direction is forged and the real production process begins.

In this scenario the risks are much higher and you'd need to establish strong controls over project phases and costs. Clients rarely agree to a time and materials budget since they cannot predict how much budget they will need to cover an unknown development time and cost. However, you will be in that precise situation if you leap into the unknown without setting up the correct parameters to cover your time and costs. Time and materials budgeting may be more acceptable if there is a cap on cost and regular progress monitoring. Agile software development methods may fit better into this payment model. (See more on Agile in Chapter 9.)

Access and use

Access and use	
The audience/users	Access to what information
Internet	
General public	
Specific market sector(s)	

(specify)		
Intranet		
Corporate/government/		
education/other:		
In-house (all)		
Exec		
Managers		
Sales force		
Other		
Extranet		
No. of sites to connect		
Who will need access		
(specify)		

This section will encourage the client to clarify their thinking even more. The benefits and achievements section will have given you high-level company and user needs, while this section will give you more detail about the content in relation to the user. The connection between the users and the reason they want access to certain types of information is the most important one to establish, whatever the medium. The type of user influences the structure and the level of interactivity. Consider how you might design information for 5 to 7 year olds to access as a resource from the web for a school project, compared to designing it for teenagers accessing information on their favourite pop group or investors checking their portfolio shares on an investment company's website.

The same information may need to be accessed by several different types of user, and this will determine its range, depth and structure. The analysis for this section can be complex and stimulates most discussion. But it is wise to raise the issues quickly so that the client realizes that, with so much on offer, it is no mean feat to prioritize the categories and match them to the reasons why the user will want to access them. This section will need to be refined and reworked at subsequent meetings in conjunction with the benefits and achievements section above.

If the client has not considered access and use in sufficient detail, ask them to make it an action point and request written replies within a specified period. They need to prioritize the range of information types and the sorts of users they expect or want to attract. Don't forget to suggest early user involvement so that they help establish the criteria.

You will not be able to do a good cost analysis until you are confident about these features and about the amount of information that needs to be gathered and structured. Don't worry if your client thinks you are asking them to do too much. Very often clients do not understand the process and have not been able to raise the right issues for themselves. This is why they may appear vague. You have to raise the right issues and then they can respond to them. Alternatively, if the client has not thought the project through in enough detail, they will probably not have planned enough resources from their side either. By raising the issues, you help them to clarify their involvement. It is at this point that the client may be receptive to the idea of using your company's information architect, strategist, marketing resource or equivalent to help with this phase – assuming you have them.

If you don't have higher-level consultants and you will be clarifying the situation yourself, then you need to have established the extent of your involvement before you commence charging. This will be easier if you have indicated to the client that you'll use the initial questionnaire to establish how long it might take to get to definition stage. Then, if the questioning process reveals that getting the project definition will take more than a couple of meetings, you can demonstrate this to them and offer to help them define their project as a paid pre-project stage. Remember, the common goal for both of you is to start the project from a clear definition of what is expected from both parties in order to progress through the stages smoothly and purposefully towards a known finishing point.

Emotional reaction considerations

Emotional reaction considerations	
Typical user reaction/first impression to main screen:	Key adjective(s)
Re the company/organization represented	
Re the content of the page	
Typical user reaction to time spent on the site	

The web is now a reasonably mature form of communication and, with that maturity, come efforts to make online experiences focused and productive. Usability issues are now taken into account from the start as opposed to the old 'build it and they will come' approach to web design. It is also true that the subjective elements have an impact, and that may be more difficult to measure. Usability principles can be applied to many answers given here regarding the use of things like colour and layout, but style and design are a combination of subjective elements that the client will want to influence. (See Chapter 8 on Usability and accessibility.)

It may well be that no strong style is indicated by the adjectives the client uses – that you are asked to produce a clear but neutral experience. However, the opposite may be true, and this helps you to understand how visually driven the client is and perhaps how much time and involvement might be needed from creatives in your team. If your client is expecting something that makes their company stand out, and the main experience from the site should be excitement or elation, then this affects the whole treatment not just the visual elements. If the client has assessed their users and their preferred behaviour, these aspects will help your design team most. By focusing on the users and what they would like or need, the design is immediately more focused and moves away from some of the other subjective responses that the people involved in the project from the client's side might hold.

When branding and image are major concerns of your client, online communication is part of their company's integrated approach that is designed to act not just in isolation but to contribute to experience over time and across communication channels. They may well have selected you, the developer, because of the connections with the branding and image market sector. Most web agencies aligning themselves to this sector have more detailed approaches to eliciting the image needs of their clients, but many other developers might recognize that it is an area they have neglected completely in the past. Check if the company have already involved their users in initiating the project and in what ways they want their involvement to continue because usability/accessibility design and testing need to be defined upfront so that they form part of your scheduling and costs.

Media mix

Media mix				
Client's media expectations	None, wants suggestions		Animation	%
	Text	%	Audio	%
	Graphics	%	Video	%
Content (existing assets)				
Written			Contact:	
Relevant databases		Spec:	Contact:	
Graphics/stills		Spec:	Contact:	
Audio		Spec:	Contact:	
Video footage		Spec:	Contact:	
Content experts			Contact:	

The client may have a vague conception of their site in terms of the media they expect to see as part of it. It is good to get these expectations out in the open, as you may well already have an indication of which media to use based on the emerging understanding of the audience and content. Allow them to state what they would like or expect, and if you think that some of it isn't appropriate or cost-effective then you should say so. Alternatively, according to what they say, you might find yourself arguing for the inclusion of some video or audio for a particular section where you feel that higher-end users would respond well to the added cachet of those media, even though the client has seen the site in terms of text and graphics only. The increased use of and access to broadband give better capacity for including rich media and has raised expectations in the public.

The cost of development in any interactive medium is affected by the number and type of suitable assets that the client already has. Perceptions of quality in integrated media are different for different modes of delivery. Lower quality is tolerated in mobiles because of the limitations of the delivery system. This is constrained by the bandwidth of the connections and the power of the handset receiving the data. At the other end, the quality of anything seen on TV, especially from a DVD, has been set very high by the broadcasters and by Hollywood.

Websites have to be optimized for a spectrum of uses, and for users who will have varying computer power and speed of Internet access. If a complete mix of media is needed, then care needs to be taken in how the media are presented, possibly with different qualities being delivered depending on how the server sees the users' capabilities. Otherwise compromises have to be made to optimize across this range. Many sites remain heavily text-driven with some graphics because of these considerations. The client may not be fully aware of the possibilities or of the compromises needed. The sooner you can contact the relevant people and understand what assets are available the better. You should be able to work out the gaps, check the rights position, and cost the reworking of existing assets and the generation of new ones. Don't forget to keep checking back to your relevant team members about the assets you find and the implications this has for them. This will help you define costs for this stage better.

It will be up to your team to make the best fit between the platforms, the media and the audience. Analysing these answers will tease out exactly what content formats will be needed for the quality level and the various platforms. This will help establish how much effort will be needed to produce the variety and so will help with the cost estimate. You can realize that if the platform is a website with text and graphics, this would lead to one production cost figure. However, if the content is needed for the website, but also some of it is to be sent to mobiles, and other bits of information will serve an interactive TV advert linked to the website, then several skill sets are needed, different formats of the content are required, analysis of exactly how the content will be treated to achieve the best for each platform will be necessary, and so on. There are some cross-platform formatting software tools and standards emerging to help with this platform mix scenario, but they may just make it easier to produce a range of versions of your audio or video. Image libraries, for example, are realizing that they have to offer their visuals in a range of formats to suit the different types of use. They are expanding their digital offerings gradually to reflect the various format needs.

Time for development

Time for development				
Client expectation		(months)	Start date	
			End date	
Any fixed dates				
(demos etc.)				
To be specified in proposal				

There is often a mismatch between clients' and developers' expectations of the development time that is needed for a project. Clients do not usually appreciate the complexity of some of the processes involved. Their expectations may be impossible to achieve, and the scope of a project may have to be reduced to meet a definite timescale.

You need to understand any factors that are driving clients in their decisions on the timescale to see if they might be negotiable. This is why any fixed dates become important. This is the right place to establish as much as you can about the client's needs for completion, because this will help to determine how much content and what media might be achievable. You might suggest scheduling completion of one component before another in order to meet their needs, or you might be able to suggest publishing components as soon as they are ready, with placeholders in the other sections, or developing skeleton pages in each component just to give a feel for the overall structure. Online delivery is more flexible in this regard than offline was, where prototyping tended to be more complex because the end result was 'fixed' .

You might also be able to 'chunk' stages of the project to achieve a certain amount to go live by a certain point for a demo or 'soft' launch. Then you can have stage two of the project where you complete the delivery while assessing user reaction to the first part ready to tighten up anything found as a result.

Special considerations

Special considerations

Database development/online transactions

Company specialist and extra questionnaire needed   yes ☐   no ☐

Client contact for this extra software analysis

Tel:

Email:

Dynamic pages required

Company server-side specialist and extra questionnaire needed   yes ☐   no ☐

Client contact for this extra server-side software analysis

Tel:

Email:

The project bias section should have alerted you if the construction of an online database, and all that is involved with that, will be necessary. This confirms if the software specialist has to perform a separate analysis and lines up the right contact to help get the information quickly. The answers to the project bias section should also have alerted you to the need for dynamic pages and the need for back-end programming. The implications for the amount of resources and work need to be assessed by a specialist. These will affect your cost and time estimates.

Testing

<table>
<tr><td colspan="2">Testing strategy</td></tr>
<tr><td>Company standard (specify)</td><td></td></tr>
<tr><td>Focus groups</td><td></td></tr>
<tr><td>Usability testing</td><td></td></tr>
<tr><td>User trials</td><td></td></tr>
<tr><td>Stress/load testing</td><td></td></tr>
<tr><td>Other</td><td></td></tr>
<tr><td colspan="2">Localization/Internationalization</td></tr>
<tr><td>Not needed</td><td></td></tr>
<tr><td>Needed (further analysis to be done)</td><td></td></tr>
<tr><td>Subcontract specialist company?</td><td></td></tr>
</table>

Testing and localization issues can be complex. Your company has to decide what they offer as standard testing applied to all projects and which will be included in the costs, and what extra categories they are prepared to support or manage as a subcontract. You need to produce a sub-set of questions to use with your clients to explain the various options and firm up the type and amount of testing that they want. Then you'll be able to cost this accordingly. (See Chapter 9 for more detail on testing.)

If there are any multi-cultural or multi-lingual facets to the project, another sub-set of questions needs to be devised to determine the exact requirements. These extra questionnaires are as much a resource for you to raise the awareness of the client as to exactly what is involved in these processes as they are to help you determine the true scope of the project. Localization and internationalization are complex specialisms in their own right and, as a general rule, work in other languages should be done by native speakers. It saves a good deal of time and money if these needs are identified and addressed at the beginning of a project. They affect everything from the coding to the look and feel, so don't under-estimate them. The 3rd edition of this book had a chapter on these. You can access it at www.atsf.co.uk/mim (see Resources) to develop a fuller understanding of the issues when developing projects for different languages if you need this.

Accessibility factors

Accessibility factors

To what standard?

Standard developer accessibility package	yes ☐	no ☐
Special considerations requested (specify)	yes ☐	no ☐
Subcontract to specialist	yes ☐	no ☐

It is now a legal requirement to take account of accessibility since everyone has a right to access information. Accessibility covers a wider range than many expect, with groups such as the visually impaired, the hearing impaired, the physically impaired and people with learning difficulties included. The standards and expectations change over time so it is important to get your products judged against the current standards and accorded a suitable rating: usually based on the A to AAA system exemplified by Watchfire's Bobby. The client should be aware of these requirements and accept that they mean some extra work and therefore cost, although those developers that have kept abreast of the standards will be used to building the requirements into the products from the start and will be more efficient than others. Accessibility is an integral part of a project such as a website – it is not a bolt-on.

(Find out more about these standards in Chapter 8 on Usability and accessibility and the Accessibility section in Chapter 10 where they are covered in more detail.)

Security issues

Security issues

Does the client's image or profile support a greater than usual risk of hacking?   yes ☐   no ☐

Is the client's web server's connection to Internet:

Direct ☐

Via firewall ☐

Is load testing required?   yes ☐   no ☐

The Internet is a major channel of open communication and, as a result, security issues have arisen. From traditional hacking and bank fraud to malicious advertising and identity theft, the security issues grow as criminal gangs recognize the opportunities and exploit them. You have to take time and effort to understand the issues and address them following the best advice you can get. Certain clients such as mortgage societies and banks will expect this as a priority but are likely already to be experts in the subject. Other clients are becoming more aware and will want reassurance. Input by your users is a danger point which has always to be controlled, but this is not the only potential vulnerability. Sometimes just having a website will prompt malicious attack. You should decide what options are straightforward for you to offer and which ones would warrant extra time and effort to achieve, and adjust the cost estimate accordingly.

Budget

Budget

£/$/€ approx

Budget holder: Position

Tel:

Email:

Project cost to be prepared and negotiated

Separate costs to be put forward for maintaining and updating

In an ideal world (for the developer), projects would be scoped and specified and clients would then pay for work done on a time and materials basis. Unfortunately, clients will usually want a fixed price agreed up front, and they will not want to change that even if circumstances change. Doubly unfortunate is the difficulty of accurately costing any software project, let alone one with as many constituent parts as interactive media. For the sake of this discussion we shall assume that a fixed-quote budget is wanted.

This can turn into a see-saw battle. It is common for the client to withhold their actual budget figure because they know you will scope to the top of that budget. Many clients prefer you to draft a few alternatives with a range of costs so that they have an indication of the quality and cost. They can then negotiate from a stronger position.

Some clients will be inexperienced in the costs of interactive media projects and will expect you to be able to give them an estimate during the first meeting. This is unfair, but it can help if you have ready some examples of the range of costs that can be incurred for projects of different length and different quality – to help them understand a top and bottom price.

You can't really work out an estimate unless the client has specified the size of the project and the expected media mix, and you know the usual production charges per hour of your company and can make a good guess at any extras such as the costs of rights clearances. Even then, considerations of content, existing assets and use will affect the costs, and we have gathered only first-level information about these in this questionnaire. You need to explain why it is difficult to cost and which factors affect the cost.

The people you are dealing with may not necessarily be the budget holder: they may have to refer the decisions on in the organization, and negotiate themselves in turn. It is important to know whether they have the authority to release the budget themselves, because if their decisions can be changed then you have to take this into account, for two reasons. First, during a project you need to be talking directly to the top decision makers to keep the decision time and sign-off time as short as possible in order to avoid delays in the project, since end dates are rarely as flexible as start dates. Second, you need to find out whether the budget holder will have any authority over the content before he or she releases the budget. You do not want to work for agreement with your client only to have their boss make changes. (See Chapter 4 for more about stakeholders, their influence and how to control them.)

Organizations work in different ways, so you need to find out how the client's authorization to spend operates and what controls are in place to control it. This can affect the turn-around time for decision-making throughout the project, and it will help if you sort out your approach to this as early as possible. If you are to propose costs for maintaining and updating the site, the person who has to accept the long-term budget costs may not be the same as the company project manager you are dealing with for the initial build, so make sure the right information is passed to the right person, to save difficulties later.

● Managing smaller projects

The principles of establishing the parameters of a small project are the same as for larger projects. You do not want to miss asking any important questions that may affect your effort and therefore the cost estimate. Because you may be dealing directly with the decision maker from the client company, you will probably get the answers you need to scope a project faster and be able to arrive at a response faster too. However, you will need the control options of change management and the time, cost and quality equations, sign-off and turn-around times for the project stages as basics even so. Unfortunately you are likely to find that the more fluid the start of a project is, the more changes are likely during it. See www.atsf.co.uk/mim under Resources for more on this topic.

● Work Breakdown Structure (WBS)

As indicated before, if you get the scoping process refined to suit your company needs, you'll find that you'll improve the next stage of WBS using your chosen project management software tool. The better your scoping, the better your understanding of the work and effort needed for the project. The better this is, in turn then the better your understanding of the staff hours that will be involved in developing the pieces of the project. The hours of development work drive the cost estimation based on your cost per member of staff per hours per role. (See the resources listed to find links to some software that may be used for this part of the work process.)

Some companies vary the hourly costs for a member of staff according to the role. If roles are collapsed into one person, as is still common in the interactive sectors, project management costs may be at one rate and the project manager's specialism (information architecture, for example) at another rate. This level of detail about how much is charged, if the rate includes a mark-up for profit or not, how your company estimates the rates per hour, what details they use to arrive at the rate – company overheads, building rates, equipment needs, etc. – all these vary so much across the interactive sectors, size of companies, market conditions and so on, that we cannot expand on this fruitfully here. You'll need to understand how your own circumstances are interpreted in the equivalent of the WBS or whatever you use to track time and cost in the project.

Emerging design and software methods: their impact on WBS

There has been strong criticism from clients concerning their needs to change aspects of the project on an on-going basis in the fast-moving interactive market. To address this, design and programming have responded by adapting their approaches to allow more flexibility. Their working practices can be made tighter by using online templates or what is called Agile software methodology. This encourages the client to prioritize what they need to be produced and enables the programmers to focus on these aspects. If the priorities change, the code can be thrown away. But the client would still have to pay for the work as agreed. Traditional project management works by planning ahead and estimating the cost of the effort. The move away from this to clients paying for the work done even if it is then re-worked or ditched remains unclear under the adoption of the Agile work practices. Some planning and the equivalent of scoping does appear to take place in practice since the risks to the developer are too high if these are missed. (See Chapter 9 for more on these aspects.) It is important though for you to adjust the scoping phase of your project according to your own company's practices, including the use of Agile methods if these prevail. A WBS may not follow on naturally under these circumstances.

Responsibility matrix

Once you understand what is needed to develop the project and you have broken the project into tasks and sub-tasks, you'll be in a position to link the responsibility for pieces of the development to named people. Having a chart that shows responsibilities – and also accountability – for sections of the work gives an incentive to the people involved and shows you if there are any gaps or overlaps. Sometimes the balance of responsibilities between the project manager and a functional head of a section in an interactive company causes confusion and even rivalry.

If you chart the responsibilities, you may sort any potential muddle upfront. It usually comes down to which one is considered to have more authority in the company, and this can affect smooth production. Actually, it is the project manager who should have absolute authority over the project, the decisions made and accountability for them. The functional heads are responsible and accountable for the quality of the pieces of the project that they and their staff produce, and these pieces should be on time and within the budget they estimated. They serve the project needs and the projects drive the company's profitability. This insight about the authority of the project manager is often lacking in a company's structure and this is to its detriment. If your company does not recognize the absolute authority for a project by a project manager, and you now understand that this has caused internal problems, then perhaps it is time to have an internal debate about it. (See more about responsibility and authority in Chapter 4, on Stakeholders.)

There are many different ways of denoting responsibility in a matrix form, and you'll be able to find various examples. The example responsibility matrix here has been tailored to suit a pitch for work in response to a request for tender to rebuild a website.

Responsibility matrix (development process)

Project 21 Jumpstar (website rebuild/makeover)

		Responsibility							
		PM	DM	PrM	APM	TM	AcM	IA	PD
WBS	**Task Description** (Initials)	GN	KT	DD	SW	MF	JW	LR	VY
1.0	Initiation – analyse tender documents	P							
1.0.1	Decide to pitch or not. Inform Project Director X with reasons	S			S				P
1.1	Pitch – (if approved) – assemble pitch team	P	S	S		S	S		
1.1.1	Assignment of roles (graphics, programming, testing, QA, etc.)	P	S	S	Su	S	S	Su	
1.1.2	Liaise with prospective client if possible for clarity on points	P					Su		
	Pitch Development — Project Team Member Initials	**PM**	**xx**	**xx**	**xx**	**xx**	**xx**	**xx**	**PD**
2.0	Pitch team briefing – high-level scope and timing	P	Su	Su	S	Su	Su	Su	
2.1	Brainstorm ideas to suit brief	P	R	R	Su	R	R	R	
2.2	Decide way forward + timing + cost estimate	P	Su	Su	Su	Su	Su	Su	Su
2.2.1	Inform project director of way forward	P							Su
2.2.2	Liaise with prospective client to check on direction	P			Su		Su		
2.3	Response to tender document – prepare and get feedback	P	Su	Su	S	Su	Su	Su	Su
2.3.1	Revise, agree with project director and send off	P							Su
	If Short-listed								
3.0	Inform project director and the team, organize meeting	P	Su	Su	Su	Su	Su	Su	Su
3.1.0	Brief the team, indicate any changes in direction, revise schedule	P	Su	Su	S	Su	Su	Su	
3.1.1	Monitor pitch development of samples	P		S	Su				
3.1.1.1	Graphics production		P						
3.1.1.2	Interface and content analysis input							P	
3.1.1.3	Technical analysis					P			
3.1.1.4	Prepare company pitch response presentation	P			Su				Su
3.2	Pitch presentation rehearsal	P	R	R	S	R	R	R	Su
3.2.1	Revise presentation	P	R	R	Su	R	R	R	Su
	Pitch Presentation								
4.0	Give pitch	P	Su	Su	Su	Su	Su	Su	P*

P = Prime responsibility   R = Responsibility   S = Secondary responsibility
Su = Support responsibility
(P* = Prime responsibility and accountability to company and other directors)

PM = Project manager   DM = Design manager   PrM = Production manager
IA = Information architect   APM = Assistant project manager
TM = Technical manager   AcM = Account manager   PD = Project director

It uses a numbered breakdown of tasks as found if you use a project management package and are used to work breakdown structures. The roles have been defined according to a fictional company and may not represent the range of roles you have in yours. Also, the denoting of responsibility into Prime, Responsibility, Secondary and Support has been used to clarify relative positions and the way the fictional company wants to work. Probably the main things to note from the example are that:

- the project director has key decision-making and key event input but a supportive role otherwise;
- the project manager has the prime responsibility most of the time, but specialisms have definite responsibility when their input is needed;
- the equivalent of the functional heads/managers delegate to their nominated team representatives and have responsibility for the quality, time and cost tracking of their work according to the needs of the project;
- sometimes there are joint responsibilities, for example the project manager is responsible for the overall quality of a pitch and the readiness of the team to carry it out while the project director has responsibility and accountability to the other directors and the company as a whole for the result of the pitch.

Look at this responsibility matrix in terms of your own company and projects and adjust it accordingly.

Prince2 and scoping

If the client has used a Prince2 project manager as part of their internal procedures to assess their needs and business case at the initiation of the project, you may well be able to ask for the documents they have generated to help answer some of these queries. Remember that in overall Prince2 terms the project can include tasks carried out in the client company prior to the search for a developer. Alternatively, working directly with their project manager might speed up the process of answering the queries. They will have defined the communication paths and the involvement of the key people as well as quality assurance plans and user involvement. The key in this case would be to show how the level of detail you are asking for fits into the quality assurance planning and business needs. They will then see the need for the answers and should help you achieve them.

Summary

Accurate and detailed scoping is crucial to the success of the project irrespective of the size or cost. It is the client's responsibility to answer the questions a developer has so they can both arrive at a fair contract for work for a fair cost. As the features and facilities of interactive work increase and mature, the range of questions that are needed to define the scope of the work also increases.

At the end of this type of exercise, the developer should be able to indicate what work they will do at what quality level and for what cost. Any extra options that are offered to the client can have time and cost attached to them. This should set the pattern that if the client asks for more, or asks for changes, then the pieces of extra work will be evaluated according to time and cost and put forward for consideration to the client. It is at this negotiation stage that the developer should establish their preferred ways of working such as use of the change management process, the time, cost, quality method, sign-off authority, turn-around time commitments and so on. The scope then will encompass the stages of work to be done in a given time for an estimated cost. It will also define the working processes to be used around the development of the project.

Top Tips

Strategy	Potential pay-off
Refine and continue to refine your initial processes for scoping to become more efficient.	Better estimates of time and cost for development of a product to a known quality level.
Educate your client in the ways you will work – your project control factors – change management, sign-offs, turn-arounds, time/cost/quality relationship.	Less feature creep, better relationships, easier justification of extras = cash, smoother projects.
Establish the communication paths, or find out if they have been identified and established.	Improved communication with the right people at the right time. More efficient use of time.
If you are forced to start a project with too little information, make it clear and in writing exactly what you will do based on your present understanding, but that you will revise the schedule and costs according to further information in agreement with the client.	Sometimes you will be pushed into work earlier than you'd like for a variety of reasons. This approach will provide some insurance for things changing – as you know they will.
Involve the whole of your team and each of the specialist functions in establishing the information they need to estimate their work effort better.	Increased appreciation of what others are doing across the project and how their work impacts others. Improved teamwork, more efficient estimates, better WBS (Work Breakdown Structure).
Attention to detail during a project – extracted with a 'scoping questionnaire' – keeps you on top of the development process.	Credibility with all. Objective criteria to use for evaluation of success by all. Better projects.

Application Task

Developers

1. Use the copy of the scoping questionnaire with your colleagues/team. Ask them to refine it according to their experience and your company's needs. Then use it the next time you start a project and see if and how it makes a difference.

2. Keep refining the questionnaire after every project.

Commissioners

1. Apply the scoping questionnaire to yourselves. Are you ready to answer such questions from the developer? It will be useful for you to inform each internal contact of the type of queries that might be raised for interactive projects. If you understand the need and pre-empt it, you will save time and effort in your interactive projects later, you'll increase the quality threshold by giving better information to your developers and you will be able to recognize a fair quote for the amount of work.

● References/Resources

Scoping projects, D. Keith Robinson, 16th Nov. 2005
http://www.7nights.com/asterisk/archives05/2005/11/scoping-projects

10 bad project warning signs, blogography, Andy Budd, 31 May 2005
http://www.andybudd.com/archives/2005/05/10_bad_project_warning_signs/

General project management software/time tracking/WBS

Ablenet Solutions – collaborative software
http://www.ablenetsolutions.com

The Turbo Project Manager series – select under Other Utilities at
http://www.broderbund.com/

Enterprise-wide project management software

MJI Teamworks
http://www.mjiteamworks.com

Ace Project
http://www.aceproject.com/

Web Spaced Project – project management software list
http://www.web-based-software.com/project/

eProject
http://www.eproject.com

Review of top 10 project management software, 2006
http://project-management-software-review.toptenreviews.com/

Creative companies

Infowit
http://www.infowit.com/index.asp

Creative Project Manager
http://www.creative-manager.com/index.asp

● **Appendix: Scoping questionnaire**

Online client-centred project scoping questionnaire

Project internal and external contacts

Project name/no:

Contact details:

Client/Organization name:

Address:

Tel/Mobile: Fax: Email:

Website:

Project contacts:

Name(s):   Position(s):

Direct line: Mobile: Email:

Previous interactive media experience

Online

None ☐   A little ☐   Fair ☐   Good ☐   Experienced ☐

Mobile

None ☐   A little ☐   Fair ☐   Good ☐   Experienced ☐

iTV

None ☐   A little ☐   Fair ☐   Good ☐   Experienced ☐

Offline

None ☐   A little ☐   Fair ☐   Good ☐   Experienced ☐

Experience description

Online

Products: Producer:

Mobile

Products: Producer:

iTV

Products: Producer:

Offline

Products: Producer:

Client's initial statement of what they want

Online project type

Internet site (new) ☐   Hybrid (Web/DVD/CD/Mobile/iTV) ☐

Intranet ☐   Mobile ☐

Website Make-over ☐   Other (stipulate) ☐

Set up new facility

(If yes, domain name suggestions?)

Add/change existing facility

Market sector

Commercial ☐   Corporate ☐   Government ☐   Education/Training ☐

Advertising ☐   Marketing ☐   Entertainment ☐   Games ☐

Project content bias

	Importance ranking	Size of section (large, medium, small)
Company profile	☐	
Information gathering	☐	
Information dissemination	☐	
Retail (products or services description)	☐	
Database access/development	☐	
Marketing/advertising	☐	
Redesign site front end	☐	
Online transactions	☐	
Redesign site	☐	
Branding	☐	

Others (specify)

Functionality requested

Site personalization ☐

Registration ☐

Site search engine ☐

Profiling ☐

Content management system ☐

   Total ☐

   Partial ☐

Catalogue ☐

Survey/Quiz facilities ☐

Mapping/location identifier ☐

Newsletter/Online journal distribution ☐

RSS feeds ☐

Advertisement spaces ☐

E-commerce transactions ☐

■ Home country only ☐

■ International ☐

■ Including paid-for downloads ☐

Others (specify)

Client's database

None ☐   SQL flavour ☐   Access ☐   Other ☐

Server-side technology

PHP ☐   ASP ☐   Perl/CGI ☐

Other (specify)

Browser/platform expectations

Either:

Developer policy accepted i.e.

Development only for X browser and X versions on X platform   yes ☐   no ☐

Or:

Client wants:

Browser(s).

Versions supported:

Plug-ins.

Platform(s).

Allow Flash?   Yes ☐   No ☐

Allow Java?   Yes ☐   No ☐

Allow JavaScript?   Yes ☐   No ☐

Allow ActiveX?   Yes ☐   No ☐

Or:

Client does not know ☐

Client contact name for answers

               Tel:

             Email:

Site maintenance

Client to maintain:

You to maintain:

Search engine optimization

Client to organize:

You to organize:

Log analysis

Is this needed?

On server?

Client to do

You to do

If yes: How much is wanted? Subcontract to specialist company?

Benefits/achievements wanted

Not applicable   (Reason)

Through this application the organization wants to achieve:

1.

2.

3.

4.

5.

6.

7.

8.

The users of the site will benefit from or fulfil needs by:

1.

2.

3.

4.

5.

6.

7.

8.

If you were a user what search words/phrases might you use to locate the site?

Access and use

The audience/users   Access to what information

Internet

General public

Specific market sector(s)

(specify)

Intranet

Corporate/government/

education/other:

In-house (all)

Exec

Managers

Sales force

Other

Extranet

No. of sites to connect

Who will need access

(specify)

Emotional reaction considerations

Typical user reaction/first impression to main screen: Key adjective(s)

Re the company/organization represented

Re the content of the page

Typical user reaction to time spent on the site

Media mix

Client's media	None, wants suggestions		Animation	%
expectations	Text	%	Audio	%
	Graphics	%	Video	%

Content (existing assets)

Written   Contact:

Relevant databases   Spec: Contact:

Graphics/stills   Spec: Contact:

Audio   Spec: Contact:

Video footage   Spec: Contact:

Content experts   Contact:

Time for development

Client expectation   (months)   Start date

                                                    End date

Any fixed dates

(demos etc.)

To be specified in proposal

Special considerations

Database development/online transactions

Company specialist and extra questionnaire needed   yes ☐   no ☐

Client contact for this extra software analysis

                    Tel:

                    Email:

Dynamic pages required

Company server-side specialist and extra questionnaire needed   yes ☐   no ☐

Client contact for this extra server-side software analysis

                    Tel:

                    Email:

Testing strategy

Company standard (specify)

Focus groups

Usability testing

User trials

Stress/load testing

Other

Localization/Internationalization

Not needed

Needed (further analysis to be done)

Subcontract specialist company?

Accessibility factors

To what standard?

Standard developer accessibility package   yes ☐   no ☐

Special considerations requested (specify)   yes ☐   no ☐

Subcontract to specialist   yes ☐   no ☐

Security issues

Does the client's image or profile support a greater than usual risk of hacking?   yes ☐   no ☐

Is the client's web server's connection to Internet:

Direct ☐

Via firewall ☐

Is load testing required?   yes ☐   no ☐

Budget

£/$/€ approx

Budget holder: Position

Tel:

Email:

Project cost to be prepared and negotiated

Separate costs to be put forward for maintaining and updating

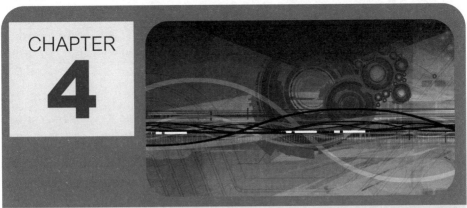

CHAPTER 4

Stakeholders and their influence

Industry Insight

Realize that when a development project fails, it's not necessarily due to the technology, but rather that all the people involved haven't been brought together in the right way to create and support the project. Stakeholder analysis is a way to identify and understand the needs and interests of people affected by a project.

Stakeholder analysis: perspectives on development, Amy Smith, Kurt Kornbluth, Prof. Mitch Resnick, MIT OpenCourseware Special Program 722, Session #4 Notes, Spring 2005

http://ocw.mit.edu/NR/rdonlyres/Special-Programs/SP-722Spring-2005/53C36AA3-9449-4D22-8250-9391CF0F43F1/0/lec_04.pdf

 Overview

Project management of the development of interactive projects has tended to concentrate on the production process and the efficient use of software tools that will aid production. Development managers are gradually understanding how wider project implications can have a real bearing on the success or failure of their projects. As the interactive sector matures, the production project management roles are blurring with traditional project management roles. These have had a wider remit of responsibilities. The initiation of a project and the identification of the people who can have an impact on a project – the stakeholders – have been part of that remit.

You may have to help win projects, deal with the clients directly and nurture the project to the production stage, or you may manage the project as it is carried out, or both. A lot will depend on how your role and responsibilities pan out in your present job. But even if your own role remains rooted in production, the project manager depends on inheriting a project from others in the interactive organization – such as account managers or directors. In this case you'll expect certain project parameters to have been tied down. By understanding the context of stakeholder analysis, you will be able to determine the situation and understand if you or the people around you – either in your own company or in your client's company – should use it to help stabilize the production process.

Stakeholders and interactive projects

So, what can we say about stakeholders? In a broad sense, the stakeholders are any people who can influence a project, and this influence can change according to the stages of the project. The IT manager in your client's organization, for example, can have strong influence at the implementation stage of a project, especially if the project needs to fit inside the organization and its infrastructure. If this IT manager has not been kept appraised and involved during the project initiation and development, it may prove difficult to work with them during implementation.

Exactly who the stakeholders are will depend on the project and the client. You need to understand how to identify stakeholders generally in order to be able to apply this to your specific projects. What you are trying to understand is the power, influence and interest of the various people. Power can be equated with authority and responsibility. These are often related to being a budget holder, but not always. Some people may have the authority to make decisions but may have to win budget approval from others in their organization. Others may have the authority to make decisions but may not clearly be held responsible or accountable for the outcomes.

'Authority' and 'budget holder' may be easier concepts for you to work with. You can immediately understand a situation where your client's representative, the person who has signed off all the stages of a project for you, suddenly turns round and explains that they don't actually have final sign-off authority but rather a committee does. You might feel gutted. The more people who have input on a stage, the more differences of opinion there will be, and the more changes there will be as a result. These are the things that we're trying to avoid by using stakeholder analysis. From the example, you can see that knowing the people who will be involved is the first stage. Checking if their power and influence can change during the project will keep you in a stronger position than if you don't check. Finally, understanding what to communicate to each of the key stakeholders becomes important so that they feel comfortable with the project and how it is progressing.

Stakeholders may come from wider sources than you'd immediately imagine, and you need to take all of them into account so that there are no surprises. If your client has a marketing section, and they will be involved in promoting the interactive product, they can have an impact on the success of the project. Their perspectives will need to be taken on board. In talking to them, it may become evident that they will not back anything that has not involved the users at several stages. Their stance may well be that they can only be successful and meet their own business targets if the products are easy to sell to the users. This will happen if the users have been involved in the design process so that the end product better matches their needs. So, from this example, the marketing perspective might have appeared to be significant only at the end of the project but, in reality, they have strong demands during all the development stages. What is better for your project: that the end product is stifled by the internal politics of your client company, never marketed properly and so is deemed a failure, or that the product has far greater user involvement and marketing backing so is marketed effectively and has a better chance of being successful? (See Chapter 8 for more on user requirements and Chapter 12 for more on marketing.)

Perhaps now you are beginning to get a feel for how important it is to identify the stakeholders in a project. It may be that doing this is more the responsibility of the couterpart manager you are dealing with in the client organization. They may already have done a stakeholder analysis as part of their own project management process and have decided who to keep informed and how. It will help you to know if this has happened so that you can use the information. Alternatively, the person who worked to win the project for your company – if this was not you – might have already carried out a client stakeholder analysis. Again, you need to know. It is better to cover it at some stage than not at all.

If your interactive company is large, you may need to consider stakeholders in your own company rather than just in that of your client. There may be several key internal stakeholders who can influence the progress of your project, from the production manager who will allocate resources, to the testing manager who may quality assure your product to client standards, and your own boss whose unconditional backing you'll need in order to establish and maintain your own authority. If your company is small, you may have the requisite power and influence to direct the project without interference from your colleagues.

Whichever analysis you feel applies to your situation – client stakeholder analysis or internal stakeholder analysis – there are several ways in which stakeholder analysis has been undertaken. The most common way is to work with your project colleagues:

- brainstorm who might be stakeholders on a project;
- make a list of these;
- use a matrix to analyse these for their power, influence and interest;
- put the people's initials in the respective boxes.

Don't be surprised if the stakeholder list is a long one. You will prioritize those that can have most impact on your project by using the grid matrix solutions outlined below. Also, don't forget to add a group that you feel may have an impact but who may not have a named contact. This might be something like 'users' or 'sales team'. Someone may need to represent their interests in your particular project. Proceeding with a representative might give the project a greater degree of success; proceeding without may cause problems due to internal politics later. This perspective might prompt a fruitful

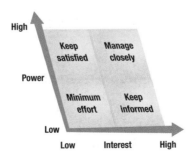

Power/interest grid for stakeholder analysis (client and own internal large organization)

discussion with your client's representative if he/she has not conducted a stakeholder analysis for their company and you are conducting the entire analysis.

From an interactive and a production management point of view, more readily applicable information might be yielded if this matrix used slightly different criteria about the client as in the following version.

Power/interest grid for stakeholder analysis (client from production perspective)

To interpret these, in the first matrix 'power' is seen as authority within the company and 'interest' means how the project will serve the person's own needs. If the project is not going to act as an aid to important figures of authority in the company, they may well take no interest in it and warrant little involvement. Alternatively it may be that while the project does not directly aid these people, it does act in the interests of and raise the profile of their colleagues. In this case, these authority figures may well perceive it to be in their interests to act against the project within their company. In other words, their 'interest' is high but negative. Some people have used colour coding to show if a person's position on the matrix is positive, negative or neutral to help decide how best to communicate with them and how often.

In the second production matrix, these perspectives of power and interest have been refocused to have more direct relevance to the production part of the project for the interactive media project manager. The people who control the release of money for the project and the people who can sign-off the various stages are crucial to the production. Anyone who can drive changes to the scope can also have a strong impact on production if they have influence over the sign-off and budget holders. So it is advisable to know who these people might be and what they might be thinking in order to understand the possible changes that might be requested. Forewarned is often forearmed in the production process.

● Who are the key stakeholders in the project?

In this way, the key stakeholders are those that you identify as having the strongest potential impact on the project – those high on both indicators of the matrix. As a result, you should concentrate your time and attention on these people. Remember that there may be both positive and negative people in the one box and you'll have to work harder with the negative ones to understand their concerns, try to accommodate them and steer them towards being neutral.

Where one factor is high but the other is lower, these people have less influence. But the biggest danger to you is non-payment, so you may tend to give any budget holders in this category more weighting in how you choose to deal with them. If there are many people who could put forward changes that would impact the project, you should have a change management process in place and make sure that they are all made aware of it. Then they will have to follow the process in order to agree the changes and get the budget and any extra time attached to them, and it will be easier to control them. If you have not put a change management process in place from the initial discussions and agreements (see previous chapters and Chapter 5 for change management), this exercise should demonstrate more than most why it is essential to have one. Without one, you are allowing many people the chance to have an uncontrolled impact on the project.

Although the last group, who score low on both indicators, appear to have little chance of impact, they can still try to influence others around them and might emerge as a stronger influence than you'd imagined. This is why it is important to revise the stakeholder analysis during the project to reflect any increased intelligence you have, and the stage of the project you have reached, since both of these can change the stakeholder mapping. You don't want to be caught out.

● Authority and responsibility

Where does an interactive media project manager stand in terms of authority and responsibility? This becomes complicated depending on the type of project and how it was initiated. If you are working with a project manager in the client company, then it is more their responsibility to have identified the stakeholders in their company and assessed the degree and type of influence that they possess. This client project manager can be very useful to you since it is in his/her interests to keep the project running smoothly and the right people in touch with progress. The client project manager should be able to help you reach the right people at the right time and either explain how to influence them, or influence them on your behalf.

But if you do not have the equivalent of a client project manager and work with just a nominated contact, then you may need to put in time and effort to try and understand the power hierarchy of the client's company, identify the stakeholders and communicate the project's progress to them. It is possible that none of the project management procedures and processes for project initiation have been carried out and you may have to try and rectify this to get a grip on the project. If there isn't a high-level project champion, a clear business case for the project, the right mix of key people involved and so on, you are in for a rough ride. Try to sort these out as soon as possible in order to make the directions for project success clearer.

You may also have to identify the stakeholders, their responsibilities and communication needs for your own company if it is medium to large and has the equivalent of a hierarchy. That's why, if you can work in partnership with the equivalent of the project manager in the client company, your role should be smoother. Perhaps the first matrix type might suit you better for an internal company matrix. You will need to adjust the matrix and the criteria according to your circumstances.

● RACI responsibility chart

Another tool that might help you is the RACI responsibility chart. If you have looked at the responsibility matrix from Chapter 3, Page 68, for the project management team, you will understand that the one used here is for the higher-level management functions across a company. You'll see that the way the type of responsibility is denoted has changed. Here there is a greater emphasis on accountability since this, more than just responsibility, is what drives people in a company. There is also an emphasis on the type of communication – inform, consult – that serves to keep the right people on board at the right time.

The example matrix here assumes that your account manager has landed this project via an established contact and the contract has been won. At this point the account manager is passing the development of the project to the project development team in your company. It is hoped that the initial scoping was carried out by the account manager with input from the project director and whatever input from the other managers was needed to agree to the cost of the proposed work. Projects arrive at development from different sources as we have seen, so it is feasible that the project manager has just become involved and is establishing this matrix as part of sorting out the parameters. The development team needs to be established. The functional managers agree who will be available for the team. Your company may not have all the roles that are used here. You'd need to adjust the chart accordingly and decide how the roles you do have would deal with responsibility, accountability, consultation and the need to inform.

With this as background, note the following to help your interpretation of the chart.

- The account manager is accountable for the parameters as he/she has had most to do with landing the project. At this point the responsibility for development is being passed to the project manager.
- The production manager becomes responsible for the scheduling of the work with the team members, but the project manager is accountable for the work being performed and so should be actively involved rather than leaving it to the production manager.
- Often the role of consulting then informing people of the outcomes is a pattern of communication designed to keep people involved and up to date.
- The project manager has most responsibility and, even if the main responsibility passes to a specialist for a particular development stage, the project manager is accountable for the work being done to time and standard.
- In this case, the role and responsibilities of the account manager are clearly not related to the development work. But when the project involvement overlaps with the client at key stages, the account manager does have responsibilities.
- The project manager needs to keep the project director informed since he/she will ultimately be held accountable by the client for the work at the key cost points, and they will expect top management involvement if there are any problems. Equally, the project team needs to know that this level of support is present if required.

RACI matrix

Project 25 ChillZone (specialist e-commerce site)

Task Description (initials)	Client CC	PS	PD	Developer PM	PrM	DM	TM	AcM	IA	QAM
Project meeting (post contract award)	C,I	C,I	C,I	C,I	C,I	C,I	C,I	R	C,I	C,I
Establish project parameters from brief				R				A		
Managers nominate team members	C	I	R	C	C	C	C	C	C	C
Refine schedule and milestones		I	I	A	R	C	C	C	C	C
Establish team with kick-off meeting	I		I	R					C	
Set up project working website	C		I	C	C		R			
Establish online contact information points (client + internal)			I	R						
Inform all concerned	I	I	I	R	I	I	I	I	I	I
Begin development work	I		I	A	R	C	C	I	C	I
Establish working practices	C,I	I	I	R	I	I	I	C,I	I	C,I
Post specific work in progress for client comments	I		I	R	C	C	C	I	C	C
Set up meetings of client specialists and own team specialists to refine scope	C,I	I	I	R	I	I	I	C,I	I	I
Testing ready for 1st milestone				A	C	C	C	I	C	R
Delivery of 1st milestone of project (1 week turn-around)	C	C	A	R	C	C	C	C	C	C
Sign-off 1st milestone	R	I	I	A	I	I	I	C,I	I	I

R = Responsible   A = Accountable   C = Consulted   I = Informed

CC = Client contact   PS = Project sponsor   PD = Project director
PM = Project manager   DM = Design manager   PrM = Production manager   IA = Information architect   TM = Technical manager
AcM = Account manager   QAM = Quality assurance manager

You will have to adjust this to suit your company, the way that you work and the roles that you have. This should indicate the gist of what a RACI matrix can offer, but it has to be tailored to work for each project.

If your client project manager has done an equivalent RACI matrix in the client company, you might be able to help each other in the communication process. You may find that you can work together on monthly progress reports for both his/her management and your own, saving time for both of you because you each write contributory pieces. If you have to work alone across both companies at project management level and keep all informed, you may well have had to increase the numbers of project management hours expected for the project.

● What form of communication is best?

The action words inside the boxes of the stakeholder analysis grid – closely, satisfied, etc. – demonstrate how much time and effort you might need to put into the communication process but do not indicate how often or what type of information to give the stakeholders. The RACI chart will give some more guidance but, in the end, you'll need to get agreement from the stakeholders from both companies on how they wish to be informed and how frequently they want to be kept in touch concerning the project status. This needs further analysis and is particularly applicable for interactive projects, since the number of ways to keep people informed has expanded precisely because of the use of technologies. However, what is natural and comfortable for you may not be so for others. Some clients prefer phone conversations backed up by emails with attachments. Others prefer printed copies faxed through. Whatever system each stakeholder prefers, you should try to match. Internally you might have to conform to a company standard of documentation for the project, your team and the extended project team.

Communication chart

Stakeholder	Type	Format	Frequency	Method
Client				
Client main contact + suggestion list	Progress status report	Pro-forma summary generated from online headings	Weekly summary of team's online status	Email + Word attachment as agreed
	Issues + resolutions	Minutes of meeting	Fortnightly meeting	Face-to-face
	Status report	Summary, key points, outcomes, progress, changes and budget extras, graphs and charts where appropriate	Monthly – end of month	Email PDF attachment
Client's project board	Status report	Summary, key points, outcomes, progress, changes and budget extras, graphs and charts where appropriate	Monthly – end of month	Email PDF attachment

Internal				
Project director	Status report	Summary, key points, outcomes, progress, changes and budget extras, graphs and charts where appropriate	Monthly – end of month.	Email PDF attachment
	On-going	As per enterprise-wide project system	Access to online real-time status	Online project web space
	Issues report	Minutes of meeting with client rep	Post client meeting fortnightly + oral update at weekly meeting	Email + Word attachment as agreed
Functional managers	Status report	Summary, key points, outcomes, progress, changes and budget extras, graphs and charts where appropriate	Monthly – end of month	Email PDF attachment
	On-going	As per enterprise-wide project system for management	Access to online real-time status	Online project web space
Project team	Progress status	As per enterprise-wide project system for team	Access to online real-time status	Online project web space
	On-going	As per enterprise-wide project system section	Access to issues reports (copies online)	Online project web space
Other stakeholders				
Finance director	Financial report	Summary, key points, outcomes, progress, changes and budget extras, graphs and charts where appropriate	Monthly	Email PDF attachment
	On-going	As per enterprise-wide project system for management	Access to online real-time status + timesheets	Online project web space
Testing subcontractor	Briefing document	Follow in-house document template headings	Month prior to starting work	Email + Word attachment
	Progress status	Pro-forma summary generated from online headings	Weekly summary of online status when work starts	Email + Word attachment
Marketing subcontractor	Briefing document	Follow in-house document template headings	Month prior to starting work	Email + Word attachment
	Progress status	Pro-forma summary generated from online headings	Weekly summary of online status when work starts	Email + Word attachment

This chart is an example of how some of the main forms of communication might be defined for a project with a main client, a developer and a couple of subcontractors. The developer company is relatively large and has an enterprise-wide project management system that they have tailored to suit their practice. As far as possible, they try to use template reporting for the various people and their needs to minimize admin time and effort. The real-time processing of the work data (timesheets, tasks under development, progress, issues, changes in scope and extra budget agreements) in the system frees the project manager from processing the data and allows a good overview of the project by the management. These systems are becoming more widely used in interactive media now, but they are not currently the norm. We have used the example here to demonstrate how potentially useful they can be if they suit the working practices.

The communication chart tries to capture the main means of keeping clients and a developer company informed throughout the project. These are not meant to be the only methods since the client contact and the project manager will have frequent phone calls or meetings not listed here, and the project manager will see the members of the team daily. But the chart ensures a minimum communication system that everybody understands. It is not necessary to show the whole chart to the clients as they might decide that they would like real-time online access to see the progress on a daily basis. You may not be ready for that, although some companies do allow this for long-standing clients who know and agree the work processes and have a good partnership approach to project management.

Many companies are now finding that taking a common approach to documenting projects makes sense. The project manager is responsible for creating a project file (probably in both electronic and print versions) of the key points, changes in scope, time, cost, agreements, budget, reports, emails, attachments, records of communication and so on, so that they can archive the project clearly at the end. Equally, the functional managers may be responsible for recording and archiving their section's contributions to a project both electronically and in print. This makes it easier for other teams and other members of staff to pick up the project later for a re-work or make-over. It also helps for other teams to know what has been done in one project that might help in another project of a similar type – given that the end results need to be clearly different and unique for each client. But, increasingly, the portability of pieces of code and web design templates is allowing re-work of this nature and leading to faster and cheaper production. Previous work is of no use if it hasn't been well documented according to a known system and isn't accessible to the other members of staff when needed. Don't forget that some of this documentation may be in the code itself in the form of comments.

Essentially, it is up to you and your company to define the working practices regarding the range, frequency and type of communication that happens in a project. The communication chart might prompt some thinking around this and could figure as a tool for you if it fits. For the client, it is reassuring to know that agreed written documents will reach a named set of people at a certain time and frequency. This alone makes you look more professional and on top of the project's progress.

Industry Insight 2

As a final point about stakeholders, it is important for a project manager's morale to remember that it is essentially impossible to please all the stakeholders all the time... Project managers need to forget the idea of maximizing everyone's happiness and concentrate instead on maintaining satisfactory relations that allow them to do their job with a minimum of external interference.

Lessons for an accidental profession, Jeffrey Pinto and Om Kharbanda in *The Human Side of Managing Technological Innovation*, page 186, 2nd edn, edited Ralph Katz, OUP New York, 2004

Summary

Stakeholders influence the progress and outcome of a project. They need to be identified and involved in the project in ways that suit them. Because there can be many people who are stakeholders across the life-span of the project, you need to rank the attention the key stakeholders want from you so that you can make best use of your time and effort. Using a stakeholder analysis grid to define your client might help in interactive projects. It maps the power to pay for the work versus the power to change aspects of the project.

The interactive project manager can be at a disadvantage in applying stakeholder analysis to a client precisely because he/she is an outsider. Ideally, stakeholder analysis would be done by the client's own project manager, and the interactive project manager would apply it internally in the developer company. A RACI matrix that maps responsibility, accountability, consultation need and information need may be a useful tool to apply here.

If both halves of the stakeholder analysis have been completed, then it is important to set up clear forms of communication between all the interested parties in a form that fits their needs. Communication charts may help decide on the type, format, frequency and method of communication that each stakeholder might prefer from a selection offered by the project manager. These ensure that the stakeholders will be kept involved and informed; they build trust and confidence in the project process and can smooth the production paths to a successful project.

Top Tips

Strategy	Potential pay-off
Check if your client's representative has done a stakeholder analysis for his/her company.	Saves you time and effort. Swap information to help each other with the control processes and lead to smoother production paths.
Carry out a stakeholder analysis for the project for your own company and the client's if necessary.	You need to know who the 'influencers' in the project are from both companies to pre-empt difficulties.
Make sure you line up with the people in the client's company that have the authority and responsibility for the project development.	You all want the project to succeed and will help each other. Saves misplaced time and effort.
In interactive projects the budget holders and the stakeholders who can change the scope of the project are key stakeholders to define.	Saves re-work time and effort and cost if you satisfy the budget holders who have the most authority over the other stakeholders. Their decisions are difficult to over-throw and should reflect what the majority wanted anyway.
Revisit the stakeholder analysis because the relative power and influence changes over the course of a project according to its stage.	No surprises. You are on top of the dynamics and can take appropriate steps to keep the right people fully involved.
Define the range and type of communication you will use with the client's stakeholders and internally with your own company.	Clear communication paths. You look professional and organized. Inspires confidence in the project – so don't let it slip!

Application Task

If you have not used them already, apply the tools used here to one of your current projects:

● stakeholder analysis matrix

● RACI matrix

● communication chart.

What insights do they give you into the communication process?

What insights do they give you about your current work processes?

Will they be useful for your company/projects for the future or not?

References/Resources

Books

Katz, R., ed. (2004), *The Human Side of Managing Technological Innovation*, 2nd edn, New York, USA: Oxford University Press.

Horine, G.M. (2005), *Absolute Beginner's Guide to Project Management*, Indianapolis, IN, USA: Que Publishing.

Web links

Ask these questions to reach your stakeholders, Lauri Elliott, TechRepublic, 14 Nov. 2001
http://techrepublic.com.com/5100-10878-1048762.html

Stakeholder analysis, Will Allen and Margaret Kilvington, Landcare Research New Zealand, Nov. 2001
http://www.landcareresearch.co.nz/research/social/stakeholder.asp

Communicate with project stakeholders, Jeffrey F. Barager, Point B Solutions Group, Microsoft Office Online, Work Essentials, no date given
http://office.microsoft.com/en-us/FX011466281033.aspx

Project Management Part 2 – stakeholders, Walter Storm, Nitron, The Code Project, 24 June 2005
http://www.codeproject.com/gen/design/ProjectMgmt_Pt2.asp

2.2 Project Stakeholders. A Guide to the Project Management Body of Knowledge – derivative developed and reproduced by the Project Management Institute, TenStep Inc., 2003–4
http://www.tensteppb.com/2.2ProjectStakeholders.htm

Stakeholder analysis and stakeholder management, Rachel Manktelow, Mind Tools, no date given
http://www.mindtools.com/pages/article/newPPM_07.htm

Understanding organizational stakeholders for design success, Jonathan Boutelle, boxesandarrows, 5 June 2004
http://www.boxesandarrows.com/view/understanding_organizational_stakeholders_for_design_success

What is the stakeholders' bargain with the project? Susannah Finzi, Suzanne Robertson, Aidan Ward, The Atlantic Systems Guild Inc., no date given
http://www.systemsguild.com/GuildSite/Stakebargain.html

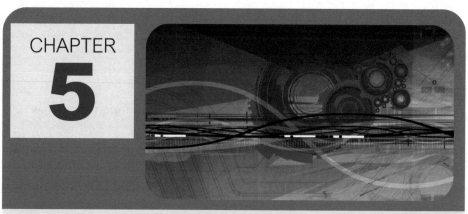

CHAPTER 5

The client/developer partnership approach to projects

Industry Insight

Every good client relationship must be built on some basic understandings or agreements between client and contractor. Start with these:

- *The client has value to me, in the form of opportunity to work.*
- *I am valuable to the client, in the form of the goods & services that I can provide.*
- *As a contractor, I have financial and professional goals which I am committed to achieving.*
- *The client has financial and professional goals which he/she is committed to achieving.*
- *Both contractor and client are responsible for their own business and achieving their own goals. This responsibility extends to being respectfully assertive and communicative when those interests are being negatively affected.*

Client relationship management, Pat McClellan, Director Online, 9 August 1999
http://director-online.com/buildArticle.php?id=358

Overview

It should be becoming clear that developers need a good deal of information to help them structure a project to satisfy the needs of their client. Then, during the development process, each side should follow an agreed set of processes or protocols to ensure smooth progress. In the end, the developer should be able to demonstrate to their client how they have followed the brief to produce the interactive application that meets the defined business needs. This seems clear and makes sense, but it is difficult to achieve. This chapter offers advice to make this easier.

● The project's 'business case'

This is an area that has been shunned in the past for many reasons:

- it is complex;
- the developer expects the clients to know their own business and be able to frame a project in business and technological terms to suit the development process;
- the client feels that the developer has the knowledge about the technology and that they should use this to understand the business in question and give the best solution to solve the business problem;
- often, the project's business case has been ignored or ill-formed;
- neither client nor developer knows where to start.

This isn't completely surprising since both are often moving into uncharted territory. There can be an overlap between developing interactive projects and introducing innovation into a business. Innovation and business parameters frame a project in an intangible, more qualitative direction, whereas using technology to solve defined business problems leads to more quantitative measures and several recognized ways of forming a business case. Even this can become muddled since different industry sectors have their own preferred ways of conducting business cases – e-learning, online charities and interactive advertising, for example. The type of project can affect the type of business case so that there are differences between business to business (B2B), business to consumer (B2C) and consumer to consumer (C2C) projects, particularly when you consider how a project pays for itself in the long term: subscriptions, purchase, advertising for example. Also, a client's company can have its own in-house approach to defining a business case for all its projects. There is no set answer.

It is easier to understand that things like changing the communications infrastructure inside an international company through the introduction of an intranet, or changing the business process of corporate offline sales to allow online sales, or even introducing an e-learning management system into an organization, are large infrastructure changes and large business change management programmes in their own right. They demand big budgets and careful business cases for traditional companies. They alter fundamental business processes, and your client is more likely to have made a business case internally to win the budget. They may have asked you to help explain the benefits that aspects of technology can bring and have built this into their business case.

Smaller interactive projects for companies, or perhaps relatively small additions or changes to an existing online interactive process – like a website make-over or move to online sales from an online information catalogue – these seemingly have fewer risks and lower budgets. Often there may be little incentive from either side to make a real business case.

However, this does not mean that with these types of project each side can bury its head and pretend that they are doing the project for its own sake. Since the 'dot com' debacle many traditional businesses have been nervous of digital technology and the hype that they assume surrounds it. This now means that when people in a traditional business put forward an idea for a technology project, they are often pressed to justify the cost to the business just as they have had to for non-technology projects.

Justifying costs in business terms is usually done through developing a cost/benefit analysis and looking at the return on investment (ROI).

Some companies need to prove the ROI over a defined period of years and quantify the profit margins expected after the pay-back period. Other companies use a different investment appraisal format to identify all costs and evaluate the full cost recovery. TCO, which stands for 'total cost of ownership', is a common acronym. This includes the costs of hardware, software, support, professional services and on-going administration of the system, among other things, but it hasn't proved a good indicator for high-technology projects.

There are various ways of working out the ROI so you need to see if your client uses one method in preference to another. In general, it is true that figures can be re-worked to help make a case or not – by delaying the kick-in of some costs until a later stage of the project, or by phasing the pay-back over stages, or by trialling it with a key group before general roll-out so that it has a smaller but faster initial impact. You have to know what you are doing and the factors cannot just be manipulated without a sound cost basis. Involve your business analyst if you have one or take advice if you are placed in a situation of making a business case without the requisite knowledge and skills. The business case solution for emerging technologies begins with a solid evaluation of the client's business processes, their business environment and the contribution that a proposed solution can make to the business objectives they consider important.

If you want a starting position, an ROI might be formed from some key indicators.

- Breadth of use of the application/main tasks – the numbers of people that will be affected by it inside and outside the organization, since the greater the number the greater the ROI.

- Repeatability – how often will the application/main tasks be used or seen, since the greater the use the bigger the ROI.

- Cost of performing the same tasks without the application.

- Re-use of the knowledge/content/structure/templates in the application, since the greater the re-use the greater the potential ROI.

- Communication – whether the application improves the communication between people in the client's company and with their customers or equivalent. Communication is usually costly, so the greater the increased collaboration or communication, the greater the potential ROI.

- Usability – ease of use for all and customer satisfaction improve interactive application use and task completion among others. (See Chapter 8 on Usability and accessibility including ROI factors.)

These indicators might help with your particular project and your client, but they might not help if the client is looking for other indicators or is unsure which indicators make sense to them for this type of project. There is no blanket approach worked out yet that everyone accepts for e-projects. A marketing perspective drives other business needs in terms of the technology solution, increasing customers, sales, leads, brand image, place in the market and recognition, for example. (See Chapter 12 for more on this perspective and its impact.)

It is important for you as a developer to know if a business case has been made and won inside your client's organization prior to you winning the development phase of the project. The projected benefits or return that won the project budget in-house will be the core of the business' evaluation used as a measure of success for what you produce. You need to know this and be sure to line up with it.

On the other hand, if you as the developer are expected to demonstrate the worth of your proposed development to the client, it will help if you use the business processes and terms that they understand. Alternatively you could explain why you use the process you use. It is often raised as a criticism by clients that the developer does not understand the client's business and so does not realize the full potential benefits for the business by matching the technology and its functionality to the business goals. From the developer's point of view, they often feel that the client cannot or does not answer their questions about the needs of the project in e-business terms. This lack of clear communication lies at the heart of any impasse between them.

In your first attempt to understand the client's business, perhaps you should ask questions about the type of data the senior management uses to make decisions about investment spending or budget allocation to projects. You need to recognize that this is how projects are viewed and budgets won or lost for that particular client. The definition of a business case we'll use here is:

> *A business case sets out the information needed to enable a manager to decide whether to support a proposed project, before significant resources are committed to its development. The core of the business case is an assessment of the costs and benefits of proceeding with a project.*

Victorian Government Purchasing Board: Glossary
www.vgpb.vic.gov.au/CA256C450016850B/0/073B1893942AC1C9CA256C5C0006AC1D

Notice that this doesn't mention anything about the use of technology to implement the project. In high-level management terms, it is irrelevant what a project is about or what it utilizes; the management may only be concerned with the cost, the pay-back and the time to ROI. This might help explain why some clients don't appear to care about the technology or even want to understand it. Developers do find this daunting since they themselves are driven by and committed to interactivity through various technology platforms. But if you speak in business terms, the business benefits should be placed upfront, with the technology implementation aspects supporting the business assertion. This may become clearer for you by looking at the business benefits table later in the chapter.

The business case definition used here shows us strongly where clients' priorities might lie. But we also need to take account of the following too:

> *A business case is a reasoned argument for a recommended change, considered against the 'do nothing' status quo. A well-argued business case can help convince senior management, finance officers and elected members of the need for change and the consequences of inaction.*

Information sheet 13 Making a Business Case
www.defra.gov.uk/environment/waste/localauth/practice-guidance/pdf/infosheet13.pdf

Considering the 'doing nothing' position can work well for winning e-projects. You can use the example of a company that is too late adopting an e-business approach and misses the opportunity to win a large segment of a market. Banks and insurance companies that entered the online market late have found it hard to win online market share and have found that they lost a proportion of their traditional customers to online facilities because these saved them time and money but were only available through a rival company. Early technology adopters can suffer from the opposite problem where they are ahead of their potential customers, and the market struggles until enough people have access and awareness of the services. From this you might gauge that early adopters might need a longer pay-back equation for the initial investment. It all comes down to client expectations and how these are managed in the project process. Amazon is often cited as the leader in online retail. It got in early, 1995, but did not start making a profit until late 2001. Its early dominance of its market sector has resulted in it developing a complete online channel branding and image that many others now aspire to.

Here is not the place to explain the ins and outs of making business cases for your work since the complexity, including matrices and models, would need a book in itself. We want you to understand some of the main concepts and take them on board to help with your projects. It is important you recognize that addressing the business case is an expected part of projects. So whether your client has already made the case and won the budget, or you find you are expected to make a business case despite the client having the budget already, understanding the wider process of making business cases for your e-projects is important.

If the client has not already made a business case, or the business case does not ring true for e-projects, you may need almost to back-track at the stage you become involved. You'll need to lock down some strong business benefits to work towards and cost into the development. A business case that you are comfortable with needs to be put in place, preferably before the development work starts. Then you can develop in the knowledge that you'll be able to prove the business benefits to your clients. This is not as unobtainable as you might first imagine and it will give you more credibility with your clients as well as with your colleagues. The marketing perspective can help here. Using it to assess the client competitors, to analyse the use of technology (client's website logs perhaps) and users' wishes can give a strong measurable baseline from which to work. You'll be able to define where you'll improve the service, how and why, in terms that will make sense to the client. (See more on this approach in Chapter 12.)

● How to talk in business terms

Industry Insight 2

You are not working on interactive media-based ... solutions, you are working on interactive media-based business solutions – and that requires an altogether different approach and mindset.

Bob Little, Interview for Managing Interactive Media, May 2006 – see full text at www.pearsoned.co.uk/england

In decision-making, business people are primarily interested in business benefits, their costs and the returns expected within a specified timeframe. Even when we are innovating with new technology and new functionality in a new market space, there are arguments that make more business sense than others as in the 'cost of doing nothing' examples given above. But as soon as we have quantifiable data about a market and the likely behaviour of the businesses' customers, we can base our arguments on that.

The trick is to understand what makes sense to your client in business terms and what also serves you so that you can demonstrate that you have achieved the business benefits you have stated. There are several key areas that make sense to any business, and these are captured in the table overleaf. You need to use these and decide how you can shape the development you offer to fit some of these business issues. It will get easier to do this project by project, and gradually you'll define what benefits fit which project type and which market sector. Notice the active verbs that tend to start the points and imagine how you can use them and tailor them to suit your own projects and the businesses you serve. Do not promise benefits you can't fulfil. The table is generic and some of these benefits apply to one type of project more than another so you can't promise all of them.

The statements in the table should immediately have an impact on you. They address business areas that all businesses relate to, including your clients. They make business sense. If you use this approach, your clients will notice the difference. However, you will only be convincing if you match your technology solution to some of the business outcomes in the table. This is where your expertise, your market segment, your project parameters and your clients will affect how you intend to achieve these business outcomes.

Some people refer to hard and soft benefits. The hard data can usually be measured and accounted for in financial terms. Soft data include more intangible benefits such as happier customers, global presence and better competitive edge among other things. Even if some of your benefits are 'soft', many clients will consider these vital for their businesses. Soft benefits can usually be demonstrated in tangible ways; it just takes longer to trap and analyse the data in order to make the case. However, it is often difficult to show that the effect relates solely to your application. The client will be used to that and tolerate it because, overall, soft benefits make a deal of difference to their company despite the poor track record of definition. Soft benefits can make more sense with using the 'cost of doing nothing' scenario. Often it can be a good idea to contrast the present company processes and their operation against those proffered by the project, and to analyse the competition and see what they are doing. This contrast can help make your case stronger too.

The business case is like the 'objectives' for the project, and the better objectives are framed the more measurable they are. If you can state some points for your project beginning with the type of action verbs listed here, you should follow through by imagining how this will be brought about – often made easier through using 'by' as your prompt. For example, 'we'll increase this BY doing this and gathering this, so that we can be better informed and make informed decisions faster'.

Over time you'll learn which triggers work better for which clients and their related market sector. If the client is in manufacturing, then improving processes, production efficiency and time to market may be the strong business triggers. If the client is in retail, then improving sales, improving the real shopping experience by online stock-checking and reserving before going to the shop or such like, generating solid leads, offering new experiences and giving access to better sales/marketing data may be the triggers.

Generic Business Benefits for e-projects utilizing interactive media components

People	Processes	Technology	Design	Business	Marketing	Infrastructure
Increase skills	Centralize core services	Reduce on-going support costs	Increase the time users spend on the site through readability of content	Create new revenue streams	Improve branding	Decrease facilities and management costs
Increase span of responsibility	Reduce transaction/business function processing time	Increase reliability and quality	Increase task completion/sales through clear layout	Increase productivity and user performance	Improve image	Enable incremental changes at lower cost
Reduce headcount	Eliminate replicated tasks	Reduce complexity by streamlining	Improve/add to company's image through appropriate use of media techniques	Increase lead conversions	Improve market position – by competitor, SEO and log analysis	Increase scalability, flexibility and agility
Reduce salary costs	Minimize errors/re-work	Lower future development costs	Increase the time and use of users through media techniques	Increase return business	Increase customer satisfaction and loyalty	Enable enterprise-wide solutions that streamline processes
Increase professionalism and motivate staff	Standardize processes	Drive business decisions through web log analysis	Attract and retain people through media techniques	React faster to business changes	Segment customers in new ways (niche markets) to sell more or allow better uptake	Improve digital asset management supply chain
Empower staff to be proactive through better information flow	Implement best practice standards	Web analytics allow better customer information	Meet accessibility criteria to increase use to new people	Increase efficiency	Allow the opportunity to create customer communities	Enable online surveys and other two-way communication capture
Focus time on critical tasks/revenue generation	Shorten product development	Increase people's access to the business offerings	Faster selection for users through clear navigation paths	Create new business opportunities	Capture better and more useful feedback from customers – web analytics	Open up company-wide communication
Create learning opportunities and records through a centralized resource	Avoid costs from unnecessary re-work	Increase traffic by optimizing metadata and search terms	Enhance customer/user experience and satisfaction	Distribution of consistent content/messages on demand	Establish a global presence with 24/7 service	Integrate electronic systems to streamline admin processes

Generic Business Benefits for e-projects utilizing interactive media components *continued*

People	Processes	Technology	Design	Business	Marketing	Infrastructure
Strengthen business relationships	Speed up review and sign-off across the necessary people	Lower costs for future platforms and updates if programmed for interoperability	Increase web page use – enhance the content through 'stickiness' analysis	Reduce costs of development and content production	Shorten time to product launch or marketing campaign	
Decrease customer support costs	Improve collaboration between people	Lower maintenance time and costs	Increase user interest by expanding content that shows in site entry statistics	The cost of doing nothing will have a negative impact on the business	Take faster advantage of emerging market opportunities	
	Increase production and efficiency by re-using centralized knowledge store	Reduce development time	Redesign common web exit pages to retain users longer	Improve partner relationships	Completion of meaningful tasks online faster than offline	
	Reduce operational costs		Expand the use of the site to less used features	Provide 24/7 global service	Enable customers to research products online before buying offline	
	Increase access to information		Decrease user errors and use of help/ support features	Reach more potential customers including users with disabilities	Demonstrate social responsibility through meeting legal and policy requirements	
				Reduce risk of legal action through meeting legal and policy requirements	Validate advertising campaigns through log analysis and/or ad server statistics	
				Monitor and improve web log statistics for unique visitors, stickiness, conversion rates, etc.	Increase market understanding through log analysis	
				Increase site traffic		

The benefits table headings will help direct you towards making the business case for your particular project. They indicate key functions that all businesses use. If you can demonstrate how your project lines up with these business functions your case will get stronger. You may not use them all – the infrastructure column is only applied when your project includes introducing infrastructure changes/additions to the client's technology mix. Introducing an e-learning management system as well as developing or sourcing some e-learning courses has impact on the client's interactive infrastructure, for example, whereas developing a specific bespoke e-learning training course will line up with other columns but not infrastructure.

In many ways, this chapter is about relationships between clients and developers. If you become good at establishing a business case that the clients relate to, don't be surprised if they ask you to explain and demonstrate how you have achieved these benefits for past clients. This will be key to them deciding to trust you. So consider your business success track record carefully and be prepared to back up your present claims to bolster your credibility.

 Development process controls

Once your client or yourselves have made the business case successfully enough to win the budget for your project, you'll have clear ideas of how your efforts will be evaluated in business terms at the end of the project. Now you just have to develop the goods. The development process for interactive media demands a structured approach from all involved while allowing the creative, technological and innovative aspects to flourish in the appropriate ways to serve the business needs. It is this balance between structure and creativity that is problematic to achieve. Without a structured approach chaos and client/developer misunderstanding are more likely and the development is more likely to falter.

Time, cost quality equation and project management

If you get just a few core processes in place that define the general working arrangements between you and the client, this will keep you on an easier path to successful completion. After all, successful projects are the result of successful partnerships. You need one another to succeed. The most important process to agree is your project management approach. This will give both of you a defined, professionally endorsed way of working with each other that works to mutual advantage. It operates at a high level, defining the boundaries of the project and indicating what lies inside the project scope and what, therefore, is outside the scope. The project is defined for all in terms of the time it will take, how much it will cost and what the product will do. This is the **Time, Cost, Quality** equation that lies at the heart of the project management process. The scoping questionnaire process outlined in Chapter 3 helps you arrive at the firm cost and time estimate. It is accepted here that the project also addresses a sound business case that was developed internally by your clients prior to you being involved, or that you have tried your best over the scoping phase to identify and line up with key business directions.

Time, cost, quality

You arrive at the equation by assessing what resources (including internal staff and maybe external contractors) you'll need and how much time they estimate it will take them to complete the set tasks to reach defined phases in the project (milestones). You also need to build in time for communication across the client and the team as well as admin involved with project management and general management. You'll need to assess how many project assets (graphics, music, photos, etc.) you'll produce to achieve the project phases and whether these will need licensing or sourcing from others, or will be developed through the people you've identified.

Each person should have an hourly or daily rate attached to them so that the cost can be worked out against the time estimated for the people. In a larger company there will be accepted rates for charging for people. The daily rate for a person is usually calculated from their salary, allowing for weekends and holidays, any taxation due by employing them and a proportion of the cost of giving them a desk, a phone, computer equipment and a roof over their head. There is also an overhead cost for some of the people in the company who are not directly chargeable to the projects but are essential to them, and these can range from the finance director to the office receptionist. The final component of the rate card is a percentage for profit.

All this should have given you a daily rate. You will probably assume that a day is seven or eight hours, although creative people tend to have very flexible attitudes to what actually constitutes a day. Then you may want to add in contingency – or tolerance as in the Prince2 methodology. Sometimes this is a figure added in the planning stage and sometimes a company will add a suitable figure at the end of the process, under the control of senior management.

This is a bottom-up approach to working out a rate. You should also consider the going rate for the task in your market and make sure that if your rate is higher than most, there is a good and justifiable reason for this. So estimating the time and cost can be quite complex.

Timesheets

Creative people are notoriously bad at estimating the time it will take them to complete a task. Most interactive companies now use electronic timesheets where employees have to identify the task and the project they are working on and the data is automatically trapped and allocated to the appropriate project so that the project manager has a clear view of progress. The way in which a company introduces a timesheet system and how it is managed is important. It can be regarded as positive when employees realize that they will improve their own skills of estimating by watching and analysing their own time expenditure. Also, they need to feel that the system is not being used to police their effort since creative ideas happen in and around the normal working environment, not just when an employee is sitting at a desk.

Time-tracking systems do not work unless they are a fair record of the time expended on a particular task. Companies also need to recognize that their employees spend quite a lot of time just being part of the company, with such things as company-related meetings, colleague networking, skills improvement, breaks, travel and so on. Many companies monitor their ways of working and take into account how many hours a week are not attributed to any clients. Then they use this to indicate a range of how many chargeable project hours they expect an employee to log. It seems that the larger the company the fewer chargeable hours are expected since more time is spent on general company business. A time system is not working when employees just fill out the sheets unfairly in order to conform to an expected minimum number of hours they are meant to log weekly. Neither is it working when people log effort to an 'admin' number because they don't want to run up costs against the client. This serves no-one, neither themselves, the clients nor the company. Used well, timesheets are an invaluable resource across all people in the company.

There's now a trend towards the integration of time-tracking and company-wide project management systems so that better data is available all round for the project manager and other management. (See the references at the end of the chapter for more information on these.) Take the time to look up some of the systems to see how they approach capturing project information. Clients seem to be expecting better data at sign-off points. They want this to demonstrate where the time and effort has gone for the money being requested. Increasingly too, clients want to be part of the on-going process so that they can log into the developer's system and see the state of the project at any time. This is what integrated project management systems and shared access to project-dedicated web space allows. These are trends in interactive development, and you should keep abreast of these if you haven't embraced them already.

Sign-off and paid stages

Cash flow through a company is vital in order to sustain the ability to pay employees and bills. It is important to decide the payment stages and mechanisms with the client as part of the project management system. By using the time, cost and quality mechanism, you can break the project down into phases (each ending in a milestone) and ask for payment at these stages subject to the clients' agreement and sign-off. You can ask for a percentage payment upfront as well. Some companies agree a payment on signing a contract, for example. Some clients ask for a percentage to be held back at the end of the project so that they can make sure that it conforms to what they expected before they will pay the last part. There is room for manoeuvre in payment schedules to fit in with company practice and needs.

Sign-off by the client is a project management stage of its own. You need to consider the number of days turn-around you are prepared to give the client when you hand them a piece of work as a milestone. You may have stipulated the number of days for them to reach a decision and get back to you, but the time you'll need for reacting to any feedback that may delay sign-off is an unknown time factor that has to be planned for and absorbed. You both need to consider how to encourage sign-off smoothly in the client's company and put in place the conditions to make that happen. You'll also need to consider what to do if slippage occurs here. Who is responsible, how will the timeline change, what about downtime costs of the development company? Sign-off is a sensitive time where the project can go off plan quite easily. You'll need to agree how to address revisions, changes or additions as a result of the scrutiny over sign-off. If you get your working arrangements for these sorted out upfront, the project will run more smoothly.

Change management

This time, cost, quality equation not only sets the boundaries of the project but also sets up a mechanism for any changes that either side decides to make. Anything that lies outside the agreed definition of the project can only be incorporated into it by using the time, cost, quality paradigm. Each extra piece, or change in the quality of what is to be produced, is looked at in terms of how much extra time it will take and how much extra it will cost. So the project management approach includes the change management process too.

This process can be introduced at the beginning of the project; at the proposal or pitch stage. When you put forward a solution to match the business needs, it is likely that there may be several options; some that may take a bit longer but will have different features (quality), or some that use more expensive attributes (quality) – animation, etc. If you present these as options that have their own time and cost attached to them, the client will see that extras are possible but that they cost more. This can be used to educate the client in the equation mechanism and set expectations for the project management approach during the project.

What is quality?

Quality has been the most difficult item in the equation for interactive people to define in a way that clients and employees can understand. However, it is straightforward to say that if you can't place a label of 'time' or 'cost' on something your client or team members are saying to you, it must relate to the quality of the project. The quality can be anything, including navigation, look and feel, features, functionality, content and testing. Most often during a project when the client wants to make changes, they are asking for additions or changes to the content in some way. While this may be easy and straightforward in some cases, in others it is not. So don't be fooled into agreeing a change without considering the consequences for your company.

For example, when a client's marketing department suddenly hears about your project for a customer-facing website, they decide they want to have some web pages of their own in the site. You'll need to listen to your client but invoke the time, cost, quality equation, saying you'll need to talk to the marketing department to understand if what they want is straightforward and will fit into existing agreed templates, or if they will want a new section operating rather differently. The first is more straightforward while the second could be problematic. Even a few web pages might take a long time to agree from a new department. Sourcing and signing off content usually takes longer than expected. So you may warn your client that even a few pages might add a time delay to the main project that will affect the agreed deadlines. You can indicate that you'll talk to the department if you can have a contact name, assess the implications and get back about the time, cost and quality impact of this request.

Of course you'll want to have a good relationship with the client, so you will endeavour to give them small extras and absorb these into your work and tolerance levels. This is good practice. But keep a record of the items you have done for nothing and then use these to explain that you will have to invoke the time, cost and quality tenet for the later requests because you have used up all your tolerance with all those things you have done for nothing. This type of approach will help the relationship and mitigate the feeling that you are just applying a formula blindly.

Variations on time, cost and quality

There are several models of the time, cost, quality equation for project management. They are variations on the basic theme, but it is good for you to recognize them since your clients or new employees may refer to them. The time, resources/assets, quality is easy to understand since in interactive terms you need to work out the time and cost estimate from the people and processes involved (the resources and assets) that indicate the quality level.

Time, resources/assets, quality

Another model covers time, cost and scope. Again it should be easy for you to recognize that defining the scope of the project, as covered in detail in Chapter 3, is defining the quality of the project as well as contributing to the cost and time estimate. They are all inter-linked.

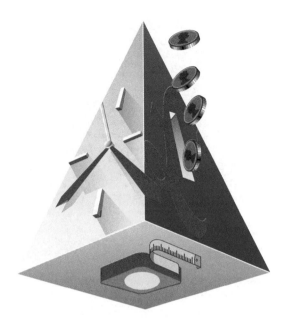

Time, cost, scope

Finally, the last model we'll cover here does have an addition that is worth considering in its own right. This is time, cost, quality and customer satisfaction, and seems to have grown from a com-bination of insights from software production and accounts/marketing.

Traditional software development took the time, cost, quality project management approach from engineering where it originated and tweaked it to suit their working practices. They spent a long time refining the scope of a project in their 'specification' stage. They realized that, unless they had a solid specification, the project tended to meander out of control and be hard to finish. Also, their development cycles were usually longer than interactive projects. So once they had the mechanics of a project management approach they applied it and even used the time, cost, quality and change management processes. However, they found that more and more projects were fulfilling the specifications agreed, but the clients were not satisfied with the result. The market and the business had shifted in the time during development so that the project did not serve its original purpose as well as it should, or the purpose was no longer appropriate. The clients probably paid for the projects but may not have pursued return business – and you can understand why.

Similarly, during interactive project development where account and marketing managers are often more closely involved with the projects, they are in a position to pick up

Time, cost, quality, customer satisfaction

on trends in the marketplace both from technology-driven innovations and from changes in patterns of their clients' business practices. They, as well as the project manager, can match the project solutions against the fast-moving market to know if they are on target or not. Because market conditions and business practices are changing faster in the digital age than ever before, development cycles tend to be shorter in order to counteract the possible mismatch. Developers are expected to be more flexible. So it is this combination of circumstances that has raised the stakes of customer satisfaction. Of course it is part of quality – and the time, cost, quality equation could encompass this shift if you identify and scope the solutions and revisit these during the project. But, by making customer satisfaction more visible in the example, it keeps it upfront in the developer's mind and there is less likelihood of the project being successfully completed to specification but not suiting the client or market as well as it might.

This shift touches on development practices for design and programming in interactive projects. These are refining themselves to become more flexible so that changes that occur in the course of the project do not have such drastic consequences for time and cost. The moves towards template design and object-oriented or Agile programming techniques are responses from design and programming to adapt to changes. The consequences for an interactive project can mean that projects line up better with the faster market shifts and changing needs of the client. Both design and programming can be affected by a marketing perspective. If competitor analysis, present technology use by the client and user analysis or market analysis are known and used to define the business case, then it is more likely that the project will line up better with the market and therefore serve the client's business needs. (See Chapter 12 for more on these.) It is important for project managers to recognize the wider context as outlined here.

The client and the project management process

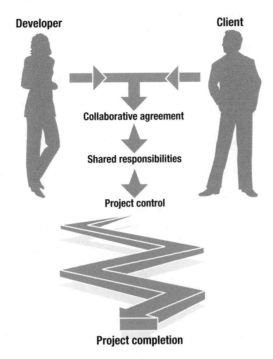

Working together

The project management approach works for both developer and client. This chapter is about the partnership relationship between them and how this helps achieve a successful project. Having a strong, clear business case helps the two sides, as we have seen in the first part of the chapter. Defining and agreeing the project management approach and working practices also smoothes the production path. Although it might seem that the time, cost, quality equation serves the developer more than the client, this is deceptive. The client is often represented by their own project manager or equivalent and they have their own set of concerns in a project. (See Chapter 7 on Troubleshooting: commissioner perspective for more on this).

One of the most common difficulties that a client representative has relates to the internal politics of their own company. Their section may have won the project budget, but they may have to work with and through other sections to help develop it and implement it in the company. Content for the website may need to be sourced from different sections and different people. The IT department may have to approve all the aspects of the interactive project because they control what happens technically in the company.

So how can the time, cost, quality approach work for them? Well, if you take the example of the marketing section of the client suddenly asking for a presence on the new website in the middle of the project, as outlined above, your main client will probably not want delays to the schedule that has already been agreed, and they will not want to pay extra costs for the development either. However, politically, the marketing section may be more influential than your representative and may have more power in the organization. Under these circumstances, your rep could have off-set the marketing department by using the project approach. The rep could have agreed with the marketing section about needing a presence, but indicated that under the change management process the developer would assess the impact of the request and come back with a time and cost estimate. Then, the marketing section could see if they had the budget available and the rep would have to assess any impact on the main project's schedule and clear that with the head, the project steering committee or whoever. The project approach has given the rep a negotiating tactic.

Often, asking a department for money – to match their request for the additional work – results in them backing off. The rep will know if his or her head of section will agree to a delay in the completion date and so, even if the money is available, the impact on the project might be too problematic to bear. Recognize that you as the developer have been out of this loop solely because of the project management approach. The rep is in fact protecting you from changes to protect their own interests. Without a clear approach to dealing with such situations, many of the additions and changes that originate outside your main client contact will land on you.

In fact you can use these situations to your advantage. If you educate your client that revisiting the interactive product every few months to tweak it to suit new market, technological advances and business interests is a recommended process, then you might suggest that you discuss the marketing needs with a view to incorporating these into a second phase of the project at a later date. This allows you to scope and cost the marketing department's needs (to continue our example) while protecting the integrity of the present project. Their needs will become part of another project. The same approach to delaying and hence containing certain additions and changes can be applied to your main client. You can protect the present project by moving their concerns to another project or phase of the project.

There's another way in which clients can be helped by adhering to the project management approach. If they recognize from the beginning of your relationship that things will change during the project, they should make financial and time provision for these changes upfront. Then, there will be no surprises. If they request changes, they know they will have to pay for them and that they might affect the timeline for development as well as the overall quality. When you are both working from the same process, the relationship is more transparent, more co-operative and solid.

Summary

Making the business case for interactive projects is not straightforward, but many more clients are expecting developers to talk in business terms. Although clients should have made their own business cases prior to involving you as the developers, this may not always be true. In this set of circumstances, you may be expected to outline your proposal for development including a business case.

A business case lines up with the expectations of the senior people in the client's company – people who control the budgets and are accountable for the project's results making a positive contribution to the business. This chapter explored ways in which developers could make a business case across the functions of people, processes, technology, design, business, marketing and infrastructure by using terminology that, in turn, uses business language.

Once a project is being developed, the partnership approach to working is established by defining the project management approach. This involves understanding the time, cost and quality equation and using change management procedures arising from these in the project. A developer and client also have to establish sign-off stages and procedures and payment stages to smooth the project path. If both use the project management approach, it can strengthen their relationship, protect the project from undue outside influence and improve the chances of success.

Top Tips

Strategy	Potential pay-off
Check if a business case has already been agreed for the project inside your client's company.	You can line up with this in your proposal and development to achieve your project's success criteria more easily.
If you are expected to make the business case, work with the client's in-house approach or find which indicators they prefer. Use these to make business sense to them and their market.	Avoid the criticism that developers don't understand their business. Both of you have a clearer sense of what the business needs are to frame the project.
Refine the business benefits table here to suit your projects, their types, markets and your clients.	You'll have good resources to help you in further pitches for business for particular sectors and products. It can give you a competitive edge.
Define and use your project management approach upfront in the proposal. Offer a small range of options so it is clear that pieces cost more and take more time. Your approach embodies the time, cost and quality relationship.	This sets the way of working and change management parameters for the project. Extras are possible but will come at a cost, affect the time for development and have an impact on the quality.
Use your electronic time-tracking positively for the project and your company.	Improved time and cost estimates from your team, clearer invoices for the client.
Establish sign-off stages, payment stages and sign-off processes.	Sign-off = money in staged phases is good for cash flow and morale.
Do small extras for nothing when you can for your client by absorbing them into your tolerance or contingency time for the project – but make a note of these and add up how much time/cost they represent.	Your client relationship improves when you work like this. The client will trust you not just to invoke time, cost, quality as a mechanism for more money. You will sound convincing when you do evoke the equation by citing the total number, time and cost of extras done for nothing.
The time, cost and quality approach to project management works well for both client and developer.	Establish a good working relationship and have smoother project development.

Application Task

1. If you are a developer, did you or your company make a business case for your present project? If so, can you fit it into a table like the business benefits table above?

   If not, how would you make the case for your present project? Use the table above and the knowledge you have of the client's business. Ask the account manager and your boss to help out.

   Does this help you see where your project could be evaluated in business terms?

   Does it make sense to the other people in your company?

   Would this be a useful tool for future projects? Educate others in your company if you think so.

2. If you are a commissioner of interactive media or a client in the developer's terms, did you make a business case inside your company for your present project? If so, can you fit it into a table like the business benefits table above?

   If not, how would you have made the case for your present project? Use the table above or your own company methods for putting forward business cases.

   Does this help you see where your project could be evaluated in business terms that would help your company?

   Does it make sense to the other people in your company?

   Would this be a useful tool for future projects? Educate others in your company if you think so.

 ## References/Resources

Business case related

Developing a web accessibility business case for your organization: Overview, S.L. Henry, ed., World Wide Web Consortium (MIT, ERCIM, Keio), Aug. 2005
http://www.w3.org/WAI/bcase/

Client relationship management, Pat McClellan, Director Online, 9 Aug. 1999
http://director-online.com/buildArticle.php?id=358

Five keys for getting your IT initiatives funded, Michael Sisco, TechRepublic, CIO and IT Management, 4 Dec. 2004
http://techrepublic.com.com/5100-10878_11-5180920.html

Make it clear, Jack Keen, CIO Magazine, 1 Dec. 2003
http://www.cio.com/archive/120103/value.html

Make them walk your talk, Sally Whittle, Computer Weekly.com, 28 Sept. 2004
http://www.computerweekly.com/Articles/2004/09/28/205405/Makethemwalkyourtalk.htm

The business case for business cases, Mary Wilson and Brad Marshall, Concept Marketing Group Inc. no date given
http://www.marketingsource.com/articles/view/1319

Understanding web logs and why it matters, Sharon Housley, Concept Marketing Group Inc., no date given
http://www.marketingsource.com/articles/view/2048

South Carolina Budget and Control Board, Division of the State Chief Information Officer, Business Case Template, no date given
http://www.cio.sc.gov/cioContent.asp?pageID=719

ROI 101: making the business case for technology investments, Rebecca Wettemann, CIO.com, Industry Experts, Analyst Corner, Nucleus Research, no date given
http://www2.cio.com/analyst/report1344.html

A business case for managing the digital media supply chain, Susan Worthy, DM Direct Newsletter, 28 Oct. 2005
http://www.dmreview.com/article_sub.cfm?articleID=1040148

Integrated project management systems

Enterprise-wide Project Management Software. Ablenet Solutions
http://www.ablenetsolutions.com/www/homepagef.nsf

The Turbo Project Manager series. Select under Other Utilities at:
http://www.broderbund.com/

MJI Teamworks
http://www.mjiteamworks.com/Site/index.asp

Ace Project
http://www.aceproject.com/

Base Camp
www.basecamphq.com

Creative companies

Infowit
http://www.infowit.com/index.asp

Creative Project
http://www.creative-manager.com/index.asp

Dedicated timesheet software

Allnetic
www.allnetic.com

Time Track
www.trinfinitysoftware.com

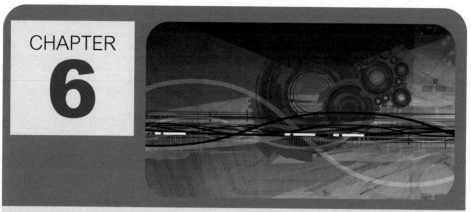

CHAPTER 6

Troubleshooting common development problems of interactive projects: developer perspective

Industry Insight

Manage the client with the same effort as managing other aspects of a project. The relationship will be stronger. The work will be better. Your team will be happier. You and your company will make more money.

Client relationships, Blog, James Bielefeldt, 28 March 2006
http://www.jamesbielefeldt.com/dasblogce/CategoryView,category,Project%20Management.aspx

● Overview

Interactive media project managers are constantly amazed to find that other people in the profession are encountering the same problems that they do. Few want to admit to meeting such difficulties, maybe because they think it shows up weaknesses in themselves, but all development companies encounter similar problems once projects are under way. The account manager over-sold the solutions; clients don't deliver content on time, ask for changes, delay sign-offs and so on. Until someone admits that these are recurring traits within the industry, no progress will be made. So here, we attempt to define such problems and devise strategies to tackle them – i.e. get them under control. They are 'risks' in project management terms and need to be assessed as such.

However, we need to recognize that clients also have perceptions about developers. They meet recurring problems during development that they try to avoid in later projects. They determine their own strategies to counteract what they consider as risks in the development stages of projects. Developers need to understand their clients' perspective and take account of it. Is our project guilty of causing these difficulties? What can we do to eradicate these and make the project path smoother to ensure client satisfaction? With this in mind, Chapter 7 also explains risks that clients/commissioners of projects have shared with us and points to their strategies to contain these. Whichever side you are representing it is important to recognize the other side's problems too, so don't skip the next chapter just because you are a developer. The same applies vice versa of course. In the spirit of partnership, as described in Chapter 5, we should work together to iron these difficulties out.

● Developer perspective

What you have read in this book so far has looked at some of the start-up problem areas and some of the macro problem areas in detail; here we try to consolidate those difficulties met once development has started and the project is under way. The list that follows is not exhaustive, but it is representative of many of the common gripes we have heard while training the industry's project managers. Some of the proposed solutions have come from the companies themselves. The solutions form their response to a recognized problem that has affected their company and their attempts to prevent the difficulty occurring again. Other solutions come from our experience.

You need to be aware that your situation may have nuances that mean that you cannot apply the solution exactly. You will need to think long and hard about the difficulty, its project context, the company or equivalent organization's culture and your team's set of skills and ability levels. The solutions may point in the right direction, but you may need to fine-tune them to suit your particular set of circumstances. Sometimes, the solutions will not be right for your context or clients. Only you can take the responsibility to define a solution that is right for the problem in hand. In reality, the concepts of 'right' and 'wrong' are too black and white for business decisions. Usually the answers are more right than wrong, or more wrong than right. Don't worry about this. No-one can get it right all the time; but doing nothing can often be at a greater negative cost to the project than taking a decision to move the project forward. You can, and should, rethink and reposition further down the line from a better position of knowledge. Decisions do not have to be absolutes either.

● Risk exposition: developers

Staged sign-off delays

This is a common problem in projects, and it leaves the developers feeling vulnerable. They find it hard to pressurize the client into signing because they don't want to jeopardize the relationship. However, delays cost the developer time and money because the project team has to be kept intact but idle or under-utilized while waiting, and then the production schedule has to be re-worked to take account of the slippage. This in itself sometimes causes more tension as the client doesn't appear to take responsibility for the slippage and often insists on the developer meeting the original deadlines.

Spin-off problems can occur if the sign-off delay involves extra people from the client company signing off the stage. This increases the risk of re-work before sign-off, since new perspectives mean new ideas. Extra people commenting on work can cause even more complications if they are senior to the people you usually deal with. The politics of the client company then take over and the sign-offs can spiral out of control.

Countermeasures

- Identify upfront and name the people in the client's company who will be involved in sign-offs during the project.
- Take care at contract stage to agree that any slippage on sign-off originating from the client will incur downtime costs of X amount daily to compensate.

Remind your opposite number about the sign-off agreement and named people. This can work to their advantage for internal company control. Sometimes it will be beneficial for your client contact to be able to tell different departments in their organization that any downtime costs incurred for lack of sign-off from their section will be charged on to them. This acts as a deterrent and empowers your opposite number.

However, if extra people are involved and/or the named people take too long, and if the named people request additions over and above what was asked for at this particular sign-off point, then slippage needs to cover downtime plus additional paid time to do the extras. All these change procedures need to be agreed upfront before the project proper begins as it is too late to introduce them in development. They need to be part and parcel of the understanding of work processes.

Considerations

If you start the 'penalty' clause downtime initiative, take care as your client may feel that they should then put penalty downtime clauses or non-completion clauses into their agreement with you. However, rather than making this standard in all contracts, you may prefer to institute the downtime initative only in a new agreement with a particular client if this problem has arisen on a previous project

Client won't give final sign-off, project dragging on

This is similar to the problem of late sign-offs as described above, and similar procedures about penalty costs can help. But hesitation over the final sign-off can occur even when clients have been fine about other sign-offs. There is more of a psychological pressure for clients concerning the final sign-off because they feel more vulnerable about severing the relationship and their lack of come-back if they find anything wrong within a certain time after the project has been completed. They know that difficulties can emerge with electronic products weeks after completion and they don't want to compromise themselves unduly from a position of weakness. Also, the clients worry that there might be a stronger position of power for the developer if they have to employ them to fix difficulties rather than go to another source.

Countermeasures

For the sake of the client relationship and yourselves, it may be that you try to alleviate this psychological pressure by building the client's confidence in you and your procedures. You may do this by indicating clearly how you have tested the final application against the agreed criteria. Hopefully you can show that the criteria were derived from your past experience as well as from specific recommendations from the client's technical section – if they have one. This will help in getting a confident final sign-off.

Some developer companies agree a period of time for the client to use the application and will fix any errors found for free. So a month, for example, can be a time limit set for the client to find any problems after final sign-off where the developer will fix the errors for nothing. Any extra work after that will be deemed as maintenance and charged accordingly. Care is needed to ensure that errors found relate to the project specification that was agreed. If the work relates to new aspects or changed aspects of the project, because the client now wants something slightly different, then the change procedure for time, cost and quality should be used. The client needs to understand how this 'free fix' time will be utilized and that it does not relate to changed criteria, only existing agreed specifications. This approach gives you a discipline to thoroughly test the project so that there are few or no errors found relating to the agreed contract within the month. (See more on these final sign-off issues in the contracts section of Chapter 10.)

Considerations

Your testing section or your programming section, whoever carries out the testing, should be well briefed if a 'free fix' time limit is part of your contract with a client. They have to accept the challenge to test the application thoroughly under the expected conditions in order to minimize the possibility of a lot of extra free work. This is not as easy as it might at first seem. A lot of projects are squeezed at the end of their schedule and testing is the first thing to suffer. This might well contribute to the lack of trust in final sign-offs that a client has developed. So, if this is adopted as a strategy for your own organization, you need to involve the relevant people and decide how it can be made efficient to work to save your company time, effort and hidden costs.

Client does not provide content/resources when specified – causes delays

This appears to be a particular problem for interactive agencies and e-learning companies when their clients hold a lot of the content in different forms – subject experts' knowledge, print, video, etc. The developer needs access in good time to the resources to re-work them into the format needed for the project. If there are delays, it is the developer that suffers.

Counterpoint measures

Ensure that the responsibility for slippage through delayed content or expertise is well defined upfront. Indicate that the time and costs associated with slippage of this nature will be the client's responsibility. You can perhaps consider invoking 'downtime' costs as defined above, working out any extension of the project's deadlines/timescale and warning the client of the projected new deadlines. It may be as well to also state that any consequences of such delays – including extension of the deadlines and any extra costs, etc. – will have to be absorbed by the client since extension of timescales is often a sensitive issue.

Considerations

As above. Clients may well place the same conditions on you if you cause delays for any reason.

Problems understanding technological information affecting project development

However much a developer tries to explain various aspects of technological information to the client's representatives, invariably the people making the decisions about the project will not be technical people themselves and so there may be an inadvertent mismatch of understanding. On the other hand, the developer themselves may not define the complete technical requirements for the project, despite being in a position to understand the consequences. Over-looking technical requirements will result in extra costs for the developer. Projects we can cite as examples have incurred problems of this nature concerning Internet browser compatibility and the differences between development and delivery environments.

Example A Browser limitations can occur when a developer has named specific browsers that a website will work with in the contract. They might do this because they have learnt that getting the more tricky parts of the site to work across other browsers incurs a disproportionate amount of time – and therefore costs – that previous clients have not been prepared to pay. In this cited case, the clients may have agreed to limit the browsers because they have little information about the needs of their company and the company's market. But late into the project, the marketing section of the company might insist that a particular browser is included because an active set of their customers is associated with using that browser. You can imagine that adding in an extra browser capability late into the project is often more costly than planning it in from the beginning.

Example B Unexpected differences between development and delivery environments can be very costly for the developer company. In one instance, the project had been completed satisfactorily, demonstrated and accepted by the client. Unfortunately, when the application was loaded onto the client company's server it failed to work. In the end this was because the client's company had a non-standard firewall for protection and the application would not work through it. Worse than that, it took a few weeks of hard work to diagnose the problem and adjust the application for this configuration – at the developer's cost.

Countermeasures

Example A Explain to the client that, although you have tried to explain the limiting factors of some technological decisions implied in the agreement, it may well be a good idea for them to retain some contingency money to release if necessary for extra technical considerations later in the project. Reasons for this might be: that their market might shift, some technical aspects will become more important than they are at this time, the client's company may make fundamental changes to their system such as a change of service provider and server platform and so on. These things do happen and are frequent causes of difficulties so you need to try to contain them in some way that appears transparent to both you and the client.

Example B When you find that work extras are caused by things your team overlooked or did not consider, your company needs to find a strategy to help minimize these for the future. You need to take action to tighten your work processes. So taking the non-standard firewall as such an example, your company would have to decide that for future projects the definition of where and under what conditions the application was to be distributed should be defined and testing procedures should also be defined within the predicted time and costs for the client to bear. This might mean adding in specific questions that your client needs to answer upfront as in the 'scoping questionnaire' in Chapter 3; these would point to the prospective problem areas that might need further investigation and definition. Or, if the client has a technical section, it may well be that your technical section representative and the client's representative should have a separate meeting to establish a seamless transition between development and distribution. There are many work practices that you can formulate as a strategy to minimize problem costs that your company does not wish to incur.

Test on the delivery platform as early as possible even if incomplete, or develop on their platform if you can arrange access. Bear in mind that sometimes your client may not be aware of the subtleties of their system and, ironically, you may not be aware of all the idiosyncrasies of yours.

Client wants changes in content to the project without extra costs

As the project develops and content gets defined for the application from various sources, it is common for the client's organization to recognize that new information, new people or even new sections from their company need to be included in the project. If the client has agreed the overall structure and look and feel of the application, they may well believe that adding in extra content will be straightforward and not warrant extra costs. This might well be the case and you need to take a common sense view on the request. You should absorb small extras for the sake of the client relationship. However, sometimes even a little extra content can mean days of time and effort.

Take the case of having to meet someone from a new section of the client's organization. They may have particular requirements in getting the most from the content they will provide. They may not relate well to the way that content has been organized for the other sections. It might mean that new functionality would serve the content best, but this has knock-on effects for you and your team. If the client is not willing to pay extra and the new section will not conform to the way the information should be presented, you are left in a dilemma that will take time and administrative effort to solve. You will be trapped in the middle of the client's politics. The situation may end up with new programming being required, the possibility of the new functionality interfering with the old and the timescale slipping. This may also incur delays in actually providing the new information and the associated difficulties already described earlier in the chapter.

Countermeasures

As you can imagine, you will be in a vulnerable position if you meet such difficulties in the middle of development. Your best countermeasure is to fall back on the standard

Changes affect time, cost and quality

ways of working and project management principles that you should have set up at the beginning of the project. These were outlined in Chapter 3 on Scoping and Chapter 5 on Partnership, and prove their worth in situations like the one highlighted here. Under those premises – that you educated your client in at the beginning of the project – changes to the project originating from the client will be assessed in terms of their impact according to time, cost and quality. You will then both agree the best way forward and how to incorporate the change. Your main client contact will also be able to use this as a control for any inside influences from the organization by warning them of the process and then passing on any extra costs to them. This should reinforce how useful these principles can be for your project partnership.

Considerations

If your relationship with your client contact is good and you can trust each other, then you need to be flexible in how and when you use this form of change control. You should also have built in some slack or 'tolerance' to allow for extras that you and your team can cover for nothing. But once it becomes clear that the change asked for has consequences that make it a medium or significant change rather than a small one, you will need the option for your client to release some extra money or time or both, and perhaps sacrifice some quality.

Client wants changes in the use of technology without extra costs

This is similar to the case outlined above. Quite often clients will keep an eye on their main competitors and, if they see some new functionality that they like, they have a tendency to start asking for it in the middle of development, even if it is inappropriate.

Countermeasures

See above. Unless you have already established the time, cost and quality partnership approach to any changes to the specification that the client introduces from the beginning of the project, you will be in a vulnerable position. You should now appreciate why getting some basics of agreement about the work processes in place upfront will save you time and money later.

Considerations

As above.

Communication in the client organization is muddled and leads to delays/unclear information

This can turn into a nightmare for you and is certainly a problem you want to avoid. It is important that you know who you will deal with, and when. You also have to understand the power base of your opposite numbers. Who will make the final decisions? Whose authority will allow payments to be made smoothly? Who will sign-off project phases, and is it the same person who will authorize the final sign-off? These are items

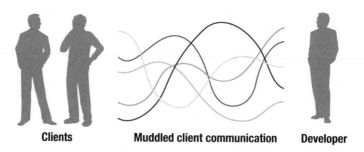

Clients   **Muddled client communication**   **Developer**

you should have sorted upfront for the project as part of understanding the stakeholders and their influence on the project. (See Chapter 4 on Stakeholders.)

Countermeasures

If, for whatever reason, your clients get themselves and you into a muddle about decisions and who is taking them – and this can be on any aspect of the project from decisions on content to functionality – you need to focus everyone on the agreement you had at the beginning of the project that named the people who had any power of veto over aspects of your work. If the client will not line back up with the agreement, you can use the time, cost and quality aspects to help you since extra or different people in decision-making will cause extra time and effort and delays. This is a change in administration as well as in project management and can be as disruptive as changes to the substance of the project.

If you did not establish named communication and decision-making lines of agreement at the beginning of your project, then you'll learn to do that for future projects. In this situation, you need to be pro-active and get named lines of communication and decision-making sorted as quickly as possible. If the people involved start changing aspects of the project development you have already completed, then you can use the time, cost and quality change process as usual, indicating that changes to the actual project are being initiated by the new named communicators.

The only difference in utilizing the change control mechanism of time, cost and quality here will be in how quickly you'll be able to apply it. In the first case, if you have established all the communication and sign-off lines at the beginning of the project, you'll be able to spot any variance quickly and take control. Otherwise the situation has to be sorted at your expense until the new or different lines of communication begin to affect the substance of the project. You can see from this example that the first saves you time and effort and therefore money. The second is a 'patch' approach and costs you time, effort and money until it is sorted enough for you to take control again. It also sets a precedent you may wish to avoid.

Considerations

You need to be on top of changes in personnel, mergers between sections of your client, or whatever has an impact on their organization in terms of who makes the decisions about any aspect of the project and who will pay for it. It is not unusual for personnel to change over the course of the project: but, if their responsibilities or authority changes as well, this can also affect your project. If you assess anything that is going on in the client's organization as a possible future risk to the project, you need to flag this with your management and put forward strategies to deal with the risks before they happen. This is classic project management. The earlier you act to control processes, the smoother the path for your team and your project development.

Extra people from client organization getting involved too late in the process causes slippage

This is very similar to the problem outlined above and is quite common. As the project becomes more mature and there is more to see and comment on, extra people from the organization want to get involved.

Countermeasures

These people may well have valid perspectives and emerge as strong stakeholders midway through the project. If you had been keeping an eye on emerging stakeholders as explained in Chapter 4, you may well have taken these into account and updated the list for the new people to be able to comment on the project milestones. Updating the list ahead of milestones that were due would have meant quiet renegotiation of comment time for the clients with your opposite number, and/or getting the extra people into the process early enough for them to be contained in the comment time allowed. Here you should notice how early intervention and foresight can keep the project running smoothly and avoid the delays that late intervention by these powerful people can cause.

If you had not been aware of these powerful extra people being involved and suddenly they emerge and delay the sign-off for a project milestone, you should be able to invoke the original sign-off list and slippage costs that you should have outlined from the beginning. There may well be a power struggle inside the client organization over this, but it will be clear that you are only doing your job as project manager and using the agreement that was in place. The resolution will be up to them. You may arrive at a position where you can recognize a compromise that will work to your advantage from a client relationship point of view while mitigating many of the extra time and cost implications that might arise from new people getting involved.

If the extra people are vocal but do not have authority over the existing sign-off list, you could point out to your counterpart that, according to your list, they have no authority and that if their comments are now to be included, the client organization will have to cover the time, cost and quality implications of any changes they request, including slippage. Often, your counterpart can then use this stance to his/her advantage to explain the procedures to the extra people in the client organization and ask them to cover any consequences to the project that they cause. Your counterpart raising the idea of transfer of funds from the extra people to cover their involvement is often a very effective means of dissolving the potential problem. Quite often they do not have access to funds of this sort at short notice and withdraw in the short term. Use the situation to your advantage – rather than causing bad feeling with these potentially powerful people indicate that these extras are useful and could be planned into phase 2 of the project when rethinking and revision are addressed. This might allow them time to find the money.

Considerations

You do not want to jeopardize the client relationship, but this cannot be used as an excuse for your company to cover the time and cost implications of extra work arising from all the difficulties encountered along the way. The use of the objective agreement on ways of working together in partnership to ensure smooth running from the beginning of the project should be making a lot of sense to you now, even if it seemed over-burdensome as a concept initially. You can use it as much or as little as you need and allow scope for the relationship element as well. If it does not exist, you have very little bargaining position and nor does your counterpart. It serves you both well if implemented as described in Chapter 5 on Partnership.

The original brief is too broad and now details are needed, no one is sure how to specify what is wanted

This is a nasty trap as you may well have committed yourself to a time and cost for a vague notion of what was needed to develop the project. If you haven't defined the content and quality levels well in the agreement, you have given the client the leeway to walk all over you. This happens more often than developers would like to admit. If you can't point to something documenting that what is asked for now is different from the original brief, you cannot make the case for more time and money.

To win projects, developers are often put in this awkward position. They know that they will need a clear definition but, if it is not forthcoming at the beginning, then they have to work with what they are given. However, they do need to build in strong parameters to indicate what they will do for the time and cost so that there is enough to show strong deviance later.

Countermeasures

Companies are increasingly taking note of this problem and have devised a strategy to counter it. If the brief is too vague to be of use but the deal has to be struck, then the developers are building in a phase to define and refine the project parameters for a specified time and cost. This allows them to move forward with some known time and costs with a proviso that if the parameters emerge to be x, y and z, then they will complete the project in such and such a time for such and such a cost subject to the usual time, cost and quality measures. This allows the developers to specify the project better and gives them markers to show that if the specified project varies a good deal from the original conception as given in the original brief, then the time and cost may be varied accordingly. However, the client still benefits from a much clearer understanding of what was needed by following this first paid stage, and will be in a much better position to understand what they will get for the money to be spent. This reflects the partnership arrangement we have been advocating during the course of the book.

Considerations

The client needs to understand the implications of this approach fully and the reasons behind the paid first stage. If they do not, then if the developer company alters the time and cost attributes this will cause conflict and jeopardize the client relationship. If you can show the client what a 'good' brief is and how their original brief is limiting your decisions, then this can help enormously as long as you are not patronizing or judgemental about their original brief.

Summary

During development there are many risks that can influence the running and management of a project. It is in the developer's interest to minimize the risks. Often these can be controlled to a certain extent if the developer is clear about their preferred working methods with the commissioner from the beginning of the project.

However, if problems do occur during development, the sooner the project manager recognizes what is happening and takes appropriate action to mitigate the consequences the better. This chapter looked at some of the common difficulties that are met during development from the developer's point of view. It put forward suggestions on how to counter these and whether there may be wider considerations to note as part of the decision-making process.

Top Tips

Strategy	Potential pay-off
Outline your work processes and the responsibilities of the client upfront at the beginning of the project after winning it.	Saves chaos and crises later in the development part of the project.
Get the client to nominate their sign-off representatives for the project at the beginning.	This dissuades other people in the client company interfering in the project and gives you the lever to control the interference.
Delays in sign-off turn-arounds and the resulting consequences are the client's responsibility. Make this clear at the beginning stages of the project.	Gives a discipline to the sign-off points and a lever for time, cost and quality extras to the developer if needed.
Explain the necessity for change control during the project and your procedures if the client asks for changes.	The client knows in advance that changes are likely to incur time, cost and perhaps quality adjustments. This makes the process easier to deal with.
Explain your lines of communication at the beginning stages of the project and get the client to explain theirs.	Clear communication lines deter mixed messages and people interfering. They give the project manager a level of control if and when necessary.

Strategy	Potential pay-off
Client gives a poor brief but awards you the project. Make the specification refinement the first stage of the project and get paid for it. Firm up the time, cost and quality agreements. You should have had caveats in the first offering you made to the poor brief such as 'if this is true, then we will do this, for this cost and time', for example.	Trying to move forward on a poor brief will lead to problems. Refine the brief and what you will offer for certain time, cost and quality scenarios. Get the client to choose between some options. Move forward more clearly.

Application Task

Devise your own problem-solving strategies

1. Have your project managers or equivalent meet with each section in your organization from designers to programmers, account managers to testers. The meetings should focus on the most common difficulties each section meets in developing projects with specific examples. If the people can identify how much extra impact these common problems have had on time, cost and quality, this will give better measurable indicators to prove when the problems have been solved or mitigated.

2. Once each section has defined their common problems, the project managers should work together to spot any commonalities that impact across the sections. These will be causing the most frequent problems for the company and so if strategies to eradicate them are put forward and carried through, this should make a great difference to efficiency, motivation and morale for the company. The project managers may well find that they can use this chapter's structure to help them decide their strategies under the headings, Problem definition, Counterpoint measures, Considerations.

3. The project managers should take their findings back to each section, or maybe a gathering of the sections together, and allow discussion about them. They should try to establish a form of consensus on how to move forward in the best interests of the company and the projects without over-burdening the staff. It might mean that phased implementation could ease the burden of changes and allow the staff to adjust to new procedures.

4. If the problems have been defined in terms of time, cost and quality measures, the company will be better able to quantify how it has benefited after the strategies have been put in place.

● References/Resources

Client relationships, Blog, James Bielefeldt, 28 March 2006
http://www.jamesbielefeldt.com/dasblogce/CategoryView,category,Project%20
Management.aspx

Managing client relationships, Patty J. Ayres, WebDevBiz.com, 2005
http://www.webdevbiz.com/article.cfm?VarArtID=9

Bulletproof web design contracts, John Tabita, sitepoint, 28 Oct. 2005
http://www.sitepoint.com/article/bulletproof-web-design-contract

Interview with Kelly Goto, Carolyn Wood, WISE-Women, 25 May 2005
http://www.wise-women.org/features/kelly_goto

How to manage the monster, Kevin Airgid, Creative Behaviour, Issue No 9, 2005
http://www.creativebehavior.com/index.php?PID=194

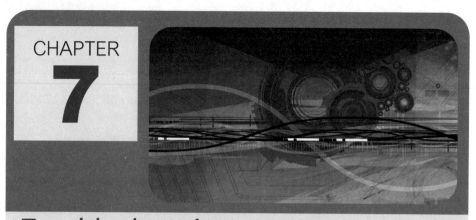

CHAPTER 7

Troubleshooting common development problems of interactive projects: commissioner perspective

Industry Insight

Too many client dissatisfaction issues occur because the client's expectations aren't managed up front. Start every project venture out on the right foot by stating the project's scope clearly and you'll reward yourself with fewer problems down the road.

Managing client expectations with a project scope document, Michael Sisco, Techrepublic, 25 July 2002
http://techrepublic.com.com/5100-10878_11-1044366.html#

● Overview

Taking the alternate point of view to the previous chapter and listening to the equivalent of our 'customer's' perspective may involve hearing things that, as developers, we really don't want to hear. However, as we'll see in Chapter 12 on e-marketing, a business won't get as far as it can unless it listens and responds to its customers. If you demonstrate to your clients how you have realigned your strategy to take account of any weaknesses you have noted in the development processes, you can only increase your credibility.

● Commissioner perspective

It is important that both developer and commissioner try to understand each other's difficulties in achieving a successful project and work to resolve these for mutual benefit. Chapter 5 on the Partnership approach to projects recommended this stance. We need to learn from experience, so the difficulties presented here indicate the most common grumbles that we have heard from commissioners about their developers.

Some of the suggested solutions have been initiated by commissioners themselves as a response to circumstances, and others we have put forward from our experience. If you are reading this as a commissioner, you need to look at your company, its culture and the details of your relationship with your developer, to decide if the solution would suit. If you are reading this as a developer, you should be trying to understand why your client is demanding certain conditions and work to accommodate these in a way that fits with your company practices.

● Risk exposition: commissioners

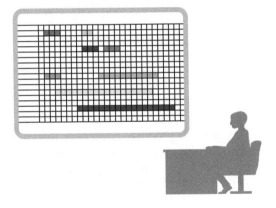

Deadlines not met

Deadlines/milestones are not met by developer

This has 'unfortunately' been reported as a common problem. If the developer fails to meet a deadline without due explanations or, worse, states that the company has met the deadline but the product does not match the level of quality that was agreed, this undermines any trust in the relationship. In this case, it will affect the partnership that is needed between the commissioner and developer for a successful project.

Countermeasures

If your developer is failing to meet your defined and agreed deadlines and you have not been satisfied with their reasons why this has happened, then you have good cause for concern because slippage is extremely hard to contain. You can try to work with your developer contact to get explanations so that you might both devise strategies to alleviate the problem. There could have been misunderstanding about the specific quality level that was expected for the particular stage, for example. You may revisit and revise the agreement to make it more precise.

If your relationship with your counterpart is good, you may get an admission that resources and/or staff have periodically been pulled from your project to work on other projects, or that a key skill set that is needed for your project is lacking. Often you'll find that your counterpart is not happy with the situation either but is suffering from internal politics in their own company. You might consider instigating a meeting with the developer's management where you ask them to name and define the relevant skill sets of the people that work on your project. This will encourage them to take stock of the project and your concerns. You might indicate that you will expect to see relevant timesheets for these people at each milestone stage so that you can assure your management of the quality and quantity of the work in reaching future milestones on time.

However, if after trying to understand the situation, you feel that the developer has not been giving your project its due attention, you might wish to consider stronger measures to bring the project back on track. Theis problem could have been addressed by the initial agreement establishing that the developer might incur cost penalties for late milestones and deadlines without your prior consent. If this is not the case, then you could consider introducing this feature to provide a focus for the developer to readjust their stance on your project.

Considerations

You have a responsibility to your company to ensure that the project progresses as smoothly as possible and that it is produced according to the agreed specifications, time and cost. The relationship with the developer is central to the project's success so if they are not maintaining their part of the bargain, you do need to take action.

If you move to put penalty clauses in your initial agreement, the developer may well ask for the same. As we have seen in the last chapter, many commissioners have their own internal difficulties meeting sign-offs and/or getting the right people to provide content on time and this causes delays. So, it is likely that each of you would incur costs for delays over the course of the project. It may be that if each of you gives yourselves the option of penalties upfront, then whether you follow through each time can be dependent on other issues as there are quite often mitigating factors. Reminding the developer of the threat of penalties, if agreed, might be enough.

Even if you allow yourself some room for manoeuvre in this way, if the developer still does not satisfy you as to why the deadline or the quality of the product for the stage is less than expected, you need the option to be firm. If you had not agreed penalties upfront, this may be the time to add them formally, in writing, to the agreement, covering subsequent milestones/deadlines. You are the customer, and the developer should respond to you or risk losing your custom. In these circumstances they should find a solution that will suit your requirements for the future and their own that perhaps avoids penalties.

Developer appears to have own agenda – creative and/or technical – so wants to push development practices for their own sake, not for the project

This dilemma can arise because some staff in the developer company wish to keep on top of their specialisms rather than use their talents to serve the needs of the client. It is up to the developer company to contain this so that it does not interfere with a project.

Countermeasures

You can off-set this by indicating to your developer from the beginning of the project that you expect well-designed solutions refined from their experience and therefore better than past products that they have produced. You need to state that you do not want innovation at the expense of extra time and costs. You can also state that you have seen this practice creep into previous projects and that you want it controlled well from the beginning – perhaps through careful selection of the staff that are to work on the project.

If you notice this happening once the project is under way and your company is purely interested in tried and tested solutions that will aid the smooth running of a project to time and budget, you must make your position clear. It is up to the developer's project manager to control the project staff to produce the interactive product within the parameters that have been agreed. You may well query the cost of development of one or two features that seem to add little to the main objectives of the product and negotiate these down or even out. This will give a powerful message to the project team that the team manager may use as a control measure with the team over the rest of the course of the project.

Considerations

However, this question of specialist self development and new trends is not straightforward. Interactive media is an innovative emerging sector, and some of the brand new options may well serve a project better than the recent options, precisely because they will have emerged from refinement practices. Also, some clients want to see added value in terms of innovations to keep on top of the trends. It is a difficult balance for the developer's project manager. You need to ask yourself if you want a safe but conventional product or something that has an edge but might be less stable under some extreme conditions, for example. You will need to pay for innovation, but controlled innovation where a couple of steps forward are planned into the project rather than many leaps being taken may offer the best of both worlds.

Wrong use of a medium or technology for the wrong reason, e.g. flash animation for the wrong reason

This is a bit more problematic. When the developer explains their approach to your brief, they should indicate what features they will use and why. You need to be convinced that the solutions are appropriate for the users and for what you are trying to achieve. Sometimes, the developer team might be influenced to push in a certain direction because of a strong personality or a charismatic specialist with awesome skills in a particular field. The team may have been convinced for other reasons. It is up to you to represent your company and its needs and the needs of your users first and foremost.

Countermeasures

If you have research about your users, or you have representatives of the users on the project board (see the earlier discussion about stakeholders, Chapter 8 on the users' contribution, and the extra material on Prince2 project management about user representatives on our website at www.atsf.co.uk/mim), then you will be in a better position to challenge the proposed solution and better shape it to your needs.

If you believe that there is an imbalance in the use of a medium or technology then you should indicate this and ask for it to be addressed at the negotiation stage. If you did not realize precisely how much one feature would dominate from the early description, then you need to indicate this as soon as you become aware of it. Trialling with users is the best way to receive feedback that will drive the developer. They will find it difficult to argue against user feedback and will use it to refocus. If the developer and yourselves had not incorporated such trials into the project plan, you should consider doing so at this point, and certainly in any future projects. If it is too early to trial with users and you had not had this as a feature of the project plan, you might consider bringing in a usability specialist to see the early aspects and comment. However, recognize that extra people being involved without prior understanding may well add time and cost factors for you to bear in the project, but this could be off-set by the increase in quality.

Considerations

The issue of innovation in a project can cut both ways. Sometimes the developer company is accused of not alerting the commissioner to emerging trends and not utilizing features or technology that would have been relevant to the project. The developer, from a position of experience, needs to make a difficult judgement here as to how far it is appropriate to try and influence the commissioner. Also they may have had their fingers burnt by another project where they had tried to exert influence to their detriment. The feature that they may have pushed inappropriately for your case may have worked well for them in a previous project. However, the requirements for that feature in that project and for those users may have been very different. You have the responsibility to act as the judge as to what will work for you and your users, although the developer should try to make themselves aware of what works where, for their own professional development.

If, independently of the developer, you do bring in usability experts or instigate trials with the users during the course of development, and this wasn't made clear up front, you may well cause resentment in the developer because there will be many more changes than they had bargained for. The project will take longer at your cost.

Lack of contingency/planning by the developer

Sometimes it appears that the developer has been over-optimistic about reaching milestones and that, with no obvious reason for delay, the team has not achieved what it should. If your confidence in the team wanes because they meet unforeseen difficulties that you feel are the result of their inexperience, then action should be taken to bring the project back on track. In extreme cases, perhaps, the project may have to be given to another developer.

Countermeasures

Institute a meeting where you draw the developer's attention to the slippage that has occurred for no tangible reason and indicate your dissatisfaction. Ask what happens as a matter of company procedure as soon as it becomes clear that they are falling behind. Their management should be aware from the frequent project monitoring process that the project is in danger of slipping and take appropriate action. They could, for example, attach more experienced specialists in the weak areas to monitor the work more often, or even add them permanently for the course of the project. If the procedures to remedy the slippage are not clearly stated to your satisfaction then you should increase your own monitoring. You may also start to hint at possible penalty costs.

Considerations

Interactive media development is more an art than a science, and developers can run into problems that are not of their or your making. Quite often they will meet bugs in third party software that need work-arounds. The company may not have project management processes in place because they have always more than satisfied their clients in the past. If they have over-stretched themselves with promises of innovation in your project without allowing due time for the experimentation and the 'unknown', that is down to their inexperience and should not be at your cost.

If the company you employ has not convinced you with a sound work plan outline at the beginning of the project, or has come across as light in work process but talented in output, you should raise the concern there and then. Initially, you can ask the queries outlined here in the 'countermeasures' and get assurances faster. This would enable you to recognize the deficiency more quickly and decide on your strategy earlier.

Overspend

Overspend

There is nothing worse than you being landed with a bill that is far higher than the project plan led you to expect. Even if you had a time and materials contract with the developer that had no maximum limit, you should not receive bills that vary from expectations. If time and costs had shifted during the project stage for whatever reason, you should have been made aware of this and agreed to the changes before they occurred.

Countermeasures

You need to take action immediately. You should state your expected costs according to the plan and that you have not been made aware of, or authorized, any extras. You should ask for a detailed explanation at a meeting that involves management from both sides. You may decide to stop the project and avoid it incurring more costs until this has been satisfactorily resolved. You can ask for a breakdown of the costs to see where and how extra expense has arisen.

Considerations

Make absolutely sure that other people from your company who have sign-off authority have not authorized extra work and costs without you knowing. Check that the developer knows that all changes and cost agreements need to go through you and that this has not been the case. Often these anomalies can be traced back to not using proper communication channels, which is why it is important to specify and agree these in the project plan.

Lack initiative – don't come forward with ideas for the users

This has featured as a complaint more often than we would have expected. The developers are equally confounded by it and reply that sometimes clients won't listen to them. It does appear strange that if clients want advice from those experienced in the interactive sector they then find them lacking in ideas. It would seem that there is a communication problem here that needs sorting.

Countermeasures

At proposal stage, make sure you specifically ask for ideas about features and treatment that will suit your users' profile. Discuss them with the developer to be sure that you're convinced of the wisdom of these ideas. Recognize that such treatments and features may well have extra price tags attached because the developer knows what it will cost to achieve them.

You may well have decided to choose a developer who has dealt with your market sector before so that they can contribute ideas based on their prior experience. Alternatively, you might have decided to have a radical change of style from your competitors and so chosen a developer with a lot of interactive experience but which is not a specialist in your sector. In the former case you can take your lead from them; in the latter, you are expected to lead them with your knowledge of the market and users. Have you defined your role in these terms?

Check that the developer has built in time and cost for testing ideas and different stages of the development on the users. If this is important to you, are you prepared to pay for it? It raises the quality but it does add time and cost. During the course of the project, constantly focus the developer on the specified needs of the users and check how they believe that the feature they are working on will meet those needs.

Considerations

The developer may well expect you to know your users, understand their needs in relation to your business and interactivity and know your competitors and what they are doing with a similar interactive product. They may expect a clear business case from you on what they have to produce and what needs they have to satisfy. Do you know your users and market to this extent? Can you brief the developer with enough salient information so that they can respond with ideas to suit the users? (See Chapter 5 on the partnership approach and Chapter 12 on marketing, for more on business cases.)

Or, in their proposal, the developer may well have included analysing your users, profiling your competition and checking that your interactive product will be well positioned from a marketing perspective. These activities will take time and money, but they will feed the decisions for the interactive treatment.

This is an area where communication may be lacking between developer and commissioner. The developer does not want to sound patronizing to their client and they assume that they know their own users and market. The commissioner may want help to focus on how interactivity and a particular platform can serve them best for their users. You both need to check what is expected from each other from the beginning.

Sometimes the developer finds that the commissioner won't listen to them so they stop raising issues. This may be because they are not talking a common language. The developer may be too 'techie' while the commissioner is too 'vague'. Another reason for non-communication is that the developer knows that they cannot mention anything that will cost more because the client has apparently reached their budget limit. Ensuring that the correct level of communication takes place across the project is the responsibility of the project manager or equivalent on each side. If there is a hiatus, keep talking to each other until you understand what the core reason for it is, and decide how to sort it.

Own IT department blocks progress

You, as the commissioner, may be part of a large organization that has its own IT division or section but you are expected to outsource any interactive projects. However, to be effective, the interactive product will need to operate across your organization and so will be subject to partial implementation and maintenance by the IT department, and they may have some control over how it will be set up.

This gives the IT department a good deal of power over the finished product. There may be a history of difficulties in instituting any system from outside the company for a variety of reasons, often stemming from IT's responsibilities towards the existing network and the kinds of software you are allowed to use on it. Whatever the reason, the IT department in this type of case can effectively make it difficult for you and the developer to achieve the project.

Countermeasures

Involve the right people from the IT section from the beginning of the project. If you have a project board or the equivalent project steering committee, you'll need someone from the IT department on it. Whoever your project champion or top internal project sponsor is, he or she needs to help you manage the internal process of getting agreement and staged sign-off involving the contact from IT.

Make sure that the developer and the IT department have a named contact and regular meetings with you present. It might be harder for the IT section to cancel meetings if this affects others internally as well. The developer will need to take into account any of the concerns from the IT section and work to address them.

Understand that 'blocking' tactics from internal sources adds time, delays and costs to the project so decide how you will absorb these, or how you will present them to the appropriate people to pass on the costs incurred. Make this clear to them upfront before the project begins. You will have to help the developer get through the internal political hoops as part of your job and for the success of the project. You need to identify this as a risk and deal with it accordingly.

Considerations

The IT department could have very good reasons to fear outside systems that may interfere with security, their reliability of service agreements or any other quality levels they have as targets. Often, once they can talk to equivalent technical specialists from the developer and find that they understand the difficulties and will work together to make the new system transparent to them, they relax.

Own management give impossible deadlines

This actually comes up quite often as a difficulty that commissioners meet originating from their own people. They feel they have little choice in passing on the deadlines to the developer even though they know that they are impossible to achieve.

Countermeasures

If you know that this is a risk, try to set up an internal education seminar about interactive projects, their risks and strategies to overcome them. If you have a training section, ask them to help by identifying it as a training need. Make it clear that this core problem of false deadlines means loss of quality and extra costs for the organization. Often the message is more effective if it doesn't come from you directly.

At the beginning of the project, use the time, cost and quality mandate to your management to show that if there are any changes requested in the project, this process will be used to evaluate the impact. You can show that changing deadlines is a common source of extra costs and loss of quality that should be avoided. Explain that the time, cost, quality equation is standard project management procedure and that the developer will be implementing it. Ask your management's advice on how to deal with this and similar issues to keep the project on track.

From the beginning of the project, specify and work to achieve the project in smaller chunks and in more phases than usual. In this way, you can demonstrate progress more often and you can set up expectations about what your management will see and when.

Considerations

As long as you have set the expectations about the use of time, cost and quality, if your management forces you into a position where you have to lean on the developer, then there will be no surprises if the developer comes back with the consequences of the changes in time, cost and quality terms for your management to choose. It will be a hard lesson for them if they have ridden rough-shod over deadlines before but, if it is in the contract, they will have to comply. Often, once they fully consider the options, they themselves will find a compromise.

Sometimes your management is in a position where the impossible is needed, or else their willingness to try to achieve it is needed. Your developer should also be able to offer options so that the best is achieved short of the impossible. They will work harder on your account for a period but can't do this all the time. And, it will come at a cost.

Summary

A successful project results from a good partnership between clients and developers. If clients have experienced difficulties with interactive projects in the past, they will try to take actions to make the path smoother for the future. This can affect the way that they want to work, and it may look at first as if the client is a demanding one. The developer needs to understand the reasons behind the client's way of working so that they can reach the common bond of trust that underlies successful projects.

This chapter has outlined some of the difficulties that clients have met when working with interactive developers and summarizes the countermeasures they have been known to take. Both sides can learn from this. The developers should take care not to cause the difficulties and to devise ways of working to ensure this; the commissioners may take note of these difficulties and take measures to avoid them or, by being aware, they will be able to recognize them earlier and take prompt action if necessary.

Top Tips

Strategy	Potential pay-off
Check the proposed work schedule to see if it has clear, logical stages or milestones that you'll need to agree, with the dates or timeline of expected delivery. Check that there is clear agreement of what should happen for the developer to inform you of slippage as early as possible.	If the developer is late with a stage, you'll have a clear understanding of what should have been delivered and when. If the developer has not informed you of slippage and given reasons, you will not be under any obligation, but it is likely that they will be.
State upfront that you do not want creativity or innovation for its own sake or for the developer's self development. Indicate that you want creativity and innovation tied firmly to the needs of the business and the users and you'll expect development ideas to be expressed in this way.	Control the type and amount of creativity and innovation to the extent you need by focusing the developer on the business needs and users' needs. This should also help control the use of the right medium for the right audience and purpose.
You need to understand exactly how much development will cost you and under what circumstances the costs will be varied. You need an agreed way for extra costs to be ratified by you before they are incurred. This is known as change management.	The developer cannot exceed the spend on any stage of development without your knowledge and agreement.
There can be many reasons why a developer does not appear to come forward with ideas. Often it is because the implementation of the ideas means extra time and charges that they feel you will react negatively towards. If you want to be sure that they offer up ideas for improvement from their experience, you need to encourage them to do so from the start of the project, keep some time and money in hand for such occasions and make decisions accordingly.	There will be more open communication between you where the developer will put forward many ideas for changes to the project while in development. Even if you cannot implement them at this stage, it may be good for you to know how to improve on follow-on revisions of the project.
Your own internal politics can make achieving projects harder both for internal interactive sections and outsourced developers. You as the representative need to try to control and protect the developers from this as much as possible. Examples of this can be blocking from your IT department and your management asking the impossible.	Only you can influence the internal workings of your company. This may be a slow and difficult process but you can take some steps to mitigate the risks. Refine the ways of working with the people around you that can influence your project. Look at Chapter 4 on Stakeholders for more information and tips.

Carry out the task as outlined below to tap into your company's prior experience. Devise strategies to deal with internal difficulties. Involve the IT department in the process of specification, agreement and sign-off deadlines or penalty costs for over-run to be passed to them if they hold the process up. Educate your management about the risks of interactive project development and ask them to come up with strategies to avoid the common internal difficulties.

You'll gradually minimize the internal risks to successful development of your interactive project. Use project management work processes to your advantage, explaining that it is your job to carry these out for the sake of the project.

Application Task

Clients: Devise your own problem-solving strategies

1. Identify, and meet with, any people in your organization who have been involved with managing interactive media projects. The meetings should focus on the most common difficulties each has met in working with developers and on any internal issues. Note specific examples and if any successful actions were used to off-set the difficulties. If the people can identify how much extra time, cost and quality impact these common problems have made, this will give better measurable indicators to demonstrate the worth of the exercise.

2. Once you have analysed the findings, write them up and perhaps post them on your intranet or equivalent, as part of your company knowledge management process, if you have one. Invite people to suggest actions for any difficulties that had no solutions put forward. You might post these under a table with headings like:

Project name	Difficulty (internal and external)	Time and cost implications	Action to redress	Notes

3. Use this knowledge and the prior experience to help you with your interactive projects.

● References/Resources

The web design business kit, Chapter 11 – Handle client complaints, sitepoint, no author or date given
http://www.sitepoint.com/article/handle-client-complaints/

Brendon Sinclair interview part 2, Kirstan Czupryna, SiteCRITIQUE, 30 March 2004
http://www.sitecritique.net/articles/art_details.php?ID=12

Working with angry or dissatisfied clients, Rich Brooks, Flyte Blog, 25 July 2005
http://www.flyteblog.com/flyte/2005/07/

Do you have a bad SEO company, or are you just a bad client?, Stoney deGeyter, Search Engine Guide, 25 Aug. 2005
http://www.searchengineguide.com/degeyter/005478.html

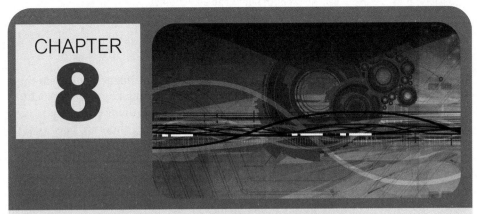

CHAPTER

8

The users' contribution; usability and accessibility

● Overview

The users (also known as viewers, visitors, end-users and customers) are the reason for producing an interactive product and so should be part of the business case analysis, design and development. This is true whether we are working on a website, mobile phone, PDA, iTV, DVD or any other platform. It is now easier to get users involved than it used to be. Their input depends on the commissioner acknowledging their importance and the developer then building in specific processes to the development phases that involve the user community.

The users should be an integral part of the design and development process. In the past, many projects ignored the users' contribution because the client, the developer or sometimes both of them believed they were already acting on their behalf. The perceived high cost of usability testing has also been a strong factor against employing it. These considerations are now being challenged. There is a much stronger case for involving the users to ensure that the interactive application suits their needs, not just for better site use in general and the returns this can bring, but to make sites accessible for all.

● Who brings what to the party?

The client has a perspective about an interactive product that might suit certain functions of their business. Their perspective might have been formed by their competitors or as a result of feedback from their customers. Or they themselves might have invested effort in a market opportunity to gain understanding about it. They operate in a market sector and have both tacit and business intelligence about it.

The developer has experience of interactive functionality, ways to produce products using this, and an understanding of some aspects of how it is used under various conditions. They are part of their own emerging interactive market, have tacit understanding about it and business intelligence about it. They may specialize in an interactive market segment: advertising, web design, e-learning, publishing, broadcasting, mobile and so on.

The user/customer can be relatively new – even naive – to interactivity, but may span the whole range up to being experienced and dexterous. They use interactive products for a purpose; they want to complete a task such as research some information, buy something, sell something, pay someone, communicate with others, contribute information or be entertained. They may also want to be seen to keep up with the trends, to know the latest on a topic, to be seen to use technology – or other 'lifestyle' aspirations.

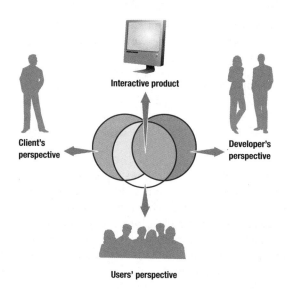

Perspectives affecting development

Each of these three groups has a perspective that can affect the development and use of an interactive product. So it would seem a 'no-brainer' that all should be involved in these processes as our industry quote suggests. Why doesn't this happen as a matter of course?

● Usability: its history and pre-disposition

Businesses have learnt that they need to understand their customers and satisfy their requirements. This is taken as given for non-interactive products. Products have evolved and been redesigned according to customer feedback. Businesses have also influenced the perception of their customers through advertising and marketing. These affect their pre-disposition to want certain features that are on offer. Both feedback and subjective appeal have contributed to design.

When interactive technology enters the mix – or any innovation for that matter – the clients and customers do not really know what they can expect or want. The business has to build its market by first trying things out and then refining them once the customers begin to establish what they find attractive about the new services or products. This uncertainty about how a product will be received fuels investment in innovation at the beginning of this production stage.

Mainframe software developments were the leaders in interactive developments. These giant infrastructure developments belonged to large corporations, and they took a long time to spec and a long time to develop. Their users were limited to people inside the corporations and the general public were not part of the mix. A lot of projects were based on faith from the decision makers. Any trials with system users occurred late into the development when enough of the final system was in place to use.

The user trials in these circumstances were highly structured, conducted in experimental conditions and monitored carefully through observation, video recording of use, recording of computer screen use, interviews with users and detailed documentation and reports. They were often conducted in usability labs specially designed for the purpose. The results were fed back into the design and development process and implemented then re-tested in another usability lab test over several iterative processes. Because of the statistical approach prevalent at the time, an appropriate proportion and cross-section of users was needed. This comprised a relatively large number of people. As a result, usability testing was time consuming and expensive. It needed specialists with the right training and experience.

These projects laid the groundwork for concepts of usability in interactive products, and this is also where some of the present dilemmas arose.

● What is interactive usability?

Usability is the measure of the quality of a user's experience when interacting with a product or system – whether a website, a software application, mobile technology, or any user-operated device.

US Department of Health and Human Services, Usability Basics.
http://www.usability.gov/basics/index.html

The user experience is affected by the ease and speed of completing a task, how easy it is to remember the system, the type and number of errors and subjective satisfaction, among other considerations.

Users can be naive in coming to your system and have no expectations, or they can be experienced in the use of interactive technology and so have prior expectations about tacit conventions. In web terms this could mean they expect:

● a company logo near the top left of the page;
● that clicking on the logo takes you to the home page;
● that navigation occurs along the left side or the top of the page;
● that links highlight and change colour on use;
● that shopping basket or trolley icons indicate a buying process.

These are some of the current 'conventions' that are common, although it is as well to note that tacit conventions change over time. For example, web links were always underlined when the web started, but this is less common now. However, underlining a word for emphasis may still make people think it's a link.

As the users within a market segment build up experience with aspects of interactive technology their expectations grow. Then they can be more focused on what works and what doesn't, what features make sense to them and which don't. At this point their opinions naturally help lead specific design and development. Prior to this, developers might have tried out some concepts for an innovative product with naive users and refined these as a result. As the product moves from innovative to accepted, the users' feedback will change accordingly and so it needs to be monitored frequently.

If the product is to be used internationally, or if it is successful in one country and so expands to others, localization and internationalization become important. User behaviour may vary according to country, culture and experience. This has not featured strongly yet in the usability debate, but it is likely to increase in the next few years as the online market grows and matures.

The usability debate

Interactive technology gets closer to the users than many other channels of communication. Users have to interact with the products, and this interaction can be monitored in numerous ways. Because usability has been seen as a migration of mainframe thinking and related processes to the new products and services, the old ways of usability testing have lingered. Traditional usability testing also added loops of quite considerable time and cost to development. However, the speed of interactive production, the use by the general public, the real-time use and the faster redesign time all change the nature of the interaction processes. These factors call the traditional approach to usability analysis into question.

Previously, selecting the right users to form an acceptable test sample was thought to be a specialist role. This may well be true for certain offline and specialist interactive applications. A piece of mobile phone e-learning on English for immigrants is best trialled with a usability sample taken from the target audience. A museum visitor information kiosk has a wide range of potential users and testers may need to fit the representative sample. But online shopping can be used by anyone from the general public who has access to the network and an acceptable means of payment. Self-selection through those that actually use the online site may be a viable option here.

In the past, for interactive software applications – particularly offline products – there needed to be enough of the whole system developed to allow the users a fair session of use. This delayed the involvement of users until a working prototype was ready, which often happened late in the project. Also, with traditional tests in usability labs, the selected users had to be booked to attend a venue at a particular time and place.

Online applications work on platforms that people are now used to seeing and using as a matter of lifestyle. It is easy to have several web pages mocked up and given a special allocation of space for nominated people to access. This can be true for clients to see and react to, as well as for users testing out some tasks or relating to some concepts. Easy access to the system can change the way users are involved in the development process, and this can happen quickly and frequently.

There are now online tools to record remote screen entry and to video live users for online usability testing. The users can select themselves to appraise the system/website because they are using it. They can be involved at every stage of development to react to features that come on stream. Google, the web search engine, has operated in this way, trying out added extras and refining the offerings according to feedback from their users.

Smaller numbers of people – apparently even as few as five or six – are now accepted as being able to find the main errors in an application. These main errors will give the biggest pay-back for user satisfaction if they are fixed. Some argue that specialists are not needed and that embedding frequent usability tests into the development process improves the skills and understanding of the designers and programmers.

Today's users still need to be clearly directed to follow particular tasks or assignments during the trial so that similar patterns of use are captured across the whole set of people. Defining the tasks to be done and interpreting the data collected does need to be tightly controlled still. People in your company can learn how to do this if they are given training and they have the aptitude. So whether a testing specialist needs to be involved is debatable. (See the references for more on this debate, but online usability testing is changing the perspectives held about traditional usability and opening up the area to a wider set of implementers.)

What aspects are covered in usability?

All aspects of interactivity are included as concerns of usability. The important overriding consideration is that this is interactivity from the users' perspective not from the designer's, programmer's or client's perspectives. Sometimes these will match but, in the end, the users' perspective should prevail until they are ready for the next stage of interaction when the design might be re-worked to line up with the users' new expectations.

Users come to an interactive product for a reason. It is up to the commissioner to understand what they want and to provide this for them. It is up to the developer to help the users achieve what they want. Anything that interferes with the users' experience affects the usability. With this wide approach it is easy to fit any of the design and development features into the purview of usability. We'll discuss usability from a website perspective, but this can apply equally to other interactive platforms.

Look The first impression or the 'look' of the application will affect the subjective experience of the users in arousing either appeal or lack of interest. It will make an implied statement about the site and the products that will be found there and it will make an implied statement about the lifestyle of the expected users. The subjective design elements are some of the hardest to determine. The client will have a strong opinion about this in terms of their current image and branding and their positioning

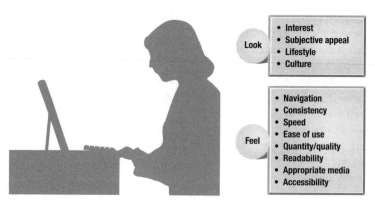

Usability and look and feel

in their market segment against their competitors. Designers will know the favoured latest image approach from their expertise in the area. The users' opinions may not line up with that of the experts. Cultural differences and the use of colour will feature more as localization and internationalization of online products continue to grow.

We all appreciate that the general look of websites appears to evolve about every six months and so redesigning the site is recommended. However, it may not be wise to jump on the design bandwagon unless the design is suiting the users and the purpose of the site. The debacle of Boo.com, which was design 'glitzy' but user unfriendly, springs to mind. The users could not figure out how to buy the goods, left the site and the company folded. The once prevalent Flash splash screen web has almost died out. But it took ages for designers to realize that people would not wait for the screen to load, didn't value the intrusive experience and so they went off to competitor sites. Surely it is relatively easy to try out some of the design concepts for the overall look with a group representing the users.

If you are redesigning a site, it is sensible to appraise the present site to understand what is working and what can be improved. This will require good information from the users and the web logs, and it will need people who have the skills to convert this information into design structures and advice.

The 'look' relates to the use of colour, general layout, use of media, impression of how much material there is, how clearly defined it looks and how easy to access it is. The home page of the website is crucial in forming the users' impression. This sets up expectations for the services offered on the site and even of the image of the company.

Feel This relates to the navigation structure, its consistency, the selections offered, speed of performance once something is selected and how easy it is for users to get to what they want. To encourage navigation through the site, the way the titles/headings and initial text are treated will set up expectations of the ease of use for the users. The number of categories as well as their titles will indicate the overall structure of the content. The structure will indicate the importance the company gives to the content that lies beneath them. Next, the quantity and quality of the content in terms of its appropriateness for the users' needs becomes important. The readability, amount of text, fonts used, size of text, relation to other media like graphics, animation, video and sound will all have the capacity to affect the users' experience.

People become frustrated if anything interferes with their concentration, so links that are broken or otherwise out of date cause negative reaction. Links need to be clear and consistent in appearance and change to show they have been accessed. People would like to know if the links are internal and so keep them within the site or if they are external and will exit the site. If this is clear then the users can make better decisions as to whether to use them for their purpose or not. Similarly, external links can be made to open in a new browser window so as to keep to original site 'on hand'.

If users have to scroll a lot looking for the particular item they want, this has a negative effect. This applies to both horizontal and vertical scrolling. There is a dilemma for designers in that if they try to avoid scrolling by having many layers/levels of pages instead, users can quickly get lost drilling down through pages and forget where they began the search. The rule of thumb is three levels or less is best.

The way that users read on screen is different to the way they read print. Research has shown that people scan and skim more to make decisions on what to drill down into and spend time on. Reading is a slower process on screen – about 25% slower than in print. This used to equate with poor screen resolution, but this has improved. Now reading practices have changed across media because people are under more time pressure. So skimming and scanning to decide on interest and then exploring to get deeper into content is even applying to print. We need to be aware that most of the research into reading of text and screen has taken the Western perspective while other cultures approach the basics of reading differently. Therefore the tacit commonalities of Western structured websites may not line up for international or global use of applications. More research is needed on these issues.

Jacob Nielson is considered to be one of the gurus of usability on the web. He has been looking into users' behaviour for many years and gives strong and useful guidelines about all forms of usability for different market sectors and for different types of website users – teenagers and the elderly, for example. His own site at useit.com is a useful touchstone for all aspects of usability. Among other reports, he lists the top ten common trouble spots on sites annually.

Use cases or user scenarios

The need to get closer to the users and their behaviour in order to determine how to develop interaction has prompted designers to draft use cases. These are scenarios of typical users performing the most common tasks for the site or equivalent interactive product. They are easy to understand and clients appreciate them. They allow a description of the high-level functionality of use that can then be translated into more technical and functional requirements.

If we consider a cinema website, a use case might describe a person trying to identify which films are on at a local cinema and then wanting to book some seats. Another use case might describe a person needing to get more detailed information about the films that are on to make a decision before deciding whether to book. The precise level of detail and what is considered important – such as if the film was a winner or nominated for film awards, critical reviews, biogs of the actors and so on – may need to be researched to see which are the most appreciated factors and lead to sales. Usability tests might show considerable difference in the categories that are effective, depending on the genre of the film and the age of its audience among other considerations, so that different categories might feature for different films. A third use case where competitions for free tickets/ice-creams or popcorn for children are offered as an incentive might be put forward, especially if the client has indicated that their market is affected and driven by children influencing their parents to buy film tickets. Finally, a fourth use case might relate to addressing the top incidental enquiries that come through as phone calls or emails to the client.

This mini use case study should be enough to show how the market and client needs can be determined and served clearly in business terms while the more technical requirements can be deduced from any agreed use cases. In many cases, the use cases feed into formal usability testing of the site, since users can be tasked to achieve the specifics of each use case as the site is constructed with the appropriate functionality. Then the hypothetical cases can be adjusted to actual user needs.

● Accessing the site/ease of search

Search capability has been added to usability in the last couple of years. The behaviour of users has changed so that they use search engines as their first port of call to find relevant sites for their purpose. This accounts for the push to improve the site's rating and therefore its prominence. This involves several usability criteria that are hidden from the users, but these allow the site to be linked to a search engine more efficiently. The metatags in the web page header, used to describe the gist of what the site contains to the search engine's software, are getting more sophisticated. (See Chapter 12 for a marketing perspective on search engine optimization: SEO.) Registering a site to make sure that the search engines actually recognize its existence has also become more complicated, since the number and pre-disposition of search engines has grown.

The more content that is added to the Internet, the more competitive it becomes for information to float to the top of the listings in a search engine. Things that helped improve ratings in the past – like the number of links a site had from other sites – are now interpreted in a more sophisticated way so that they are, as much as possible, less open to abuse and 'fixing' and reflect a 'peer review' of the site. As soon as search engine operators recognized that there was competition to get a site seen, they realized there was a market for people paying to be put at the top of search lists or to have small ads listed alongside the results by 'buying keywords'. Things change quickly in the Internet marketplace so the best ways for optimizing searches are being refined all the time. It pays to understand what the trends are in order to keep up.

Searching has become the favourite way for people to find sites that they want, so the ways people use to search, how they define what they want, how they refine what they want, what they do when they can't find what they want, all drive a new industry in search engines and the way they analyse and sort through the massive amount of information on the web. The search mechanism that users find better than another (because of its usability) will win custom away from one search engine to another and improve access to sites of interest to the user. The search engines become the guides for the users. They represent big business opportunities.

However, this hidden manoeuvring is only one part of 'search'. Many sites offer their own search facility to help users find what they want within the site itself. This is particularly true for larger sites where it is recognized that people might get lost. Sometimes these search facilities only serve to confuse users. Generally people are not good at predicting terms that others have used to classify chunks of material. The skill of 'searching' online is now being recognized and taught in its own right. People are impatient and seem to give up quickly if they can't find what they are looking for. They don't appear to have many varied ways of searching and often don't try refining their searches by using advanced techniques if the site has them. Common tricks include putting quotation marks around phrases (to search on the phrase rather than individual words) and using boolean logic terms like AND and OR.

It is now quite common for companies to include their website URL on their brochures, newsletters, letters and other forms of communication or advertising. Each method helps the other because people have preferred ways of finding information and may want to cross-reference between digital means and traditional means. It has taken a long time for retailers to understand that many customers research products and prices online before going to a traditional store to actually buy them. Companies need to try to understand the users' behaviour while they're using the website, so that they can blend the online and offline experiences to suit the behaviour.

● Usability: return on investment

It was difficult to make the case for usability testing previously because, as we've seen, many believed you needed dedicated facilities, carefully selected triallists and skilled staff, and that it was an iterative process of refinement. Things have changed in the online environment, so it is becoming more straightforward to measure the results of employing usability criteria. This makes it easier to make a case to include usability in the development process. (See the references for this section.)

If we remember Chapter 5 where business cases were discussed, ROI (return on investment) is a strong driver for those making business decisions. Although the business cases for interactive media appeared embryonic, the data on usability is more tangible. Jakob Nielsen conducted comprehensive research into the returns on productivity from websites that had applied usability testing in their development in late 2002. From that, he recommended that 10% of a project cost should be spent on such testing as it doubles usability of the application, and he saw this figure increasing to as much as 20% over several years. Because cost and use are different measures, he acknowledged that these ROI numbers were not a classic use of the concept. In this context Nielsen described usability as increased use, more efficient use or higher user satisfaction.

He explains the difficulty of trying to compare like with like in terms of use. Project size and complexity have implications for the data Nielsen uses, but he explains how he has reached his conclusions taking all these factors into consideration. In those websites that had employed usability, they saw:

- the sales conversion rates for retail sites increase by 100%;
- the traffic/visitor count increased by 150%;
- the user performance or productivity increased by 161%;
- the use of specific features on the site increased by 202%.

The benefits of usability have also been put forward in terms of:

- decreased user error;
- decreased training costs;

- savings made by capturing design flaws early in the development stages;
- decreased need for user support;
- reduced maintenance costs;
- reduced development time;
- higher rate of customer satisfaction;
- increased customer loyalty;
- stronger branding.

If users find a site easy to use, it is more likely that they'll return and build a relationship of trust with that site and its goods and services. Return customers are apparently also more likely to spend more.

● Where does accessibility come into this?

Accessibility

Since 1999 it has been a legal requirement for websites to be accessible to everyone regardless of ability. In the UK this is governed by the Disability Rights Act and the US equivalent is Section 508 of the Rehabilitation Act. Now, because this has not been followed as widely as hoped and because there has been some confusion about achieving this equality of access, the UK Disability Rights Commission has indicated that it will start taking action against sites that do not comply. Other organizations that represent the rights of people with special needs, such as the visually impaired, hearing impaired, disabled or those having a low level of literacy and poor reading skills, have been becoming more active as well. (See Chapter 10 for more on the legal implications of accessibility.)

If we say that an accessible website is one that provides equal access and opportunity to people with disabilities, this expands the concept of usability to everyone, and the things that make a site accessible also improve its general usability. This is why we have included strong reference to accessibility in this chapter as well as covering it in other places in the book.

Users with disabilities may use tools such as screen readers, magnification software, voice recognition devices, a head-operated mouse and an on-screen headboard among others to aid their use. Some will have fine motor skill difficulties for positioning the mouse and clicking to select; dyslexic users may need more time to read, for example, so animated text will be difficult for them to follow. Others with learning difficulties can be aided through better and clearer writing of content. Colour – especially the readability of text on a coloured background – is problematic as well since many people have defective colour vision. The use of tables for page layout, text rendered as a graphic and even the ubiquitous Flash have accessibility implications.

Companies may have different reasons for instituting accessibility guidelines on their websites. It might be part of their ethical policy for equality, it might be to demonstrate social responsibility, or it could be part of meeting international standards and technical quality initiatives. All of these can influence company decisions to comply with guidelines for accessibility; but being able to reduce the risk of legal action being taken against you is a strong business case.

PAS78 is the Publicly Available Specification and set of guidelines for Accessibility (March 2006), developed by the British Standards Institute and sponsored by the Disability Rights Commission. It covers the whole process of websites from commissioning and designing to building and maintaining. There is also guidance for contracting web design companies and accessibility auditing services. It outlines levels of conformity for different reasons so that sites can balance the needs of their key target market against those of users with disabilities who may wish to use their site.

Both commissioners and developers need to recognize the amount of accessibility and therefore usability that will be needed in the interactive application. This does affect the design and development process. There are three levels of accessibility defined in the guidelines, and the client should consider which is most appropriate for them. The developer will then design, develop and test the application against the proper criteria to follow conformance procedures. There are websites that offer tools to help test conformity to A, AA, and AAA levels or their equivalent Priority 1, 2 and 3. (Follow the Watchfire reference below to understand these requirements.) Some of these tests are free, but increasingly the online test facilities are beginning to charge fees for testing and constructing reports.

Including usability and full accessibility testing will make development more expensive but including them in the whole process from the beginning will bring strong benefits to the applications, increase user satisfaction and will be cheaper than taking remedial measures later.

Where does testing fit into this?

Usability and accessibility are just part of a testing plan that each company should develop. Testing is part of the total quality assurance package a developer can offer. The range and type of testing should be divided into standard testing, which will be performed on any development, and specialized testing, which can be available at an extra cost to suit particular clients, the market and application. The client will have a choice of how much will be employed and how much time and cost it will incur. The three perspectives of 'business, technology and the user' mentioned in the initial industry quotation above all need to be tested to a defined quality level. The range and types of tests are many because each has its own standards. It is up to the developer to educate the client on what is available, what is recommended and what is obligatory. Chapter 9 concentrates on the technology aspects of testing while Chapter 5 outlined some of the business aspects that need consideration.

Relation to Prince2 methodology

It is worth mentioning here for those that need to line up with Prince2 methods of general project management (more prevalent in Europe for the moment) that the users are involved from the beginning of the project and built into the whole process of design and development. Even if the first part of the project (the initiation) has been carried out by the client prior to contracting the developer, the involvement of the users or the users' representative is recommended from the start-up (SU) phase.

The users should be represented on the project board, if one is to be established. If there are several user areas involved then they may be formed into a user committee where the chairperson reports the findings/needs to the board. We can immediately see this applying for the design and redesign of a corporation's intranet, for example, where the end-users are diverse sections of the corporation itself. But the needs of the general public – as in many Internet sites – and then the needs of market segments within the general public for more specifically targeted sites are rather different, and it is harder to see where the Prince2 guidelines can be followed stringently. However, the spirit of representation of the users from the beginning of a project is sound. This is reinforced by the premise of employing usability and accessibility in this chapter. They both offer measurable potential benefits.

If the client/commissioner has not included the concepts of usability and accessibility in their brief, nor tabled the involvement of users in the development process, then the developers should raise the issues and explain how they may be addressed. User testing in stages throughout the design and build may be appropriate. Conformance to a defined level of accessibility as per the standards mentioned above should also be raised. Then, it becomes the client's responsibility to determine what they expect from these areas. The developer has educated them by informing them of the issues and offering set ways to address them. The questions about usability and accessibility should be raised at the scoping stage if not before, but they should not be forgotten. (See Chapter 3 on Scoping, for more on this aspect.)

Summary

The user perspective can influence interactive design and development, and it has not always been taken into account. Both the client and the developer might have believed that each was representing the views of the users when in fact both have their own bias in the equation.

Usability testing has long been part of IT software development processes. It involved lengthy, iterative testing in a special laboratory using careful procedures and triallists. Because of the legacy from this, many have perceived implementing usability criteria as costly and time consuming. It was also difficult to prove that the processes had added value to the interactive application in terms of the business case.

This has evolved with online usability where faster, easier and so cheaper methods of usability design and testing have emerged. There are better measures of the impact that usability can have on the business as well. Increasingly, the case for involving users in the design and development process is getting stronger.

Usability and accessibility are intertwined. Access for all users is an extension of usability criteria. The more users who react with satisfaction to the interactive product, the better the use, and the more likely it is that the product will achieve what the business stated in its business case. Designers can educate clients about the value of usability/accessibility. They can build these into their initial design processes at a smaller cost than would be incurred by applying them retrospectively.

Top Tips

Planning	Potential pay-off
The users hold the answers to effective use of the interactive product so involve them in the design and development process.	Better use of the application, increased user satisfaction, increased performance on tasks or equivalent.
Approach online usability with a fresh perspective. Appraise new methods of testing.	Online processes drive new forms of usability that are faster and cheaper than older methods.
The 'look and feel' of an interactive product affect the users and their satisfaction. Appraise your design and build procedures from the users' perspective and change if necessary.	Your designers and programmers will improve their skills from both a users' and a business point of view since the client is happy if the customers are happy.
Users change their opinions/perspectives according to experience so keep checking their prevalent wishes.	You keep on top of changing trends in user behaviour and can offer strong cases to the client to restyle their sites accordingly.
The users' behaviour is driving search engine optimization, because they are using search engines to narrow their search and save time.	Knowing the trends for the use of search engines and which are most popular will affect what you offer to your client and why.
Return on investment cases for usability are available and make business sense. Find them and use them.	This will be convincing to your client and affect their perception of your skills. It gives you both objective measures to develop for.
Accessibility is part of usability and is now a legal consideration for developers and client. You need to educate yourselves and your client if necessary in this.	Accessibility offers the potential for more satisfied users. More satisfied users make business sense. You'll both fulfil your legal requirements as well.

Application Task

If you feel that your company might improve their record on usability and accessibility follow the task below.

1. Identify if your company has a designer and a programmer (or someone else, preferably in a position of authority) who has expertise in usability and accessibility.

2. Give them the task/project to update their expertise and present their findings to the whole company at a meeting or seminar. (Have a defined date for this seminar for them to work towards.) As part of the recommendations they will need to incorporate the principles into the design and development processes of the company – from the pitch for work or equivalent through to the design, redesign, build, etc. They'll also need to attach costs to the offerings for the client to know what they'd get, why it was important (business case) and what it would cost.

   Create the time and opportunity for this for these people or it will not happen. Have a 'champion' for this high up in the company to protect the initiative. Take the role yourself if appropriate.

3. Get the company to buy in to the proposed changes and make usability/accessibility a natural, costed part of your work offering.

 References/Resources

Definition

US Department of Health and Human Services, Usability Basics
http://www.usability.gov/basics/

Traditional against new usability methods

The culture of usability: how to spend less and get more from your usability-testing program, Janice Fraser New Architect, Aug. 2002
http://www.newarchitectmag.com/documents/s=2450/na0802b/

Remote testing versus lab testing, Bolt Peters, 3 Feb. 2005
http://boltpeters.com/articles/versus.html

Conduct your own remote usability study, Bolt Peters, 16 Feb. 2005
http://boltpeters.com/articles/tutorial.html

General usability

Usability News, Newsletter of the Software Usability Research Laboratory, Wichita State University, Vol 8 Issue 1, Feb. 2006
http://www.usabilitynews.org/

Criteria for optimal web design (designing for usability), Michael L Bernard Software Usability Research Laboratory, Wichita State University, 30 March 2003
http://psychology.wichita.edu/optimalweb/

Getting started – what is user centred design? Usability Net, no date given
http://www.usabilitynet.org/tools/gettingstarted.htm

Growing a business website: fix the basics first, Jakob Nielsen's Alertbox, 20 March 2006
http://www.useit.com/alertbox/design_priorities.html

Time for a redesign: Brad Wieners interviewing Jakob Nielsen (re 10% spend on usability), 1 June 2004
http://www.cioinsight.com/article2/0,1397,1612183,00.asp

Choose & use the best colors: the psychology of color, Andrew Eaton, Concept Marketing Group, no date given
http://www.marketingsource.com/articles/view/2629

Research-based web design & usability guidelines, Sanjay J. Koyani, Robert W. Bailey, Janice R. Nall et al., National Cancer Institute, US Department of Health and Human Services, 2003
http://www.usability.gov/pdfs/guidelines.html

Return on investment

Return on investment for usability, Jakob Nielsen's Alertbox, 7 Jan. 2003
http://www.useit.com/alertbox/20030107.html

Usability ROI, Foraker Design – Provider of Usability & Web Design Services, no date given
http://www.usabilityfirst.com/roi/index.txl

Usability return on investment, Nielsen Norman Group Report, no date given
http://www.nngroup.com/reports/roi/

Return on investment for usable user-interface design: examples and statistics, Aaron Marcus, President, Aaron Marcus and Associates, Inc., 28 Feb. 2002
http://www.amanda.com/resources/ROI/AMA_ROIWhitePaper_28Feb02.pdf

Usability ROI: measuring return on investment, Foraker Design – Provider of Usability & Web Design Services, no date given
http://www.usabilityfirst.com/roi/

Accessibility

Watchfire webxact online testing
http://webxact.watchfire.com

Web Accessibility Initiative (WAI)
http://www.w3.org/WAI/

Developing a web accessibility business case for your organization, S.L. Henry, ed., World Wide Web Consortium (MIT, ERCIM, Keio), Aug. 2005
http://www.w3.org/WAI/bcase/

User-friendly websites for all

User-friendly websites for all, Disability Rights Commission, News, 8 March 2006
http://www.drc.org.uk/newsroom/

PAS78 Guide to Good Practice in Commissioning Accessible Websites, BSI, launched 15 March 2005
http://www.bsi-global.com/ICT/PAS78/

Web Accessibility in Mind
http://www.webaim.org

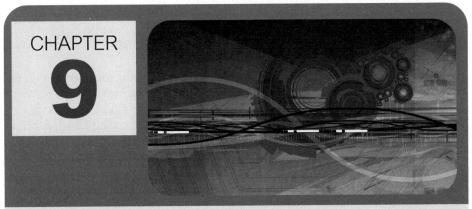

CHAPTER 9

Interactive media testing and archiving

● Overview

Whatever interactive platforms you are developing for, they need to be robust under known conditions and perform gracefully under stress, be usable by the target audience and fit your client's business needs. Essentially this splits the testing of these three areas into functional testing, user testing and fitness for business purpose. The functional testing relates to checks on the quality, performance, security and robustness of the coding, and the user testing covers the interface design, the navigation and the structure of the content. Accessibility issues need to be covered too. The business needs testing is devised for each project according to its orientation. (See particularly Chapter 5 for more around these business issues and the return on investment – ROI). Both testing and archiving can form part of the quality assurance of the product.

The archiving of digital media is receiving increasing attention as the early forms of digital media become obsolete, threatening an information gap in the history of information archiving. The responsibility for archiving needs to begin with the creators of the material to allow them to access the assets if needed again without re-engineering them. Then the assets will meet more general archiving standards for posterity in the new digital archive repositories that are emerging.

● General concepts of digital media testing

Testing is a large topic but is often relegated to being a minor consideration in the industry. It is controversial – there is genuine confusion about what 'testing' should cover, when it should be done and who is going to pay for it. When technologies are emerging and products are innovative, there are grounds for tolerating less than perfect functionality but, as the products mature, expectations of performance quality increase.

Interactive media teams very often appear to be under pressure to develop products on the fly with fluid requirements definitions. Testing requires planning, clear definitions, time, cycles of testing and adjustment to the product, its features and its market. No wonder there's a clash. Testing can cover aspects of the hardware involved, the software, the media features (text, audio, video, graphics), the navigation, the structure, the content, the functionality (including features tailored to commerce, retail, learning, finance, publishing and so on), the subjective orientation of the product, usability, security of data and performance, standards compliance and accessibility. This is not an exhaustive list either.

Chapter 8 on Usability and accessibility concentrated on the user side of product performance, the front end or, in other words, the quality assurance for those aspects. They involved their own forms of definition and testing. Chapters 3–5 gradually elicited the business requirements through scoping the project, talking to the stakeholders and establishing the partnership agreement on what the project was trying to achieve in business terms. The core business requirements were elicited here, and this set up the equivalent of the business test criteria for proving to the client that the product satisfied their business needs.

In this chapter we'll concentrate on the more functional software aspects of testing: because the interactive application relies on technology, this has to be tested. All three

Testing = examining aspects of performance

aspects of business, user and technology testing need to be considered for each application, however, just as the industry quote in Chapter 8 indicated.

Technology/Functional testing

Each platform will have its own set of tests for the software, hardware and its performance. Then, since interactive media hinges around the production of software-driven applications, this software needs to be reliable under known conditions and needs to respond appropriately under stress.

A single application is likely to be made of components from a number of sources, including ones written by the developer, and they need to work together to achieve the required end result. So a website may contain code for animating graphics, a database, for content management and e-commerce, JavaScript for monitoring form input and tracking users' behaviour, active pages to format data returned from the database ... all from different sources and all integrated with the back-end Internet server.

Each of these functions needs to work in its own right, and then work in conjunction with all the other pieces. Essentially, this is what technology testing addresses. It is the hidden end of the application that often draws attention only when it is not working. If it is transparent, it is working and is taken for granted. This makes it harder to justify in terms of who should pay for testing. The client believes that it should work and that if it doesn't work all the time it is broken. This is especially true if 'off the shelf' components are used.

Software isn't like that. Most software will work under certain conditions but not under others. It is designed for a purpose and, if the purpose or parameters change, it may lose its efficiency. It is rather like designing an engine for a small car because that is what the client appeared to describe as a requirement. That engine will be efficient up to a point and within certain parameters but, if the client then expects more than they first indicated, the designers realize that they should have designed for a medium, a large or even a racing car. The whole approach, processes and costs would have been different if they had known. To add to the difficulties, any application where users can enter data has to be able to cope with accidental or malicious input that may be outside the expected parameters. So this is the dilemma for designers and programmers developing interactive materials; most of the design is hidden from the general population, a bit like an iceberg.

Those that do not work in the programming end of interactivity, together with the great majority of clients, do not realize the varieties and types of testing that may be needed for particular applications. It is up to the developer's management to educate both the client and the rest of the team to appreciate the sets of hidden tasks that the 'front-end' and 'back-end' staff have to carry out. The roles of graphics and programming, where both deal with software and both integrate work into the application, are becoming increasingly blurred. It is recognized that they need each other to create a whole package and that there is a point at which one set of skills ends and another begins, but to most outsiders this is a black art.

The diagram below should help to indicate the types and variety of coding practices that can occur. Different configurations of these sets are needed for different projects, but they are all part of the repertoire of interactive skills.

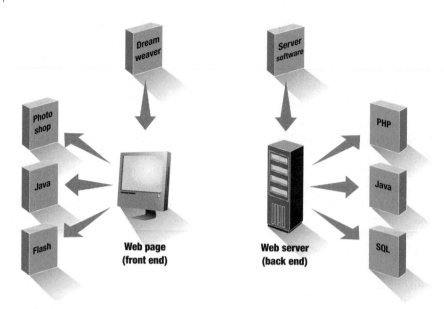

Examples of front-end and back-end programming

The interactive media approach is further complicated by the increasing use of design-led packages which can produce code so that programmers may not be needed for an application at all. Flash programming is a case in point. This can be used entirely to produce a website, where a self-contained Flash application is simply embedded in a single web page. Images for the page would be processed in an application like Photoshop. Other packages like Dreamweaver are also design-led and can produce code that runs in the browser without requiring the designer to leave the WYSIWYG environment, while Java has to be programmed but can be used to run almost any kind of application in the browser. The back-end processes are not design-led but programmer-led, and are either self-contained programs such as databases like MySQL or extensions to other programs such as extra modules added to the web server. They structure content, databases, e-commerce interaction, credit card clearance, etc. to feed information back to the front end as and when necessary. Back-end adjuncts to the web server software itself include more traditional Common Gateway Interface (CGI) systems such as Perl, integrated scripting such as Active Server Pages (ASP) or PHP or high-performance code using Java.

● The software approach debate

Core back-end programming has lined up with traditional software development and has been affected by the approaches to development used in computing/computer science and engineering until the early 2000s. There has been increasingly heavy criticism of these traditional approaches as they do not appear to work under the new market conditions of software development – and this includes interactive media. We need to address this debate here because the approach to development has included how and where the testing of the applications occurs. Testing and development have been and remain intertwined. Each interactive company will be employing an implied 'approach' to development and testing, and it is important that you can recognize which approach or version is used since it will pervade all aspects of the application development, including testing, and have implications for the project manager.

The 'waterfall' approach is the name 'retro-fitted' to the traditional model that is now being criticized. This applied a linear stage-by-stage development process and involved heavy documentation before, during and after development. So companies that have requirements specification, technical specification and functional specification documents might appear to be adopting the waterfall approach. The approach maintains that you need to pin down the absolute detailed specifications of what you do when you develop, build, test, implement and maintain the application. The critics emphasize the linear and contained nature of the stages. It would appear that testing only took place at the required time in the development cycle and that this was always towards the end. The developers controlled the process and discouraged changes from the clients after the specification process was agreed. Critics also claim that many of the projects that used the waterfall technique did not complete on time and budget, did not meet the requirements of the clients and market, because these had changed over the development period, and did not perform well from a code point of view either.

This approach originated with the large software engineering projects that took years to develop and involved large teams. They were often building the hardware as well as the software for the projects. Interactive media projects tend to be smaller, faster projects developed for an emerging market that fluctuates rapidly. The measured, strongly planned processes of the waterfall approach do seem at odds with this.

The waterfall approach evolved through stages to a 'spiral' approach, which was less self-contained and allowed iterations of design, build, test and redesign. The concepts of prototyping and mock-ups appeared. These were an attempt to collapse the process to make it faster. They tried to compensate for the client working blind and not knowing what the end result would look like, in order to ensure that the end result fitted the client's needs.

The development of the spiral approach coincided with core changes in the way code was written. Programming practices changed, moving away from large interdependent lines of code to object-oriented coding. This allowed discrete pieces of working functionality to be free-standing and was the start of a coding revolution that is on-going. Rapid Application Development (RAD) and Rationalized Unified Process, among others, have now led to Agile programming techniques and practices and the use of eXtreme Programming (XP).

These latest approaches recognize that the requirements are fluid because of the fast-changing nature of the market, and that clients change their minds during the development cycle. This equates to the interactive media environment, or so it would seem. Under these Agile approaches, small pieces of functionality are coded and tested every couple of days. The team – designers, programmers, team leader, the business representative (account manager or equivalent perhaps) – work together with frequent meetings. They devise small but definite tasks to achieve within a few days and demonstrate to the client. The project keeps moving forward with the expectation that some code/functionality will be thrown away as the requirements firm up on the fly. Documentation is almost non-existent; programmers tend to work in pairs. Code and tests for the code are worked on simultaneously with tests being devised first then code written to see if it passes the tests. This is done so that each piece is robust under known conditions and can be inter-mixed with other bits of code. Functional testing is not confined to a specific stage and occurs at the time the code is written, not as a stage late into the process. Productivity is meant to increase under this approach.

The software approach debate is continuing and interactive media is caught up in it to some extent. There are criticisms of the Agile approach too, even though it addresses the faster production cycle and changes in requirements that are characteristics of interactive media. From the project management and business point of view, when can a contract and agreement for a payment schedule for developing the interactive application be made if neither party knows what the boundaries of the project are? How can the developer give an estimate of the cost if they don't know how many resources/people and how much time it will take to reach a successful conclusion?

These are fundamentals that are vitally important. Unless the client agrees to work on a time and materials contract, which allows the developer to bill on an on-going basis based on actual work done, then the developer is at considerable risk, giving an estimate on unknowns. It is very rare in interactive media for a developer to get a direct time and materials contract. There is sometimes latitude in the interactive advertising segment of the market when the company has won a large contract to serve all a client's advertising needs. In this case, the interactive proportion of the budget will be agreed internally and the team will have to work to their own management, on behalf of a client, up to a pre-determined figure. In this way, they might effectively be on a time and materials contract as long as the total spend was within the limit set for the interactive advertising portion of the work.

Scott Ambler (see references below) suggests a middle of the road approach to cost estimates and budgeting, even if an Agile system is being used, since he finds that clients are not used to a fluid relationship with cost: it'll be ready when you've decided what you really want, when it's finished and it will cost what it costs. Management needs the ball-park estimate – just as has always been provided – even though developers know how unreliable these can be. Clients do not have bottomless pits of money and have to justify what they might be spending to their own managements. Scott's recommendations seem to make sense. They encourage an initial requirements specification at a high level – enough to have a general understanding of what needs to be achieved so that a rough time and cost can be put forward. Then the functions are prioritized through 'use stories' in terms of business imperative (these are small tight requirements, smaller than use cases, see Chapter 8) and developed in the Agile way piece by piece, unit tested as they are developed. It isn't made clear exactly how change management and extra costs are handled when clients change their requirements. But this would need to be resolved from a project management perspective and from the point of view of both the developer's senior management and the client.

This then provides some of the background about the place of testing in an approach but it cannot be separated from the project management and business issues for developers. Some aspects of the earlier approaches might seem to offer a stronger project management case, but some of the latest techniques also offer some client management latitude. As long as the approach fits the developer's business needs and is manageable for a project manager or equivalent, then any of the approaches can be tailored to suit particular cases. The amount and types of testing will be affected by the approach. In light of this, we cover a variety of types of testing in this chapter; and each company might be using some of them, but probably not all. There is no set answer to which approach will work best for a developer or a particular project and suit the developer's business needs, although Agile methods are currently gaining ground with programmers if not management.

Types of test (technology/functional)

Each developer needs a listing of all the types of testing that they might employ for the business, the user and the technology. Overleaf we'll list the technology tests and give a brief explanation of them to show the breadth and diversity. This is not exhaustive, particularly as some terms are not universal and some types of testing can be called by several different names. However, what tests you will list will depend a lot on your in-house skills. You may use this list to explain to the whole team what is available and what is recommended, and what is 'house' standard. Any tests that need to be subcontracted will have an extra time and cost attached to them. This will help the team recognize what to offer the clients and where to negotiate for additional time and cost if necessary.

Quality assurance

If the concept of quality has been defined in some way through recognized and accepted standards, then tests can be devised on the interactive product to see if it meets the quality standards. In this way, quality assurance and testing can overlap. The testing is being done for a particular purpose according to a defined standard. However, the requirements of your piece of software/code/navigation and so on may be targeted very specifically to a type of use and so you may have to formulate your own test specifications on top of some quality standards to meet the product's own requirements. The mix and match of tests and the selection and use of appropriate tools should be made by an experienced performance tester who is part of your team.

Archiving

Archiving is the process of storing a project away once it is completed so that, if necessary, it can be retrieved at a later date. Archiving shares some common ground with backing up since the final backup at the end of a project should become the archive of the project. However, it is likely that the way your backups are done will reflect your network structure rather than the projects you are working on, so there is unlikely to be a clear relationship between the two.

If the project has been a large-scale production then there are likely to be lots of loose ends that need to be tidied up at the end. This can seem like bureaucracy running amok but, once you have been caught out by clients requesting individual graphics from their application for marketing purposes, clients returning after several months to do an update that had never been mentioned, your colleague wanting to see the budget breakdown to help in costing another similar project, another colleague wanting the name of the voice-over artiste and agent, your management dealing with

Test types and definitions

Test name	Description	Orientation
Alpha and beta testing	Testing near completion (alpha) or on completion (beta). Usually done by external testers. An alternative meaning is that alpha testing tests with a small amount of possible dummy content while beta includes most or all of the intended content.	Back-end (mostly)
Archive/backup and restore	Carry out a test restore of anything backed up or archived to make sure it is retrievable, especially before deleting originals.	Back-end
Browser compatibility	Confirm that the web pages look the same on the agreed range of browsers and platforms.	Front-end
Client/server testing	Test the communication between a client (e.g. a web browser) and a server (e.g. a web server) across the network. Check both functionality and performance.	Back-end
Compatibility testing	Expand the browser testing to check other parts of the system such as plug-ins and the version of Java used (for example). Make sure the requirements match the actual performance.	Front-end
Component testing	Testing of the smallest runnable part of the software in a real world environment. See Unit testing.	Back-end
Database testing	Check the level of normalisation of a relational database, look at efficiency in terms of both performance and space used and that there are no redundant tables. Make sure that any tables are optimized.	Back-end
Integration testing	The next stage after component testing. Tests that a number of components (or one if it calls itself) work together correctly.	Back-end
Internationalization	Make sure a user can switch between languages without having to restart. May involve change of direction for text.	Front- and back-end issues
Installation testing	Check that the application can easily be installed (on the server) if necessary. Don't assume that the developer team will be the only people installing (or uninstalling) it.	Back-end
Load/stress	Simulate heavy use of the application to check performance hits and determine whether the server is likely to grind to a halt under load. Load testing usually checks for issues under normal, but intense, circumstances where as stress testing may deliberately over-drive the application or deprive it of memory, disc space or some other resource.	Back-end
Localization	Repeat any tests in every language version of the project.	Front- and back-end issues
Maintenance – links, logging, tracking, etc.	On-going tests of items not totally under your control such as broken links and of on-going monitoring of accesses (web logs) and user tracking.	Front- and back-end issues
Modem testing	Check performance for a user who has a slow Internet connection.	Front-end
Mutation testing	Deliberately introduce bugs to make sure they are detected. Particularly useful for testing test data.	Back-end
Performance (speed of download, reliability, backups, down time, updates)	Measure the response time of the system in normal use and check this is acceptable for an end-user.	Back-end

Test types and definitions *continued*

Test name	Description	Orientation
Platform testing	The software interacts with the underlying environment, such as the operating system, in the appropriate way.	Back-end
Production testing	If a number of instances of the software are being deployed, make sure they all function correctly.	Front- and back-end issues
Recovery testing	How well does the system recover from a 'catastrophic' failure such as a crash and reboot.	Back-end
Regression	If any changes are made to the system, repeat testing to ensure the changes have no adverse effect.	Back-end
Security (firewalls, passwords, encryptions, etc.)	Check that any unexpected user input is handled gracefully. If the application is very sensitive, try to hack into it.	Has front- and back-end testing components
Smoke testing (also known as sanity testing)	Simplest test after completion or after changes. So-called because it is the software equivalent of powering up a machine and seeing whether it catches fire.	Back-end (usually)
System stability	Make sure the system you are running on is functioning correctly and not generating bugs of its own.	Back-end
System testing	Similar to integration testing except that the system as a whole is being debugged for things like performance and security.	Front- and back-end issues
Testability testing	As with system stability testing, you must be sure that your hardware and system software are in a fit state for you to begin testing your application. In other words you have to be sure that you are not chasing bugs in the OS!	Front- and back-end issues
Unit testing	Testing the smallest runnable component of the software in an artificially controlled environment such as a specially-written test harness. See Component testing.	Back-end
Web server testing	Part of testability testing: make sure your server is working properly and has the resources it needs.	Back-end
Validation testing	Use W3C validators to check code against standards. This is especially important with any dynamically-produced pages.	Front- and back-end issues
User testing		
Accessibility	Use the W3C and 'Bobby' to check the level of accessibility of the pages. Look at pages with style sheets disabled and with graphics turned off to make sure they are readable.	Front- and back-end issues
Usability testing/ user testing	How well do the intended users understand the system and make use of it? This testing should be carried out with members of the target audience and not the developers.	Front-end
User acceptance	Is the application acceptable to the intended end-users (at a broad level)?	Front-end
User scenario testing	If user scenarios were used as part of the initial requirements, the application should be checked against them.	Front-end

an enquiry from the corporate client company's inspectorate about exactly who had signed off the content in the project a year earlier, a museum insisting that they are one slide short and claiming four months' penalty fees and so on, then the value of the time put into archiving in a structured manner is clear.

Chaotic archiving

What needs to be archived?

Companies may have their own policies for archiving their projects. Many have different systems and locations for storing such disparate things as documentation, audio and video files, code and graphics, as well as finished web pages. The archive should gather together all the relevant files for the project, in forms that are not encrypted or copy-protected. It is debatable whether you need to include copies of shrink-wrapped software, and this might not be legal anyway, but any documentation and also originals of any assets licensed or produced for the project should be included, even if you may use these in other projects. Ideally, someone should be able to recreate the project from the archive without searching out other files, apart from operating system or server environments.

The operating system and other system software wouldn't usually be archived with a project, even though they would be essential to rebuilding it. This is a little counter-intuitive but then you are unlikely to archive hardware either (unless the project is making hardware).

Gathering this material together is an onerous task, which usually falls on the project manager and/or admin assistant as the only ones left working on the project. So it will help to have a systematic approach to archiving. If no archive checklist is provided by the company it will be in your interest to draft one, because it is easy to forget one or two major items. It can take several days to 'box up' a commercial, large-scale project. You may also be pressured to get the project's assets off the development system to free space for other projects.

The company may have defined a set way of capturing the final version of the project – like putting a website copy onto a CD or even keeping a reference copy on a web server. Bear in mind that there may be back-end assets such as a database or the contents of a content management system that need to be archived as well. SQL databases can be archived as text files configured to automatically rebuild the data structure as they are restored.

As the range and type of projects vary so much, a project manager should know what the company expects to be archived across all projects and then devise some sub-sections of extra considerations that might apply for other projects.

Formal documents

These will include all contractual documents, such as the final proposal document, any terms and conditions agreed as per the firm's policy, any agreement to ways of work-ing, all sign-off documents for the intermediate stages and the final sign-off. They should also include all confidentiality agreements from the team members if this was a condition accepted from the client. Copies of all signed contracts drafted for subcon-tractors or freelancers should be held with the formal documents. All rights agreements for the content should be sorted and filed accordingly. You'll need an index of what the files contain for quick access later. Finally, a list showing where physical assets such as video master tapes and code backups are being held is necessary for a full formal record to be complete.

If you had to use external assets from picture libraries or museums then a similar list should have been compiled for those. Whoever was managing the rights and clear-ances for the project should have made good records showing what has been returned and what may be outstanding and why. Any outstanding items must be returned now and a record kept of what was sent back and when.

Budget information

During the project you will have been monitoring the actual time and cost against the predicted time and cost as stipulated in the final proposal agreement. These are impor-tant records, so detailed files are essential. If your finance department has been collating the team's timesheets against tasks or sign-off points, and costing according to the internal and external rates you gave them, then you should already have a file with their information. They should be able to provide you with a detailed copy for the complete project soon after final sign-off. However, for many reasons this rarely seems to happen, so often you have the best understanding of exactly where the pro-ject stands in relation to the actual expenditure. Record your understanding.

You need to rationalize the details that you hold with those that the finance section holds. For example, you will have the detailed breakdown of numbers of assets cleared from each source, so it may be easier for you to arrive at a final cost for asset rights clearances than the accounts section. A lot depends on the accounting system that is in place and how it records project components. You will then be able to match your fig-ures against the projected figures to get the final picture. You should have been on top of this type of equation all through the project, so that refining the information should be relatively easy.

It is a good idea to write a budget report to put with all this information, compar-ing the predicted and actual spend and the predicted and actual time spent. It will help you for future projects, as well as colleagues and the management, if you indicate the reasons for any overspend in any section or any extra time incurred.

It is easy to forget the causes of problems on a project, but they will help you to become better at predicting time and costs on other projects and to make sharper decisions about risk factors. Some of the factors may point towards organizational issues that should be resolved by management to help all projects run more smoothly, and some may show where you yourself might improve.

Closing the project

Once all the archiving is in place, all assets have been returned if required and your work area is probably the tidiest it has been since you started the project, then the project is properly finished. If you don't take the responsibility to do all this at the end, you will find that the project can haunt you as small requests from all quarters become harder to implement. You will have lost interest in the project, and your own understanding of the files will fade quickly.

Many organizations do not pay enough attention to archiving. You may need to fight for this as legitimate time to build into the schedule at the beginning, but it is in your interest. You need to bear in mind that by the end of the project you'll probably hate it and just want to finish at all costs. It takes mental stamina to persevere with archiving, particularly when your other team members have moved on to more interesting things. One final note: you should check that you can restore any files you have saved in an archive before you delete the originals.

Successful archiving

Maintaining a digital archive

How can a computer archive have any meaningful longevity? Any paper in your archive box will be readable in hundreds of years, unless damp or mice get to it. Can we say the same about data? In the short to medium term, the format on which the archive is held will be a bigger issue than the formats of the contents of the archive. Tape streamers are traditionally beloved of IT departments for their capacity and reliability, but over the past 15 years formats such as Exabyte and DDS have come and gone. DVDs are a good way of archiving projects now and the format is likely to be around for a while yet, since the newer high-definition DVD formats will play previous versions. However, a number of high-capacity disc formats are on the horizon, which may not be so backwards compatible. Some sources suggest that hard discs may be a better archive choice than any removable medium, especially as their price comes down but, no matter what the format chosen is, you should aim to copy the data every so often, perhaps even as frequently as every year, if you want to be very secure with your data.

An alternative might be to get someone else to store your archive and pass on to them the responsibility for material continuing to be accessible. The Internet Archive (also known as the Way Back Machine) is archiving many websites for people at their request, never mind the ones it keeps stashed away from its regular trawls through the web. However, dynamic pages, such as those from databases, still prove difficult to deal with.

Coming back to a software project after a really extended period, the most important things will be any data (and other assets) and documentation describing data structures and functionality. You may no longer have the platform to run the application, but it is likely to be the content that is most important in retrospect. That is why it is important to know the format of everything, and hence the documentation is vital. That is also why any encryption or copy-protection can render an archive unusable.

It is difficult to archive any dynamic web-based project with one eye on history, but you can never tell what may eventually become historically important and, while thousand-year-old paper documents can still be seen, we are finding that interactive media projects from the early days (i.e. the 1980s) are almost impossible to resurrect. This is because so much of the system is going to be obsolete and unobtainable: the computer itself, the operating system, the medium on which the material was held, the (compiled) language in which it was written – all these are likely to be long out of use. Early assets may be analogue, held on things like videodiscs that are virtually impossible to play and are likely to have deteriorated. One solution is to emulate the obsolete system using software running on a current computer, but this assumes you can still get access to the original data and transfer any analogue assets. Take yourself forwards 20 years and think how you might resurrect your current project with hardly any of the system you use being available. Archiving is a big issue.

Summary

The important components of testing relate to the business needs of the client, the user's ability to access and complete relevant tasks, and the robustness and reliability of the application. The three aspects warrant testing at different times and by different people in the team. Sometimes the tests spread across a couple or all of the areas, but other tests are dedicated to certain functions of the applications. Because of this, each company needs to assess what testing it is doing, what it wishes to offer, who needs to be involved with each type of test, when the tests are administered, what the purpose of the test is and how they will be paid for in the development process.

▶

There is an on-going software debate about the programming approach and the forms of testing that should be employed for 'functional' or back-end testing in interactive media projects. Developers should keep an eye on how this is progressing to inform their practices. There is at this time no clear agreement on how to do things in an interactive environment where fast development, fluid client requirements and ill-defined payment processes dominate.

Archiving is becoming a stronger consideration for digital media projects. People are recognizing that applications and digital platforms are becoming obsolete far faster than previous technologies. This can leave a permanent vacuum in history in terms of some processes and data distribution – a worrying situation and one which is already beginning to happen. Digital archiving responsibilities will be firmed up for the future as a result of this situation and developers will need to take this and the measures put forward to counteract the situation into account.

Top Tips

Planning	Potential pay-off
Testing over the project cycle should cover the three areas of business needs, user needs and functional operation of the interactive hardware and software. Is this what your company does consciously?	A clear approach to all the areas of testing shows professionalism, adds value to your products and allows better communication with clients.
Check out which types and varieties of testing your company offers. Define your company's standard offering for front-end and back-end testing. Indicate those tests that are extras with costs attached.	Clients will know what they are getting and what they might have to pay extra for if they require them.
Compare your list of tests from your company against those listed in this chapter and those implied in Chapter 8 on Usability and accessibility.	Spot any gaps and decide if they need to be filled. Can lead to improvement of quality of the product.
Educate your whole company about the practices of front-end and back-end testing. Use your experts from these areas to help.	Improvement of skills for scoping and estimating time and costs for projects. Testing is usually a hidden part of the development process. Many members of staff do not realize the breadth or depth of testing that needs to occur.
Identify the programming software approach used in your company. What are its effects on functional testing?	You may decide to change the approach to improve your productivity.

Archiving

Decide what you should archive from projects and make a checklist,	Having a systematic approach will make it easier and means you are less likely to over-look things.
Don't forget the contents of databases.	If the site used content management this can be most of the content.
Include all contractual documents.	Queries over rights can return long after the project is finished.
Check that all borrowed assets have been returned.	Penalties can be due for overdue loans.
Include a note of any problems encountered.	Can help avoid repeating them.
Check you can restore any files archived.	An archive you can't read is useless.

Application Task

What forms of testing do you employ and for what purpose?

Now you realize that the tests need to cover three major areas and be performed by different people in your team, which of your tests relate to the business needs, the users and the code? How are you assigning costs to each of these? Which are you offering as standard and which as defined extras with costs attached?

Fill in the following table for your company's present position and compare it against what you know from reading this chapter. What will you need to put forward to offer a complete service for your internal team, for your clients and for the users of their applications?

Company's present practice		
Business test	User test	Functional test

Tests identified as missing		
Business test	User test	Functional test

 References/Resources

Books

Beck, K., Fowler, M. (2001), *Planning eXtreme Programming Reading*, MA, USA: Addison-Wesley.

Andrews, M., Whittaker, J.A. (2006), *How to Break Web Software : Functional and Security Testing of Web Applications and Web Services*, Boston, MA, USA: Addison-Wesley Professional

Boehm, B., Turner, R. (2004), *Balancing Agility and Discipline: A Guide for the Perplexed*, Boston, MA, USA: Addison-Wesley Professional.

Beck, K., Andres, C. (2005), *Extreme Programming Explained: Embrace Change*, 2/E, Boston, MA, USA: Addison-Wesley Professional.

Web links

Software approaches and implications

Comparing approaches to budgeting and estimating software development projects, Scott W. Ambler, 17 April 2006
http://www.ambysoft.com/essays/comparingEstimatingApproaches.html

Demystifying extreme programming: focusing on value – how to interact with your clients to deliver the software they really want, Roy Miller, Feb. 2003
http://www-128.ibm.com/developerworks/java/library/j-xp020403/

Adaptive project management using Scrum – part 1, Craig Murphy, Methods and Tools, Winter 2004
http://www.methodsandtools.com/archive/archive.php?id=18

The Go-ForIt Chronicles: Memoirs of eXtreme DragonSlayers, Part 2, eXtreme programming: deceptively simple innovation, Willy Farrell and Mary-Rose Fisher, June 2001
http://www-128.ibm.com/developerworks/ibm/library/i-extreme.html

The Waterfall Model, Wikipedia, April 2006
http://en.wikipedia.org/wiki/Waterfall_Model

Testing tools

Software QA Testing and Test Tool Resources
http://www.aptest.com/resources.html

website Test Tools and Site Management Tools
http://www.softwareqatest.com/qatweb1.html

General relating to testing/archiving

Open source security testing methodology, Federico Biancuzzi, SecurityFocus, 29 March 2006
http://www.securityfocus.com/columnists/395

Performance & Software Testing Presentations, Scott Barber
http://www.perftestplus.com/presentations.htm

How can World Wide websites be tested? Rick Hower, April 2006
http://www.softwareqatest.com/qatfaq2.html#FAQ2_15

Some basic testing concepts: Tests are tools, Derek Sissons, Philosophe.com, revised 24 April 1999
http://www.philosophe.com/testing/testing.html

Testing without a formal test plan, Derek Sissons, Philosophe.com, revised 2 July 2000
http://www.philosophe.com/testing/without_testplans.html

Internet Archive
http://www.archive.org/

WC3 Mobile Web Initiative
http://www.w3.org/mobile

CHAPTER 10

Legal issues 1

● Overview

It is very useful to have some knowledge of the legal framework in which you operate. In some industries, the emphasis might be on health and safety, in others it might be on the duty of care that a professional has for clients. In interactive media, you will be working in a wide-ranging field embracing many legal aspects. You are not expected to be an expert in the law (unless you are the company lawyer of course) and you should always leave the details to the professionals, but what we will do in this chapter and the next is outline the areas you should be aware of to help you know when you should take legal advice and to assist you in discussing the issues when you do. That is our important caveat here: this chapter and the next are not meant to be a substitute for legal advice and must not be taken as such. Subjects like intellectual property are complex areas of the law, and expert advice should always be sought if there is any doubt. The legal framework and even the basic philosophy differ between countries. The growth of the Internet has complicated the issues even more. These two chapters are intended only as an introduction and not as a user guide.

We described the legal framework for interactive media as 'wide-ranging'. That is not to say that doctors, bus drivers or plumbers are without such a framework, but interactive media has, perhaps, more than its fair share of legal interests. To set the scene, here are some of the legal issues you face.

Aspects of task	Potential legal implications
Creativity and content	Copyright, moral rights, contracts, libel, trademarks
Programming	Copyright, patents
Staff and subcontractors	Copyright, moral rights, data protection
Selling	Distance selling regulations, tax regulations, data protection, sale-of-goods, digital rights management
Customer relations	Data protection, disability rights
Client relations	Contracts, copyright, moral rights
Data	Data protection, database right, copyright
Publishing a website	International jurisdiction
Archiving content	Copyright, database right, data protection

This list is deliberately limited in scope to the issues (in our opinion) that you should at least be aware of as a project manager working in interactive media. If the project deals with areas like gambling or financial services then there will be other specific regulations that need to be heeded. In Chapter 11 we will look at intellectual property, including copyright and patents, but let's start here with contracts.

What is a contract?

A contract is an agreement between parties that defines the rights and responsibilities of those concerned. It is said that a properly drafted contract should have 'benefit and burden on both sides'. It should also include what is known as the 'consideration', which means that when one party does something for another there should be some form of reward. The contract doesn't have to be written down, but having a written and signed copy will make it a lot easier to prove what was agreed, at a later date.

Any project can involve several documents and several parties. You will need agreements not only with the clients but with your staff (through their contract of employment) and with any companies you work with during the project. Often, a contract will consist of more than one document. There may be a standard document describing the way the business relationship is conducted which is intended to be the same for every project. This will include some so-called boilerplate clauses dealing with issues such as payment terms, liability (and limitation of liability), circumstance under which the contract will terminate (such as bankruptcy or either party being sold), force majeure (what happens if a totally unforeseen catastrophe strikes) and the law under which the contract is written; the kind of items that should go into any service contract.

Added to the main contract will be a letter describing the project and anything specific to it, such as dates and budget, and possibly naming people responsible for sign-off. One good reason for separating out the project detail from the body of the contract is so that, in theory at least, you don't have to renegotiate the contract if a name changes.

Benefit and burden

Of course this is not the only form of written contract. It may be a single document. You may also work with a kind of mini-contract, such as a letter of intent or a so-called heads of agreement, which indicates the intention to develop the project without going into detail. This might be enough to enable work to start while a full contract is drafted.

So what should the contract for developing an interactive media project, such as a website, contain?

The project description

This is not as easy as it might seem, especially if the application is very interactive. You can describe it functionally (what to do) or technically (how to do it) or as a mixture of both. A functional description would be more flexible since it gives you the option to change your plans if you find a better way of achieving the result.

Don't forget to agree the deployment environment. In the case of websites, the variety of HTML and cascading style sheet (CSS) implementations can make it virtually impossible to produce code that will appear identically on all platforms and browsers. It may be prudent to define the platform/browser combinations that will be developed for and tested on. Similarly, you should specify and agree the standards of web coding and accessibility appropriate to the project.

Budget

The cost of producing something like a website is mostly down to staffing costs. All your costings are likely to stem from how long it will take to do something, and from there you can work out how much it will cost. (See Chapter 5 for more on this.) Of course there will be some other costs that are not related to your staffing costs, such as server hosting, content licences, capital costs, consumables and the cost of any subcontracted work.

Usually your client will want a fixed price for a job, so that they can budget for it in their organization. So you have to think carefully about what the project entails, and build in some contingency. The alternative is to work on what is called a 'time and materials' basis where you bill for the work actually done as the project progresses, possibly against an estimate and/or a cap on costs. The figures for these will be specified in the contract. Don't forget to consider currency fluctuations if your client wishes to pay in another currency. This can sometimes happen even if you are both in the same country, one instance being where the work is done as part of a European project and is costed in Euro.

Timescale and milestones

There are two aspects to timing. One concerns when the project starts and when it finishes. It is not unusual for a contract to deal with time in an almost abstract way by referring to 'month 2' and so on, rather than actual dates. Bear in mind what would happen if the project started late. You should also remember that there is a difference between days and working days, so if you are supposed to respond to something in five days, think about what happens if that period includes a public holiday!

The other aspect of time relates to payments. Unless the project is relatively short, you may wish to stage the payments due under the contract. Such interim payments will usually be tied to the delivery of stages of the project, known as milestones. If nothing else these milestones, signed off by the client, will demonstrate that the project is proceeding satisfactorily. You could even agree that the first payment is due when the contract is signed and that, at the end of the project, a small percentage is held back to allow for bug fixes and acceptance. These kinds of things are options that can be specified in a contract.

One thing to consider is how to make sure the project actually finishes. This may seem a curious thing to ask, but you have a payment timed to the completion of the project, and it may be possible for the completion to be delayed because a crucial piece of content is unavailable. To address this, your milestones should have timescales associated with them, and changes to these will most likely be as a result of managed changes or delays.

Change management

The issue of change is a difficult one since it is to be expected that the requirements of a project will develop, especially if the project takes time to produce. You could include a statement to the effect that the project definition may be modified from time to time as mutually agreed and the implications of this for the budget and the timescale will be considered at the appropriate time. You may want to include timings for decisions on changes, to stop them delaying development. The bottom line is that you should expect things to change, so be sure that both parties know how this is to be managed.

Lines of communication and sign-off responsibilities

Stages of a project, and its completion, will need to be approved and signed-off by the client. It is important to know who has the authority to do this since sometimes it won't be the person you deal with on a day-to-day basis. It is a good idea to make it clear in writing who has the sign-off authority in the client company, and probably a good idea to do the equivalent for the developer company as well. The names themselves might not be in the contract, but the contract might say that names will be agreed. Allow for the possibility that the person may change during the project. There should also be timescales included for each sign-off, otherwise production will be delayed. Many contracts also include a procedure for giving formal notices and may specify something like 'in writing in a letter delivered to head office'. This is not the same thing as day-to-day management or sign-off.

Incentives and penalties

It is not unknown for clients to be slow in responding to sign-off and other time-related issues. The development team may eventually be stuck waiting for a decision. Do you want to introduce penalties for this? On the other hand, clients often see developers as being slow to respond to requests for changes and the project as a whole can over-run. Do they want to introduce penalties for late delivery? Following the maxim of benefit and burden on both sides, it is reasonable to expect penalties to be balanced by incentives. An interesting approach to this is the use of 'lane rental' in highway maintenance work, where the contractor rents the road space for the duration of the work. This automatically provides both penalties and incentives based on the time to completion. It can become critical if the project has been announced in advance and has a very public launch date already set. This is quite possible where the lead time for the launch event is longer than the time needed to complete the project.

Provision of content and clearances

One issue here is that of timing, since the client must provide whatever they agreed to provide in good time. There will be some flexibility in accepting content for web pages (for example) but, in the end, the pages don't exist without the content, not least because the structure of the site needs to take the amount of content into account. As discussed earlier, you may wish to penalize late delivery in some way but, at the very least, it should be clear who is responsible for the delivery.

The second issue is that of rights. Your client must have the necessary rights for you to include content in their website. So if the client is to provide content this should be specified in the contract, and the client should also state that they have the necessary rights and permissions to do so and possibly indemnify you. This is known as clearing the rights. If you reasonably believe that they have permission to use material, you should have no liability for what is called secondary copyright infringement. However, just because something has been used in, say, the printed corporate brochure does not mean it is automatically cleared for use on a website.

If you are to source some of the content, such as stock photos, then this responsibility should be stated as well. One thing to note is that, if you are being paid a fixed fee for the work, any rights you clear must be compatible with this. It is no use licensing something for which fees based on time or numbers are due if you are being paid a fixed fee. Websites should always be cleared for the world, if Internet use is not specifically mentioned, even if the intended audience is local.

Ownership of rights

As we'll discuss in Chapter 11, the intellectual property in something you develop for a client belongs, in the first instance, to you. Your client will need to be granted the rights to make use of whatever you produce and there will be a clause or three in the contract dealing with this. If the client needs to be assigned copyright in what you produce, so that you no longer have any rights in it, then this has to be done in writing.

We'll say more on this issue in Chapter 11, but for the moment it suffices to say that the contract should include your mutually agreed position on ownership of rights in what is produced. You should also consider access to any source code (for Flash or Java for example) and provisions to allow the client to update or maintain the result of the project in the event that they don't want to do it with you, or you can't do it. These issues are not the same as copyright and your client does not necessarily have to be assigned copyright in such cases. If there is source code and you do not allow the client to have it, it may be prudent to offer escrow arrangements (where a trusted third party holds a human-readable copy of the program source) in case your company goes into liquidation, is taken over or for some other pre-agreed reason is unable to maintain the code. Such arrangements are common in enterprise-level applications such as databases but, in many smaller interactive media applications, the relatively short lifespan of projects like websites makes escrow less necessary.

Promotion and credits

Since interactive media involves computer programming, there is no moral right of paternity (more on this later). This means that a developer has no automatic right to be credited for the work. From a business perspective, previous work is a vital promotional tool, so you may wish to include a right to be credited on the final result (like a credit at the bottom of the home page of the website) and, if appropriate, have the right to use the project for promotion, including appropriate use of trade marks. This would have to be included in the contract. The client may ask for sight of any promotional material that includes their name.

On-going support and maintenance

Even if the project *per se* doesn't include on-going support and maintenance, you should be clear as to when development ends and maintenance begins since the client may need continual small changes. It may be possible to include reference to further maintenance in the development contract.

It is reasonable for the client to expect fixes for any bugs found after completion and delivery. You may wish to limit this 'free fix' period or to agree to a hold-back of a few percent of the budget to allow for bug fixes in the first few weeks after delivery. After that, bug fixes can reasonably be classed as maintenance since they are unlikely to be catastrophic (otherwise you'd have found them, wouldn't you?).

● Clearances

This next section will outline some of the issues that arise when you are using other people's intellectual property in your project. These are often referred to as assets, and some will come from your client and some from outside the project. We've already mentioned that you should check that anything your client gives you for inclusion is cleared for such use so let's go on to look at other people's material.

When you clear any copyright material for use in your own projects, you will be asked how long you want to be able to use the material and for what purpose and audience type and in which countries. These are known as the markets and territories you want covered and, as mentioned before, the web is always a world-wide medium. This is not as simple as it sounds. Many applications begin with one purpose but evolve into others. Material licensed for a television programme in one country may be moved to a website, which is accessible across the whole world. If the rights were originally cleared only nationally, they would have to be renegotiated. An in-house training application may be released on the consumer market after a period of time in the company, so the audience changes.

The duration of rights is also established at the time of negotiation, so you need a good idea of the life-span of the project's result to determine how many years to ask for, or you may consider 'buy-outs'. This means making a once-only payment by which you get agreement to use the material indefinitely and which is the basis of 'royalty-free' licences for things like photo libraries. Exclusivity might also be a consideration, although few rights owners would be willing to give up other use of their asset and, in any case, it would be very expensive. It is safest to assume that any licence of an asset is non-exclusive, and if you or your client wants exclusivity then you should commission the asset.

You need a clear directive from the client on their short- and long-term plans for the site or application. You should state what markets and territories you will cover when clearing rights for offline, and how long the clearances will be valid for any project. If you put this in writing and have their agreement to this formally, there can be no confusion as to who should have done what and when, if circumstances change.

If the client intends to remake the website or application in another language then you must have obtained clearance for such use. In some cases a rights owner will count a direct translation as part of the original agreement, but in others they will not: check. A similar situation occurs when an update is required, to change information that has become outdated, although web use should assume an on-going programme of revision. The extreme situation in this chain is the derivative, which is another project based on the first.

● Ownership of code and other assets generated in the project

Code is often built up of fragments, libraries and routines that were written for other projects to carry out certain tasks such as drawing a picture to the screen or synchronizing sound and pictures. Part of the way developers survive is to build up a stock of code or libraries that help them in the production of other projects. This does not mean that they will produce an application that looks and behaves exactly the same as the original product for which the code was generated. Most often the code forms some of the building blocks, but is adapted to fit the new requirements. If your client is not a computer company or a developer they will probably not have any use for the code that underlies their application. It is best to try to retain copyright in the code but issue a free licence to the client for its use.

The company needs to establish where it stands on this issue so that it will not infringe any rights in re-use of the code later. There is an added problem in that the code used may well be a combination of pre-existing company code and third-party code as well as the new code. This would make it difficult to identify exactly which parts of the new code might belong to the client and which you would not in consequence have the right to sign away. With open-source code you need to be sure that you do not infringe the licence agreement if you were to 'sell' the code to your client.

It is custom and practice for software not to be sold but to be licensed. If you produce an application (including a website) for a client you should not assign the copyright in the code to the client because that will make it difficult for you to re-use any of that work. Clients ought to accept this, but it does mean that you need to state it explicitly in the agreement with your client. You will, of course, have to grant a free licence to use the code, otherwise they cannot make use of what they have paid for, but they will not actually own it.

As a developer contracting software from a programmer you will have the opposite point of view, and will probably want to make continuing use of any code written for you. This means that you will have to explicitly license the rights you need from the programmer. If you have contracted a company rather than a person, you need to be sure that they can assign you these rights because they have taken them. Should you ever want to license rights in code to your client then you have to have the rights yourself first. It's a basic rule – you cannot license rights you do not have.

● Freelancer and contractor contracts

When you need to recruit extra people for the team, you also make agreements with them. These will have separate issues that need to be covered, or you may find for example that your graphics artist's company owns the copyright in the visuals that are developed, not your company, and so you can't pass these on to your client. Employees are different from contractors as long as it has been established that all work that is created in the course of their work belongs to the company, and this would be stated in their contract of employment. Any of the team, whether in-house or external, has the same moral rights as the company does in relation to the work and the client. So the company may need to establish an overall policy for themselves and employees, depending on how moral rights are treated in their country – if at all. Note that moral rights cannot be signed away to someone else, but they can be waived. (You will find an explanation of moral rights in Chapter 11.)

The company may be comfortable with employing a contractor who then subcontracts the work, or it may not. Clauses indicating who is responsible for the work, and if and how subcontracting can be done, are necessary to cover the type and quality of the work. If you have agreed any confidentiality clauses with the client, these usually put the onus on the developer to bind any staff to the agreements, so you might need to be very clear who is working on the project to comply with your confidentiality undertaking.

● Selling at a distance

While it is beyond the scope of this chapter to go into detail about law covering selling on the Internet, it is worth mentioning two points which can affect the way a website is coded for e-commerce. Firstly, sales taxes and the way they are charged has usually worked on the basis that if a buyer and seller are in different countries then no sales tax is due: in the USA this has applied to buyers and sellers in different states. In Europe this has changed.

Value Added Tax (VAT), the equivalent of sales tax in Europe, has complex rules applying to sales between countries in the European Union (EU), and in principle, sales of goods or services to someone in the EU who is not registered for VAT (usually a home consumer rather than a business) are counted as if the buyer and seller were in the same country. In this case tax is applied in the seller's country unless the buyer is registered for VAT, in which case the buyer has to apply special reverse charging arrangements to account for the VAT.

The complication comes when you are supplying what are called 'electronically delivered services' and this includes sales of anything that is downloaded across the Internet. In this case the 'place of supply' is the country in which the buyer is, not the seller, because the rule says this is 'where the service is enjoyed'. This rule does not apply to physical goods bought over the Internet which are then shipped to the buyer conventionally.

The reach of VAT has even crossed the Atlantic since US companies (and others outside the EU) who provide 'electronically delivered services' to non-business customers in Europe, such as downloads of software bought over the Internet, have to collect VAT just like they would collect sales tax from someone in the same US state. An organization outside the EU has to register for VAT with an EU member state (only one) and account for VAT at the appropriate rate for the customer. The reasoning behind all this is that, as downloaded software cannot be checked and taxed at the border like a physical package, the government is losing out on some tax money. At the same time the *de minimus* limit below which VAT is not charged on imports (currently £18 in the UK) does not apply to electronic services.

The USA is not immune from reverse charging. Traditionally there has been a 'use tax', which has been levied on buyers of 'big ticket' items such as cars which were bought out of state. This tax is collected by the state direct from the buyer. As online buying increases, some states have decided to try to collect use taxes on out-of-state online purchases of any size, despite the bureaucracy involved.

If you are developing an e-commerce website and you or your client is selling downloads (or any other electronic service such as a phone service or hosting) into Europe then it is vital to make sure where the customer is and whether they are registered for VAT, because this affects the way the tax is applied.

Finally on the sales front, recent harmonization of legislation called the 'Distance Selling Directive' has been introduced across Europe to provide consumer protection for any remote selling, including by telephone and the Internet. It will place obligations on the seller, many of which are common sense and which should be reflected in the terms and conditions on the website. For example, things ordered have to be delivered within 30 days unless agreed otherwise and the customer has the right to change their mind about the goods received within seven days of receiving them. These regulations do not apply to business-to-business contracts but, if you are selling on a website and your customers could be either consumers or businesses, it may be prudent to assume that the same level of protection is suitable for either.

● Data protection

Data protection is a broadly European concept in law, and it is a particularly important issue for websites which have customer relations management (CRM). Basically, under UK law, anybody who controls data relating to living people may have to be registered under the Data Protection legislation. The definitions of a data controller and a data subject, and the eight Data Protection Principles, are carefully set out in the UK Act and in the guidelines for registration.

The eight principles can be summarized as follows – the data must be:

- fairly and lawfully processed;
- processed for limited purposes;
- adequate, relevant and not excessive;
- accurate;
- not kept longer than necessary;

- processed in accordance with the data subjects' rights;
- secure;
- not transferred to countries outside the European Economic Area without adequate protection.

If you produce a database that contains personal information about living people you are a data controller and must be registered. There are exceptions for data used for business marketing and personnel purposes, and for 'household' information such as Christmas card lists. The 1998 UK Act changed some of the ways that the data protection legislation worked. The use of cookies may come under data protection legislation, and we'll briefly discuss cookies and privacy issues below.

Data protection is not dealt with in the same way by every country. There is no such thing in the USA at a national level, but it is clear that not having an arrangement for transferring data between Europe and the USA would be a serious problem, as you will see from the final principle listed above. To resolve this, the EU and US administrations came up with the 'Safe Harbor' principle whereby individual companies certify that they provide 'adequate' privacy protection as defined in the European regulations.

Although it is not strictly part of data protection as covered by the legislation, you may find that during development your staff will obtain confidential information about your client and their business. You may find that there will be a confidentiality clause in the contract but, in any event, you should be careful to keep such information confidential. It can be difficult if you specialize in an industry and find yourself working for competing companies. In this case you may have to dedicate teams to the different clients to preserve 'Chinese walls' around their secrets.

● Cookies, mailing lists and marketing messages

Marketing messages are now regulated. In the UK they are covered by the Privacy and Electronic Communications (EC Directive) Regulations 2003 and the Committee of Advertising Practice (CAP) Code. They apply to email and mobile messages. To add someone to a mailing list you should ask them to opt in to the list by ticking a box. It's best not to have the box ready ticked on a web page. It is also legitimate to send mails to someone with whom you have already negotiated or to whom you have sold similar goods or services. In all cases there should be a clear opt-out instruction in the message and the message must identify the sender. This is difficult in an SMS message of 160 characters, but it must be done.

Cookies, and other data about users, also come under the Privacy and Electronic Communications legislation and a website is required to explain their use and offer users the option of refusing them. This is usually done by explaining how the user can go to their browser preferences and change the cookie settings. Of course some websites may not work correctly, if at all, if cookies are disabled. Cookies and sessions are a mechanism used to track users as they move through a site, and this is a common way of handling authentification. In this case a user who refuses cookies may not be able to log on to use restricted areas of the site, and it would be advisable to explain this before they attempt to log in.

These days most websites have both 'terms and conditions of use' and a privacy statement on their pages. As well as stating their use of cookies in the privacy statement, many sites also explain about web logging, although web logs identify a computer or router rather than the person accessing the web page.

Accessibility

Disability rights legislation has been passed in many countries of the world and gives everyone a legal right of access to places and services despite their disabilities. The challenge of making things accessible for everyone has resulted in changes to the ways our streets are laid out, our buildings are designed and our websites are built. High-profile cases such as that involving the Australian Olympic website in 2000 have raised awareness of the issues, and organizations such as the Web Accessibility Initiative (WAI), Watchfire (who produced the Bobby accessibility guidelines) and the UK Royal National Institute for the Blind have taken a lead in helping the web industry come to terms with accessibility requirements.

In fact, basic accessibility goes hand in hand with good information design. Separating the content of a web page from its layout by using semantic markup will also make the pages easier to manage. Thinking about how a web page appears to a machine reading it from top to bottom helps structure the information. Two clues to the accessibility of a web page come from looking at the page with its style sheets disabled and with graphics turned off. If the page makes sense and lacks no significant information then it is well on the way to being accessible. Although it can be difficult to make a fully-animated page or site built using something like Flash as accessible as straight HTML, you have the option of adding an HTML version which, coincidentally, would give search engines something to spider.

Current web design tools help you build accessible pages, and building a site with accessibility in mind from the start will be much easier than trying to retrofit it later. There are online tools, such as the WAI and Watchfire validators, which will help with this process. Unfortunately, unlike validating code for standards compliance, it isn't possible to fully automate an accessibility check so the validators still leave you with a checklist which you have to work through by eye. These validators define levels of compliance using terminology such as A, AA and AAA. While 'triple A' compliance is difficult, it should be easy enough to reach 'double A'.

The UK requirements stem from the 1995 Disability Discrimination Act, which brought in a legal requirement that websites became accessible in 1999. This applies to all websites that provide a service, or are related to education, recruitment or employment. Whether a purely information-based website would be covered by the regulations seems unclear, but it would be prudent to assume that any web pages being designed now should be accessible. The American legislation in this area includes Section 508 of the US Rehabilitation Act.

Libel

A libel is a malicious falsehood which has been published. It has to be untrue and it has to be malicious. Of course, if it is not malicious it would not injure anyone's reputation: calling someone a saint is unlikely to be troublesome, but not everyone wants to be known publicly as a sinner. A libel action can be taken against anyone in the distribution chain, including the author, the publisher and the distributor.

The question of libel has taken on a new importance as we move towards what is being called Web 2.0 since this involves the end-user of a website becoming an author of it. Traditional web pages were one-way affairs and, while the author and publisher needed to think carefully about what they said, they did at least have control over it. With web pages that anyone can write to, the situation becomes serious.

There have been instances where libellous content has been posted on the Internet; on websites and in Usenet groups. The publisher of the site should monitor anything posted and if anything potentially troublesome is found, it should be removed. The terms and conditions should say that posts can be removed. This would not only include libellous material: obscene and offensive language is not unknown in posts and even trade secrets and other confidential information. Certainly, if a site is notified that some posted (or indeed any) content is defamatory, the content should be removed. This is known as 'notice and take-down'. It may be advisable to keep a secure copy of the material rather than just deleting it.

● Jurisdiction

One of the more significant things that the Internet has done to communications is to internationalize it. Anything you put on your website can be seen by people in most of the countries in the world. Before the Internet, world-wide publishing involved making licensing or distribution deals with different people in different countries and arranging for shipping of items of software between continents. Now all it takes is to tell someone that your URL exists and say 'Please come and look'. Unfortunately this raises the issue of legal jurisdiction. Jurisdiction is basically the law you come under.

This could be important in multimedia publishing on the Internet, partly because everything you publish that way is available internationally. Just because your website is situated in Denver, Colorado doesn't mean that you have to clear rights only for the USA. People in the UK or Egypt or Russia or New Zealand can see what you have published. But rights are not the only issue. A libel committed on the Internet, such as in a Usenet news group, could be read anywhere, so a legal action could in theory be taken anywhere. The state of Minnesota declared that its consumer protection legislation was applicable to any online purchases – even if the purchase did not involve a buyer, seller or recipient in that state. A court in Northern Territories, Australia, put a ban on some newspaper coverage of a murder trial and this forced a British paper to remove relevant archive material from its website to avoid any possibility of being in contempt. Basically the internationalization caused by the Internet lays any web publisher or supplier – including you with your home web page – open to action anywhere in the world. So be careful.

Summary

Compliance in areas like data protection and accessibility will be mostly the responsibility of the publisher of the information, your client. However, knowing what to look out for on behalf of your client is good business practice and, if you accept any liability in the contract, mitigates your risk. Much of the legislation that comes into play when designing and building a website, such as accessibility, should by now be coming naturally out of good design practices. If you run your own website, as you probably do, and especially if your visitors can post things on your site, you need to be aware of your responsibilities.

And remember ... if in doubt, ask advice.

Top Tips

Strategy	Potential pay-off
Put your agreement with your client in writing.	Proves what you agreed in case of problems.
Make sure you know clearly when a project has finished.	Avoids delays in final payments.
Consider the role of incentives and penalties in managing delivery and sign-off.	Can provide leverage to encourage timely turn-around, but it does apply to both sides.
Be clear about who is responsible for provision of content and clearance of any licensed assets.	Makes sure content is properly cleared for use.
Give appropriate licences to your client to cover code you have produced.	Avoids confusion over what code you can, and can't, re-use.
Take necessary rights in subcontracted work and remember to ask for a waiver of moral rights.	Allows you to actually use the material, and license it on, legally.

▶

Make sure online sales are treated correctly for VAT, especially B2B downloads.	Keeps things legal and avoids mistakes in taxation when selling to European businesses.
Program email lists carefully to comply with regulations.	Keeps things legal and increases customer satisfaction.
Write web pages with accessibility in mind.	Makes the pages easier to use for everybody.
Monitor user-produced content on websites. If informed of illegal material on a website, take it down immediately.	Mitigates any liability.

Application Task

Look at a typical contract that your company issues to a client. Does it cover the points recommended here and if not why not? Don't forget that you will find other clauses relating to the business relationship rather than the production of the project itself, which is what we cover here.

Should you be raising any of the production legal issues with others in your company? Consider who should know and how you can make them aware if you feel it is necessary.

 ## References

Book

Smith G.J.H. ed. (2001), *Internet Law and Regulation*, 3rd edn, London: Sweet & Maxwell.

Substantial (and comprehensive) reference and analysis, updated to 4th edition in 2007. Free online updates to the third edition of Smith (above) are available at http://www.sweetandmaxwell.co.uk/online/intreg/index.html

Web links

Model contract for web projects, New Media Knowledge, 2 Oct. 2004
http://www.nmk.co.uk/article/2004/02/10/model-contract

Bulletproof web design contracts, John Tabita, sitepoint, 28 Oct. 2005
http://www.sitepoint.com/article/bulletproof-web-design-contract

Data Protection, Information Commissioner
http://www.ico.gov.uk

Briffa – London-based legal firm with good resources on their website
http://www.briffa.com/

UK RNIB Web Access Centre
http://www.rnib.org.uk/xpedio/groups/public/documents/code/public_rnib0087
89.hcsp

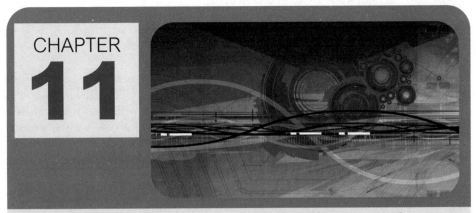

CHAPTER 11

Legal issues 2 – intellectual property

Industry Insight

Imagine the Internet as a play. The key to the plot is to identify the players and understand their roles. A player on the Internet often performs more than one role. When determining the legal consequences of activities on the Internet, it is important to identify which roles the person is performing.

Smith G.J.H. ed. (2001), *Internet Law and Regulation*, 3rd edn, London: Sweet & Maxwell

● Overview

In this second chapter on legal issues we'll concentrate on intellectual property, such as copyright, moral rights, trade marks and the like. Again, this is not an exhaustive discussion. The aim is to help you identify things that might be problematic, so that you can take proper advice. As before, these chapters are intended only as an introduction and not as a user guide.

Don't forget that you will have two roles in the Internet 'play' as Graham Smith describes it (or indeed any other media production, whether interactive or not). Your project will be a consumer of intellectual property as you build your web page, iTV application or CD-ROM ... or whatever. But the project, and the people working on it, will also be generating intellectual property.

One important point to remember is that intellectual property laws do not protect abstract ideas. They protect the realisation of the idea in the form of a work of literature or art, an industrial process or a design. We will start with copyright: not the only kind of intellectual property right (IPR), but possibly the most important for us here.

What is copyright?

In law a copyright, like most other kinds of intellectual property, is the equivalent of something tangible. It can be bought, sold and even rented and it can be passed on to your heirs. Unfortunately it is also intangible. You cannot actually touch it, and so it does not match our usual understanding of a property. There is now a whole generation who have grown up with the ability to download music and movies from the Internet, and this has often been seen as a free resource. This also obscures the value of intellectual property.

In the beginning

Copyright as a concept in English law has its roots in new technology. In the second half of the fifteenth century the invention of printing made it possible for books to be mass-produced, rooms full of monks were no longer necessary and, as a result, unauthorized copying of literature was a possibility. This was initially controlled by granting monopolies to printers, notably a royal chapter to the Stationers' Company in 1556, but such things provided no benefit or protection for the authors themselves.

The first copyright act in the UK dates from 1709, and gave the 'sole right and liberty' of printing books to authors and whoever they assigned rights to. Protection was for a period of 14 years from publication but could only really be enforced if, as before, the book was registered with the Stationers' Company.

Later revisions of the law widened the scope to include other creative works such as engravings and music. Eventually the emphasis on copying had to be extended to embrace rights of usage for performances of music and drama, and eventually sound recordings, cinematograph films, broadcasting and the Internet joined the fray, the concept of what is still called copyright extending to embrace new means of distributing intellectual property.

It is only recently that the Internet has been considered specifically in copyright law. Until 2003 a website (in UK law) was considered to be equivalent to a cable television programme. Then, a new right of communication to the public was introduced, and broadcasts and Internet 'transmissions' are different aspects of this. It is worth noting that a key differentiator is whether the 'transmission' is at a scheduled time. So it would seem that a live streaming of Steve Jobs' latest keynote would be classed as a broadcast but on-demand repeats of it would not.

The 2003 updates to the law were introduced as a result of harmonization of copyright across the EU, and there is substantial international agreement on the protection of intellectual property. This covers inventions, copyrights and designs together with the relatively recent addition of moral rights. To a great extent, the introduction of moral rights into UK law in 1988 reduced some of the differences from, say, French law. The British approach had been that protection of copyright is protection of the material benefit of exploiting that right. This is why UK law protected the rights of printers. The French perspective is that copyright is in some way a recognition of the artistic achievement of the author. In fact in French law it is not copyright that is protected, but droit d'auteur – the right of the author.

International agreement on copyright has been based on a series of conventions that are ratified by governments. Since the distribution of intellectual property is an international business, it is only equitable that a country should expect the same kind of protection for its citizens' work in a foreign country as it gives to its citizens itself – or indeed gives to citizens of foreign countries. Needless to say, some countries have taken a more 'laissez faire' view of this kind of protection than others have, as any visitor to certain parts of the Far East may have found.

● Getting a copyright

In US, UK and European law a copyright is created at the same time as the work itself, assuming that the creation is tangible and original. The situation used to be different in the USA, where you had to publish using a particular notice of copyright, or in some cases register a copyright for it to be in existence, but this situation was anomalous and recently changed, although a work of US origin can still be registered, which brings advantages relating to damages amongst other things. Registration also fixes a date to your work. However, it is possible for two people simultaneously and independently to produce the same thing. There is no official registration process in the UK.

You can have copyright in a work of art (painting, drawing, sculpture and so on), literature (prose or poetry – even the source code of a computer program), drama, music (more on this later), and in a photograph, movie or television programme. There has to have been some originality involved in creating a copyright, so that by photocopying a drawing you do not create a new copyright – you only risk infringing the original one. US law requires that some creative effort took place before a copyright is created. The condition in UK law is sometimes called 'sweat of the brow', and is less demanding.

Although copyright protection is automatic in the USA and UK, it is considered good practice to assert the copyright by printing a notice such as © 2007 Elaine England and Andy Finney. Other phrases such as 'all rights reserved' and 'if you copy this we will send the boys round and sort you out' or the prominent FBI shield that you may see on American videos are arguably a bit over the top. The reason for using them is to remove any possibility that a defendant in court could claim he or she didn't know the material was copyright. This is of course no defence to a primary infringement, but it could be considered to be mitigation since ignorance of copyright is widespread. Primary infringement is the initial production of an infringing copy. In cases of secondary infringement, ignorance can be a defence in the UK. This would happen if, for example, you imported an infringing work or licensed the work and it was reasonable for you to believe that the person who provided the material owned or had cleared the rights. Even if an infringer acknowledges that 'copyright infringement is theft', as they say, there is also an attitude that copyright owners are rich and would not miss a few bucks. But we all have the potential to be copyright owners, and deserve not to be ripped off.

When you produce a copyright work as part of your employment, the copyright usually rests with your employer. However, when you commission a freelancer or another company to produce it for you, the ownership of the copyright will usually rest in the first instance with them (although there are exceptions, for example sound recordings and films where ownership lies with the people who organized the recording or the shoot). For this reason, the developer that subcontracts another company will usually take the necessary rights in this commissioned work under the terms of the contract, and this is probably the best way to avoid confusion. This situation is complex, especially when contributors are contracted via an agency since it is possible that they are employees of the agency and, in this case, the agency may own the rights rather than the contributor.

If you have to decide about copyright ownership you should think of it in terms of future use. If you as creator will have no further use for the work then you lose nothing by assigning copyright or granting an exclusive licence. Assigning your rights means that they are no longer yours: you have sold them, and an assignment is always exclusive.

As the developer commissioning material you have to be able to use the work for its intended purpose, which may or may not require you to own the copyright. Beyond these issues the copyright in something is as much a part of the deal as the money paid, and it can be negotiated since the copyright has a value in itself that is distinct from ownership or use of the work. It is also unrelated to the time it took to create the work, since a Picasso sketch remains a Picasso sketch whether it took him ten days or ten seconds to draw. It is also, usually, unrelated to artistic merit. To be safe, all copyright assignments and licences should be in writing. In fact, under US and UK law, an assignment of copyright can only be made in writing.

● Moral rights

Moral rights are a relatively new addition to intellectual property in UK law. This provides a method in law for you to be credited for your work (called paternity or attribution) and for your work to be used only in ways of which you approve and without unauthorized changes (integrity). Given the inherent flexibility of interactive media, moral rights are quite significant, especially integrity. The British moral rights legislation is narrower than the French, whereas in the USA, moral rights are narrower than in the UK and usually apply only to visual arts. It is worth noting that you can do anything with a work if the author consents.

The composer of a piece of music has a moral right for the music not to be edited. You should not cut out the verses to leave just the chorus or change the order of the verses. If you design an interactive application that allows the user to do such things then you risk a claim for conspiring or inducing infringement of the moral rights of the composer. For this reason most music publishers will not allow you to include a song in your interactive application under circumstances where the user can change the music because they do not have the permission of the composer to do so. Music will be discussed in more detail later.

When a graphics artist builds a montage of images from many sources there is a risk of infringing moral rights. A particular photographer might take exception to having something extracted from the image or to having the image cropped. Juxtaposition of one image with another might be problematic for reasons other than copyright because it is possible to libel someone by publishing an unwisely montaged or positioned picture, so great care should be taken with this. Is it real or is it Photoshop? An extreme example would be to build a photograph of a notable teetotal politician drinking a glass of water into a montage so that he appears to be drinking in a vodka distillery. Because computer technology is now quite able to produce realistic images of non-existent objects, dinosaurs, ancient Rome and alien landscapes, in a way that is very difficult to distinguish from reality, this problem is only going to get more difficult.

Moral rights are a recent addition to UK law, so there is less guidance on what can and cannot be done than there is with more established areas of copyright. One possibly contentious area arises because the author or authors of a computer program have no rights of paternity or integrity. This is because computer programs were assumed to be written by large teams. But does this also apply to a website? As a creative person your future depends on people recognizing your past work, and it is important that credit is given where it is due. There will be instances where your client will attempt to deny you a credit. Your only straightforward way of achieving your just credit is to insist on it in your contract with the client, rather than relying on the law. Conversely, most commissioning contracts will include a clause waiving moral rights.

● Exceptions

One problem with copyright, if taken to extremes, is that while the owners have their rights, the rest of us should also have some leeway to enable life to go on; and the concepts known as fair use (fair dealing in the UK) and insubstantial portions come into play. In law, and in the right circumstances, these are two important exceptions to infringement. A critic reviewing a book has the right to quote from it without asking permission. A student studying the works of an artist has the right to photocopy illustrations to include them in a research paper as long as sufficient acknowledgement is given to the author and the work itself. You can quote a small (insubstantial) extract from a literary work, again with an acknowledgement. Reporting of current events and news gives a lot of leeway: but note that this exemption does not extend to reproduction of photographs. There is a specific exemption for decompilation of computer programs where this is done to achieve interoperability. In the USA there are also exceptions for parody, and even some commercial use may be fair if it does not injure the copyright owner.

Unfortunately, we cannot always benefit from these exceptions in websites and other interactive media productions. Some of the exceptions to infringement will not apply if you are making a commercial product. The term 'insubstantial portion' does not necessarily mean that anything short is OK. The test is always one of degree, and there are no hard-and-fast rules about what constitutes an insubstantial portion. One example to consider is in music, where it has been argued that any extract that allows you to recognize the tune is substantial in these terms.

Alongside the exceptions included in copyright legislation there has to be an element of common sense. It is very difficult to judge whether a photograph will work in a montage or on a web page without trying it out. Here, technology is actually making things more difficult for us. In the old days, to make a mock-up of a page of a magazine, you might cut out copies of photographs from the colour supplements and paste them onto a piece of paper. That does not infringe copyright in the photographs. Doing the same thing on a computer involves scanning the photographs, and so you infringe the copyright unless you already have permission to scan the image into the computer. In this case the intention is the same, but changing the means by which you carry out your intention has led to a possible infringement.

One very constructive idea to get over the mock-up infringement problem has been implemented by some stock photo libraries which give you a blanket permission to reproduce their images for mock-ups. Many even supply low-resolution images for this very purpose.

The idea of what is fair and what is not has to evolve. Now that many of us have tiny music players attached to our ears, the issue of copying recordings from one medium (i.e. the CD you bought) to another (your iPod or phone or whatever) in order to listen to it ... which was, after all, why it was sold to you ... is becoming a crucial part of the debate on extending fair use. In some countries (such as the UK, but this is currently under review) it is illegal to copy music in this way (and some digital rights management would inhibit it) since it infringes both the music and recording rights. But many would argue that this is something that should be considered a fair use.

● The World Wide Web

Copyright, and other, legislation around the world is coming to grips with the ramifications of the Internet. Recent legislation mentions it explicitly, which in itself may raise problems as technology develops further.

When you produce a website you will be exploiting copyright material, such as:

- literary rights in text of the words on the page;
- literary and other rights in the computer code of HTML markup or PHP code;
- database rights in pages held in any content management system;
- artistic rights in graphics;
- rights in photographs.

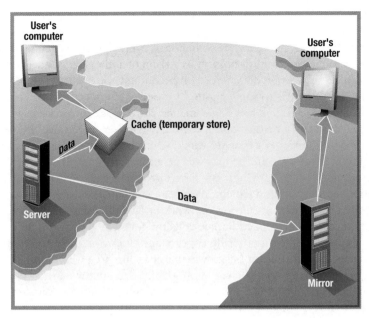

Caches, mirrors and web linking

You may own some of the content yourself, it may be provided by your client or it may be licensed from third parties. Increasingly it might be put onto the site by end-users. When you put a page onto the web you are publishing it, and to do so you must have the necessary permissions or rights. Only if you have such rights can you, in turn, grant some form of licence, explicitly in your terms and conditions or implicitly by the very act of publishing the page on the Internet, to allow others to view the page. This is what is called the implied licence and would include anything that you reasonably expect to happen with a web page. It would include all the stages involved in moving the content of the page from the server to the browser and the screen, and could even include printing of the page for personal use.

The technical way in which a website makes its way from the original server to the viewer's screen means that copies of the site can exist in RAM, in caches or proxies and sometimes on mirror sites. All web browsers use local caches to stop re-downloading of data that has already been downloaded, and some Internet service providers have proxy caches to reduce long-distance download times for pages frequently viewed by their customers. In an extreme case the original site, the cache or mirror and the viewer can be in three different legal jurisdictions.

Whereas a cache is a necessary and automatic part of the functioning of the web, a mirror is not. (A mirror is a copy of a site on another machine, usually in another part of the world, to expedite access from a distance.) This means that it could be argued that anyone publishing material on the web knows that transient copies will be stored in caches and so implicitly authorizes them. This is not so with mirrors, and explicit permission must be sought to mirror a site.

Caches and mirrors may also disrupt the usual logging of accesses of the site's pages, and if this is a crucial part of an agreement for advertising then we have a problem. In some cases a cache will check to see whether a page has been updated, and this shows on the site log in a distinctive way.

Linking from one page to another is a key part of the web, and it is assumed that anyone can link to anyone else freely. When we find someone has linked to our pages we are delighted. However, not everyone would be so happy under all circumstances. A link can be seen as an endorsement or possibly as a claim of authorship. Under some circumstances it can be seen to be defamatory or encourage copyright infringement. Also, consider the use of frames to show another website as if it were part of yours or using the image source HTML link to bring someone else's image into your page (known as inlining or hijacking). In neither case is there any copying done since the final page is assembled only in the viewer's browser window, but both of these instances go beyond simple display of a web page and so may well go against any implied licence.

Recent changes to UK copyright law have introduced 'temporary acts of reproduction' as an exception to infringement. These are incidental and transient copies made as part of the process of transmitting the work or lawfully using it. In some ways this removes the need for an implied licence to allow for such activities. The exception is actually narrower than it superficially appears and does not apply to computer programs or databases and so it isn't clear whether it applies to a website *per se*. However, it would apply to other works, such as photographs, that appear on the web page.

Domain names are a complex area in their own right. Although domain name registrars operate a 'first come first served' system for granting use of names, this has to be seen in the light of other legislation. Domain registrars now give priority to trade mark owners in both registration and resolution of disputes; but remember the same name can be trademarked several times if it is in different categories. In registering a domain name you may be at risk of infringing a trade or service mark. You might think that companies who have such rights to names have registered the relevant names, but this is not necessarily the case. Where the domain name includes the trade mark, or is deemed to be close enough to it to cause confusion, then registration and/or use of the domain is likely to attract a lawyer's letter at the very least. You need to be careful to avoid this, possibly by searching the relevant trade mark registry. But marks can be used and recognized without being registered. You should be especially careful if your client insists that you register a particular domain name and should make it clear that you cannot take responsibility for any issues arising from this.

A whole domain name can be a trade mark. If you look at the list of trade marks on Amazon's website you'll find several of these, such as Amazon.com and Amazon.co.uk. This is an example of domain names that are clearly the way the company identifies itself to its customers. There was a suggestion that trademarking was a way to pre-empt registration of new TLDs, but this might be difficult to justify.

When you mention a commercial product in a web page (or in any document) you must be careful not to misuse any trade mark. Companies register the names and symbols under which they are known as part of their brand. The marks have a commercial value and, unlike copyrights, trade marks have to be policed otherwise they can be lost. You can get into trouble if you use a trade mark in a way that the owner reasonably objects to. This is a complex issue and also includes the concept of 'passing off' where one business purports to be another.

Two contentious areas involve metatags and context-sensitive advertising. It is possible for a web page owned by Company-A to include the trade mark name of

Company-B in its metatags so that people searching on Company-B will be led to Company-A's site, and the practice can thus cause customer confusion. If Company-A is discussing Company-B's products or is a distributor, this is not likely to be an issue; but if they are competitors, it could be. Recent cases in the UK have opened the question of whether including a trade mark in a metatag constitutes a 'use' of the mark since it is machine readable and not, in theory anyway, human readable. We said it was complex.

With context-sensitive advertising, such as Google Ads, it is possible that someone searching on Company-A will be shown an ad for Company-B if Company-B bought Company-A's name as a keyword. Is this a trade mark infringement? This question is certainly reaching the courts around the world.

There are so many interesting points arising from the way the World Wide Web works (in the meaning of 'interesting' used in the famous Chinese curse 'May you live in interesting times') that it may be that the only solution is to widen the scope of fair use and fair dealing to take account of it. This is a point made in Graham Smith's book *Internet Law and Regulation*, which is in any case a good place to start if you want to explore this field further.

Databases

A database consists of a collection of items that are stored so that they can be found in a systematic way. If the database consists, for example, of photographs or articles from a newspaper then these, individually, are copyright. If there is creativity (or even just skill) applied in the selection or arrangement of the contents then the database is in itself copyright. Even if the contents are not copyright, a new European right called *sui generis* is applied, which protects the database for 15 years from publication. In the case of a living updated database this could continue forever.

A database may be protected as a compilation in the USA if there is some creative selection. So a selective list would be protected (my favourite movie stars) while a simple list (all movie actors in alphabetical order) would not, even if the latter were more difficult to produce. Until 1991 a compilation was considered to be protected if sufficient effort had been made in producing it, but a Supreme Court case involving a telephone directory (known as the Feist decision) set that aside and insisted on creativity and not effort as a key criterion for copyright protection. One way to avoid this dichotomy would be to include an annotation with each record in the database, since this note would have its own copyright and anyone who copies the database including this note would infringe that copyright.

It is worth considering the protection of databases in an interactive media context because a website is often built as a database, using some kind of content management. You might even argue that a hierarchical website structure is systematic and so even a static website could be a database. In addition, many sites include lookups for consumers where you can enter, say, your post or zip code and be given information specific to your locality. Such things are also databases, whether they use a 'real' database engine or not.

● Music

Once you write a tune it is copyrighted, and you have the exclusive right to exploit that tune. You might do this yourself, or you might license the rights to a publisher, who then 'works' the tune on your behalf for a fee. You can license the rights for either the full duration of copyright or for a limited time. You can grant a licence for performance of the tune in public and you can grant a licence for the tune to be recorded. When the tune is recorded, the recording itself is copyright but, even if it's your tune, this time the copyright will belong to whoever organized the recording. These are the three principal rights in a piece of music: the Performing Right, the Mechanical Right and the right in the sound recording, sometimes (in the USA) called the Master Right.

Note that a MIDI file of a piece of music is also a mechanical transfer and a licence is needed to produce one. Similarly, the MIDI file will have its own copyright, as with a sound recording.

In the UK, performing rights in music are administered by a body called, logically enough, the Performing Right Society (PRS). PRS collects money from radio stations, concert venues and the like. In the USA the equivalents of PRS are ASCAP, BMI and SESAC. The mechanical right is administered in the UK by the Mechanical Copyright Protection Society (MCPS) and in the USA by the Harry Fox Agency. There are equivalent performing and mechanical agencies in many countries and, in some cases, they are one and the same. Licences for use of sound recordings usually come from the copyright owner, who is probably a record company or broadcaster. It's worth saying that an instrumental tune and a song would be licensed in the same way.

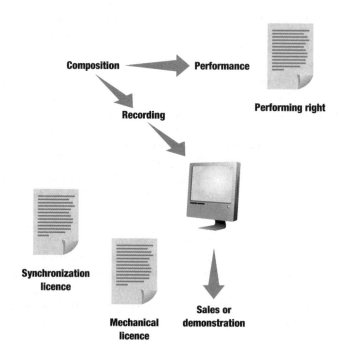

Music rights

When we discuss music on a website, we have to separate downloads of the iTunes variety, whether paid for or not, from background and incidental music used to enhance the user experience. Downloads are like sales on a CD and, if you were to produce a CD compilation of recordings, you would pay a mechanical licence fee to the composer and a fee to the owner of the recording (and a fee to whoever replicated the CD). If you were to sell music downloads on your website then you would make equivalent payments. The rights owners are, reasonably enough, very concerned to make sure that they get the appropriate payments for what you distribute and that usage of the individual copies can be controlled. While getting a licence for the music seems straightforward in these circumstances, with both MCPS/PRS and Harry Fox issuing licences, getting licences for the recordings from record companies would require individual negotiations. That's a field outside the scope of this chapter ... so let's consider background and incidental music.

Is use of music on a website a performance or is it 'mechanical'? There may have been room for debate on this when the only way to listen to music on the web was to download a file and then play it back. You could argue that since the performance wasn't in public there was no need for a performance licence. However, most sound files are now listened to using either real or quasi-streaming. Quasi-streaming is where the sound file starts to play back as soon as the player thinks it has downloaded enough to play through to the end without the file running out. The point is probably moot in any case since, in the UK at least, PRS and MCPS now issue joint licences for such things, and Harry Fox issues licences for both downloads and on-demand streaming in the USA.

The need for a dual licence and even individual negotiations covering mechanicals and recording has led to some publishers setting up special libraries for use in audio-visual media. Here all the rights are controlled by the publisher, including those in the recording, so they become a one-stop shop for music. Using these recordings is always cheaper, so library (sometime called production) music should be your first choice for music.

Another significant benefit of library music is that it is provided specifically for you to tailor to your needs. The publisher will expect you to edit it to fit your requirements. This will not be the case with a commercial recording where you would normally have to explain in some detail just what you want to do with the recording before permission is considered.

When you license a music recording from a record company, the company will probably have to pay royalties to the principal performers from your usage, depending on the contract between the record company and the artists. Use in interactive media, whether online or offline, might not be covered by their contract, and the record company would have to negotiate for the right with the artist before being able to license it to you. This may be impractical, and so the record company would have to refuse you a licence.

Use of music on websites has become easier over the years, since music rights owners, in common with all rights owners, are now familiar with what a website actually is. The copyright clearing houses now have specific categories for online music, whereas offline uses will normally fit into long-standing categories such as Non-Broadcast Audio-Visual Productions. You will probably find that permission to use a piece of music as background to a web page will be treated differently to streamed or downloaded music on demand, so you should always be very clear about what you want to do. Note that rates for advertising are invariably higher.

Alternatively you could get the music specially composed and recorded, and a surprising number of projects do this. This ignores what a good library publisher can offer, but it does ensure that you have original music, which might be very important to your application. If you do commission the music, you should make sure you take further exploitation rights. This would enable you to use the music in a sequel, or to release a record if (say) your games theme was a hit.

● The public domain and clip media

Copyright does not last forever. As the concept of copyright in law developed, so the time for which a work was copyright grew. At the beginning of the twentieth century copyright in the UK lasted only for the greater of 42 years from the date of publication or seven years after the death of the author. In the following 100 years the period has grown to allow the heirs of the author more time to benefit from the work, until the period in Europe reached 70 years after the year of death.

In the USA the duration is much more complex than in Europe. Pre-1979 works are protected for an initial period of 28 years, renewable for a further 47 years. A work that first expired after 1963 was automatically renewed, but complex rules govern who actually receives the renewal rights. The duration of most copyrights in the USA is now the same as in Europe, life plus 70 years, although in some cases, such as work for hire, it is the earlier of 95 years from publication or 120 years from creation.

Any assumption that a work is out of copyright is fraught with danger, and you should seek professional advice, but in general a literary or artistic work is in copyright in Europe until 70 years after the end of the year in which the author died. This becomes more complicated for a translated work, where the translator has rights too, and similarly for illustrators and engravers.

In Europe, copyright in a sound recording expires 50 years after publication. So if you have an original 78-rpm gramophone record from before the late 1940s in your possession – an old Caruso recording, for example – then the recording is no longer in copyright. The tune, however, could well be in copyright since its copyright lasts for 70 years after the death of the composer. Similar arrangements apply to photographs, but for movies – known as cinematograph films – the situation is complicated since performance in public was not seen to be a publication. So some movies have surprisingly long copyright lives. The situation is not simple, and you can undoubtedly imagine the complexity of rights in a production containing multiple media forms, each of which has different copyright terms and needs world rights. It is entirely possible for something to be out of copyright in Europe and in copyright in the USA, for example.

Incidentally, you should assume that a transcription onto CD of an old recording is copyright, especially if the sound was cleaned up in the process. It is possible to fingerprint digital files to identify the source, so if you wish to use an old record, you should clean it up yourself.

So now we come to the Mona Lisa. Since Leonardo da Vinci died over 70 years ago, the picture is out of copyright. It is so old that copyright did not even exist at the time. Therefore you might assume that you can include an image of the Mona Lisa in your application without permission. Unfortunately this is not the case, and the reason will become clear if you consider how you would acquire an image of the painting; stealing it from the Louvre is not an option.

If you owned the Mona Lisa you would have the right to control access to it and, as a result, to control reproductions. This is true of any collection of out-of-copyright works, usually in the hands of museums or art galleries. They will grant permission for reproduction, for a fee, as if the work was in copyright and they owned the copyright. The agreement you sign with the gallery allows you to use the image for a specific purpose. If you use it for another purpose you are not in breach of copyright but you are in breach of the contractual agreement. There will be a copyright in the photograph you receive from the library as well.

Going to the gallery or museum and photographing the picture yourself would not infringe copyright, but the museum would presumably allow you entry only on condition that you did not take photographs or that, if you were to do so, they would not be for publication. This is a contractual obligation on you, but it could be invalid if it was not brought to your attention before you bought your entry ticket. The Van Gogh museum in Amsterdam has a more straightforward approach. They do not allow anyone to take a camera inside. Incidentally, if you were able to take a photograph through an open window, you would not have infringed copyright or any contract. Whether the resulting image would be good enough to publish is another issue altogether.

In general the terms 'out of copyright' and 'in the public domain' are used to mean the same thing, but they are not exactly so. Copyrights expire after a time, but the owner has the right to give them away before this time if he, she or it (because an organization can own copyrights) so desires. The owner can also allow people to exploit the work without payment, with or without conditions attached. This is known as placing it in the public domain. However, just because an author places something, such as a piece of software, in the public domain does not mean that it is out of copyright. Often conditions are attached; so read the small print or the 'read me' file. The copyright on something placed in the public domain in this way will expire at the usual time.

NASA, like other US government agencies, places its material in the public domain. This means that you can use images from the space probes free of charge (apart from paying to get the picture itself). However, NASA does state that you cannot use the images in such a way as to suggest that NASA endorses your product. So there is a condition, albeit a relatively small one, attached. Since 1978 works of the US Government have not had copyright protection at all (Section 105 of the US Copyright Act), but this was not intended to extend outside the USA, which raises the question of European use and even of export outside the USA of finished works incorporating such material.

Some companies produce libraries of assets that are supplied royalty free for you to use on paper or in web pages and other interactive media applications. This is clip art, or clip media. The material is often still in copyright, and it is not really in the public domain either because you may have paid for a book or CD-ROM that contains it, and your use of the material is restricted. There is probably a restriction to make sure that you do not produce more clip media discs from their clip media discs, and you might be restricted to a certain number of images in a single production. But you do not have to pay anything else to use the material in as many productions as you like.

CD-ROMs of clip media range in price from tens to hundreds of pounds/dollars. You can even buy clip art in books, and the Dover Books series of clip art and design is a notable example of this. They often reproduce illustrations from Victorian books and magazines because they are, in themselves, out of copyright. If you own or have unrestricted access to hundred-year-old copies of the *Illustrated London News* or *Strand Magazine* (with its original Sherlock Holmes stories and illustrations) then you could exploit their contents because you have the actual out-of-copyright originals, assuming that the author and illustrator died sufficiently long ago.

It is possible to obtain free material such as clip media by downloading it over the Internet. You should assume that something you can download is available for you to use only if you are explicitly told that this is the case. Usually there will be a page of contractual terms and conditions that you agree to by clicking on the link to start the download. Because web pages can so easily be taken apart, it is sensible to include a copyright notice on any image on a page as well as on the page itself, but bear in mind that the attitude to copyright on the Internet is loose, to say the least, and you should assume that someone somewhere will copy. On the Internet, infringement is considered to be the sincerest form of flattery.

As a developer you must think not only of the rights you take in assets you license but also of the rights you can take in any work you commission. You could be commissioning artwork from a graphic designer, photographs, music or scripts. There is even the software written by your programmers.

As a rule of thumb you should explicitly acquire rights or a licence in any work done for you by your staff or freelancers. This would be included in the contract for the work but, for you to be sure, it has to be a contract with the person doing the work, not an agency or subcontracting company. If you are acquiring rights from a freelancer or subcontractor then he or she must be able to pass on those rights, and should indemnify you against any claims should that turn out not to be the case. You can acquire rights in future work if it is appropriate, and in Europe it is important to obtain all appropriate waivers of moral rights as well.

● Patents

You cannot copyright an idea, only the form in which the idea is expressed. The idea that a television receiver and transmitter could be put in an orbit so high above the earth that it appeared to be stationary, and could then be used to relay television signals, cannot be copyrighted. It could be patented – or could have been in 1944, when Arthur C. Clarke wrote his famous *Wireless World* article on the subject. The article itself, being the expression of the idea in literary form, was copyright, and indeed will be for at least the next 70 years since, at the time of writing, Sir Arthur is still very much alive.

A patent is a document given to you by the government granting you the exclusive right to exploit and control exploitation of a process for doing something. You have to be able to describe the process in such a way that any reasonably capable person could carry out the work from your description; so you cannot be vague and patent, say, time travel without describing how to do it. The process must not be obvious (patently obvious?) since there has to have been an inventive step in the process that you have seen but others have missed. Finally, you have to have done it first. If you were beaten to the process by someone who can prove it then your patent will not be granted, or could be declared invalid, even if you genuinely knew nothing about the other idea. This is called prior art.

Prior art can come from the craziest places. One, possibly apocryphal, instance tells of a patent examiner who was trawling through literature to see if a particular new idea had been described before. He finally found a reference, but it was not in a scientific journal or a PhD thesis: it was in a comic book.

In most countries you have to keep quiet about your invention, since disclosure can invalidate the patent as well. So do not be tempted to give a learned paper on the subject too soon. Timing is critical, and swear everyone you discuss it with to secrecy – that is, non-disclosure.

If you have been granted a patent, you have the right to control use of your process for (in most countries) up to 20 years from the date of filing. A patent does not actually have to be taken out by the inventor. Often employers will take out patents based on work done by their employees. The employee will be the inventor, but the employing company will have the patent rights if the work is done during the course of the inventor's employment.

The process of getting a patent is both time consuming and costly. It is important that a patent is carefully worded so that it can stand up to scrutiny for inventiveness. A particular kind of lawyer called a patent agent should be involved in this process. If you want to protect your invention around the world you have to file an application with each jurisdiction, but there is a mechanism under the Patent Cooperation Treaty which lets you file a single application which will then be reviewed by each of the countries you specify. You can also apply for a European patent, specifying which countries you require. This should be the countries in which your product would be used or manufactured. You have the right to stop both sales and manufacture of an infringing item – or to negotiate a royalty payment.

In Europe a computer program cannot, as such, be patented (but this has been a very contentious issue). However, a technical process can still be patented even if a program is key to carrying it out. It is the technical process that is patented, not the software behind it. But this distinction is more easily seen in an industrial context than in the kind of work done in interactive media. The UK Government Intellectual Property website explains that a program to improve translation between two languages would not be patentable because translation is not a technical process. A program to improve image manipulation would, however, be patentable.

However, since software patents are granted in the USA that would not be granted in Europe, it is important that possible patent infringement is considered when learning from other people's techniques on the Internet. The risk is probably slight, especially given how much code is freely available under open-source licences, but it should not be ignored.

A final point is that in the process of granting you the 'letters patent' the government will also publish your invention. This will happen even if you decide not to pursue the patent.

As the inventor you have the choice of patenting your invention. If you decide not to patent it you should consider finding a way of establishing your prior art by publicizing your idea. If you do this, someone else trying to patent the same process later on will not be able to gain a patent and so stop you making use of your 'own' invention. Altruistically, publishing your idea allows other people to make use of it. It is the equivalent of open source.

Although you cannot copyright an idea, and many ideas cannot be patented or would not be because of the cost and time involved, you can protect your idea by contract. If you need to discuss your idea with anyone you should get them to sign a non-disclosure agreement (NDA) in which they agree not to disclose your idea. That will afford you a measure of protection and, along with terms and conditions of trade, every company should have a stock NDA. An NDA might prove useful when pitching for work. (See the discussion of pitch protection policies in Chapter 2.)

Summary

Intellectual property laws do not protect abstract ideas. They protect the realisation of those ideas as works of art, designs, patents and the like. Intellectual property is a complex business, and it is changing all the time. In producing any kind of media project you will be using IPR and generating IPR of your own. Make sure that anything you include in the project is cleared for the appropriate use, even if your client supplies it, and, before you license anything on to someone else, be absolutely sure you have the rights to do so.

And remember ... if in doubt, ask advice.

Top Tips

Strategy	Potential pay-off
Be aware of how copyright works.	Greater ability to avoid potential problems.
Check all metatags and other trade mark use to be sure the use is justified, appropriate and legal.	Avoids risk of litigation.
Include copyright material, if appropriate, in databases. Be creative in how data is stored and presented.	Improves IPR protection if the database is not in itself protected.
Use either library music or specially-composed music.	Easier clearance and probably less expensive.
Have clear terms and conditions for any user-added content on your site.	Makes sure you have the rights to use the content (and remove it if necessary).

Application Task

Take a recent project in your company and analyse all the IPR contained in it: where it came from and what steps were taken to clear it for use in the project.

Was it straightforward to do this? If not, should a separate legal record/log be created, retained and archived for each project? How could this be achieved in your company, and in your present project? Remember that some of these documents will be printed with signatures and these have to be preserved.

 References/Resources

Books

Wilson, C. (2002), *Nutshells: Intellectual Property Law*, 2nd edn, London: Sweet & Maxwell.

Brief but easily digested run through all aspects of UK IP law intended for students. Gives the lie to all law books being expensive.

Dworkin G., Taylor R.D. (1989), *Blackstone's Guide to the Copyright Designs and Patents Act 1988*, London: Blackstone Press.

This book is a straightforward introduction with useful reference tables and a copy of the Act itself. Bear in mind that it predates EU harmonization.

Smith G.J.H., ed. (2001), *Internet Law and Regulation*, 3rd edn, London: Sweet & Maxwell.

Substantial (and comprehensive) reference and analysis, updated to 4th edition early in 2007. Free online updates to the third edition of Smith (above) are available at http://www.sweetandmaxwell.co.uk/online/intreg/index.html

Strong W.A. (1999), *The Copyright Book: A Practical Guide*, 5th edn, Cambridge, MA, USA: MIT Press.

This is a guide to US law for non-specialists.

Web links

Nolo's website is an all-round resource for US law
http://www.nolo.com

The US Copyright Office has various documents on its website including one on basics of US copyright law and a summary of the DCMA
http://www.copyright.gov

Many aspects of UK Intellectual Property law are outlined at:
http://www.intellectual-property.gov.uk/
and
http://www.patent.gov.uk

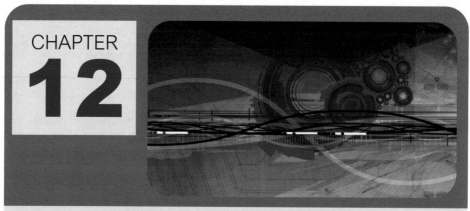

CHAPTER

12

The e-marketing revolution and its impact

Industry Insight

... the audience to whom you market is no longer a mass of demographics whose only choice is to take what you give them in the format you specify. They're individuals who know all too well that their choice of personal relevance in media is at an unprecedented height, and getting greater by the hour.

New media age explains marketing, Paul Doleman, Jan. 2006 www.nma.co.uk

 Overview

What is marketing?

For many, the concept of marketing is closely identified with advertising and selling. In fact, it concerns a wider two-way process of exchange in which the supplier identifies, anticipates and satisfies customers' wants, and the customers choose to buy because the goods or services meet their criteria. This is a continuous process since the customers' criteria change according to many influences – economic, cultural, legal, technological, social, informational and political. The supplier not only needs to recognize any shifts in requirements but also needs to anticipate them in order to satisfy the customers before the competition does, or risk losing business.

What is online marketing?

The same principles apply for online marketing as outlined in the general definition above. Your clients supply goods and services to customers online and want a clear understanding of their needs in order to anticipate and better provide goods and ser-

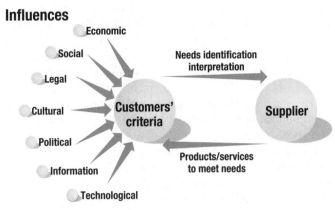

The marketing perspective

vices. Your clients want to utilize the interactive technology links with their customers and potential customers to help the marketing cycle. Web developers are actively involved in the process because the technological tools they choose to use, their approach to design and even the definition of relevant website content can be affected by a marketing perspective.

The path that links products with their target market is referred to as the marketing or distribution channel. The Internet has become a strong channel for both distribution and communications. It is an excellent example of a technological influence that has changed and continues to change customer behaviour. Mobile phones and 'texting' using SMS messages are emerging as another channel where customer behaviour is affected by access to the technology. Interactive television, iTV, is an embryonic medium at present, but it may well stabilize once it finds how its customers want to use this form of communication.

Because of its distribution strength, the web community has developed its own cultural, social and informational requirements. It has driven new legal, political and economic imperatives. The new culture and its requirements are contained in a technological framework, and web developers and marketers have to work together increasingly to achieve results. They depend on integrated processes to distribute goods and services and interpret consumer information.

Even though the web has enormous potential as a channel because of the numbers of people using it, understanding what people want or will tolerate from an interactive channel, what they will give in terms of information about themselves, how they will relate to it in terms of advertising, what they will wish from direct email marketing and so on is problematic. As more is known about the attitudes and behaviour of particular online customer groups, the informed marketing cycle evolves to suit it.

● Why are these concepts important?

The general principles apply not only to your clients but to your own business. If you apply them to your company, you may find weaknesses that you can address to help you win out over your own competitors. In particular, if your company is producing e-commerce or service sites, these concepts are useful so that you understand your clients' drive to know their customer base. They'll appreciate you being knowledgeable about their market sector and you may well need to get up to speed quickly.

You may find that many of your clients already have an understanding of marketing issues but want advice from you about the latest online trends for their sector so they can decide whether they should utilize extra techniques on their site. Many expect you to have access to specialists who can improve ratings on search engines by using SEO (search engine optimization) techniques. They may expect you to offer web analytics of the traffic on their sites too.

Other clients will actively seek interactive companies/agencies that have keen knowledge of the online advertising market and who can recommend strategies for particular dissemination of information, goods or services. SEM (search engine marketing), email marketing, affiliate marketing, viral ad campaigns, personalized search, sector search, subscription search and the use of blogs are examples of these services among others. So there may be many reasons why a marketing approach to a project will be needed.

If clients have insights into marketing and employ specialists, they will have devised an integrated strategy for their marketing mix and marketing communications. They will wish to extend, enhance and complement any offline communication strategy through the use of interactive channels as well. Sometimes the client will go to a full service advertising agency that includes an interactive section, to ensure an integrated solution across all media. At other times the client will just want an extension of their strategy into the new media channels. In yet other projects, the client may not have an integrated marketing communications strategy; they may exist only in the interactive arena or be small enough not to have embraced marketing concepts fully.

If your client has difficulty in making a convincing business case to you as part of their requirements, you may be able to firm the business needs up for them – and for yourselves – if you conduct some market research and competitor analysis for them. Collecting this type of data is part of gathering marketing intelligence.

Traditionally, market intelligence has been derived from information external to the organization. Much of this has been informal – feedback from sales, distributors, customers, trade sources, conferences, published surveys, business reports and government statistics. These have provided trends in markets, marketing new products, technological breakthrough and competitor activity. They have collectively informed you about the external trading and marketing environment.

Interactive channels of communication have made access to marketing intelligence much easier and much more affordable. Interpreting web log analysis data on websites allows access to more refined levels of data that are directly applicable to the company and the users of its site. Because marketing intelligence is directly related to business intelligence and drives business decisions, if you can talk to your clients in marketing information terms, they will see you relating to their business needs. This will give you more credibility and they will trust you more.

The marketing perspective will give strong and measurable pointers to what can improve the client's business. Its results will demonstrate clear business needs that you can use to help prove that you have developed a useful business-focused website or whatever online product the client needs.

So online-derived marketing intelligence can drive business decisions regarding interactive solutions. It can influence stakeholders in the project to your advantage. It may well be the single most important investment you make to clarify requirements, set a strong direction for your designers and back-end staff and serve you as the interactive media project manager. This chapter then should not be viewed in isolation. Marketing information can affect the whole project management process. In some cases it will drive it.

It would be foolhardy not to take the basic concepts on board to apply to your own company and website. After all, you have competitors and you need your clients. You're part of a market sector too.

● Marketing principles and new media

The concept of marketing has gradually been recognized as a determining factor that can affect the success and long-term survival of companies. If all sections of your client's company coordinate their efforts with a view to putting the customer first, this is a clear sign that the company is applying the marketing concept. There is also an emphasis on profitability rather on the volume of sales; on relationship and loyalty rather than anonymity and a quick sale.

The key principles of marketing and distribution have been difficult to apply to online media until recently. These principles are:

● know your customers;
● know your competition;
● know your strengths;
● know your market;
● know how to reach your customers with information and products; and
● know how to keep your customers.

Even when these principles are applied in a mature market, marketing is not an exact science and many predictions are wrong. But all decisions have to be made on available data, so market and competitor intelligence, and the interpretation of this information, are important aids to targeting the market or a particular part of it. Even a little information on an emerging market might allow the development of a strong product line or service ahead of the competition and establish the company's credibility with their customer base.

Interactive technology tools now allow the equivalent of trials to a targeted section of people online, automatic processing of the data and reporting to the client. They can then use the intelligence to refine their product or service and release it to a wider audience. Alternatively, the client may offer the product or service to a narrower, more specific but more responsive set of customers as a result of the intelligence. This form of survey and trial becomes more accessible to more companies as a result of the tools and the customer's access to online technology. (The involvement of the users in an online survey or test of service was covered in Chapter 9.)

Know your customers

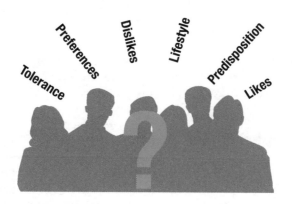

Know your customers

From a marketing perspective, it is essential to know who your customers are and what they want so that you can meet their needs and get them to do business with you, rather than the competition. It may seem an easy task, but it isn't as straightforward as it seems. Are your own customers those who commission the project from you or are they the end-users of the deliverables you produce? We've noted in previous chapters that the end-users' needs should take priority and you should be their champion whenever possible. Unfortunately the people holding the purse strings will quite often interpret the business needs without taking their users or customers into account. This can end up in the 'Z' model of projects as explained in Chapter 1.

However, if the client is market-driven, they are likely to have an interest in the users and their profiles already. They will be informed about them. They will be interested in getting feedback from them in as many ways as possible. They will be able to direct you knowledgeably. If your client does not show this awareness you may be able to influence them with your own market knowledge and advice, get them to pay you or a specialist firm for an appraisal of their online market sector to help drive their decisions or encourage them to gather the information themselves as part of their decision-making process.

In marketing terms, knowledge about the users is needed so that certain customer traits can be identified. Then the market can be divided into certain types of customer behaviour and 'wants'. This leads to products and services being developed specifically for particular segments that are clearly identified and differentiated. Marketing companies have been trying to establish new business models for the new ways of doing business online, but they need access to the same sort of information to base their decisions on as they did in non-interactive media: their customers, wants, needs, likes, dislikes, aspirations, beliefs, attitudes, lifestyles and sense of humour. Then they can work with you to design websites that provide experiences to suit the trends. Online tools and techniques allow more personalization, and this is emerging as a new business model.

Whereas traditional marketing was only interested in trends that showed large and lucrative segments, now it is far easier to tailor offerings for a smaller but still profitable segment of the market. In the end, if you satisfy a single customer who you then retain and who comes back for more later, this customer is more valuable than the unknown casual shopper.

Knowing and understanding your customer base is still the most important driving principle from a marketing point of view, even in interactive media. If you have this information from your client then you can tailor the website accordingly to reach the right people with the right messages. Just because it is easier to retain large amounts of data on customers via interactive channels, this does not exempt companies from local and international legal requirements concerning data protection and privacy rights. It is important to have proper legal advice when devising your online marketing strategy. (See Chapter 10 on legal issues for more on this.)

How to get to know your customer online

As the online environment has matured, techniques to find out who is using the technology – where, when and how – have firmed up as well. Interactive professionals have had to come to terms with the drive from their clients for gathering data on potential customers. The use of cookies – small strings of data that a web server can lodge on a visitor's computer to tag that visitor – allows businesses to track who is using their Internet site at a particular time, allows tailoring of their experience in real time as they use the site, offers more of what they appear to be interested in based on their previous visits (tagged by those cookies) and so on. Web access logs capture information about hits on the site. They gather and collate data about what pages people look at most, how much time they spend on the site and on which pages, what information they seem to prefer and what products they research and/or buy, among other information. These two features are technology-driven but are useful marketing tools as well.

Increasingly, information that was once offered freely on sites is now being aggregated into a semi-closed section where people have to register before they can access it. Online newspapers often follow this pattern. Sites that have developed a large enough following have started to charge for some information that used to be free – often this is coupled with registration so that they can email more offers that they think you'd find appropriate. So registration can be a means of getting to know more about your customer; email address, phone numbers, company address, reason for visiting the site and perhaps other aspects. It depends on what is asked, what information is deemed compulsory and what information the customer feels comfortable giving away.

Sites collect the information and the data can be analysed by web log software. There are many web analytic tools available. Which set of tools will give a better analysis for a particular purpose depends on the nature of the client's business. Companies can find web logs confusing because there is so much data, much of it technical. Developers can help clients understand which figures might be most useful and which to interpret to gain the best picture for their purpose. They might include a monthly or weekly web analytic report tailored to the client as part of their on-going services. It is easy to ask for feedback online – online surveys might be one way to do this. You'll get to know about your real customers and their opinions of your service in this way. Analyse the feedback and act on it to tighten up or improve the service.

All these techniques add to knowledge about the customer – a traditional marketing stance. In fact, traditional media are finding that they know more about their customers through the company's websites and even mobile phone interaction than they did before. Enhanced TV is a strong case in point. Increasingly TV series and programmes have a website attached to them so that viewers can be motivated through the programme then follow up on their interest via the phone or website. Because of the online interaction, different information can be offered from that in a linear programme – the backgrounds to the actors, writers, etc. Competitions and quizzes are popular and the answers can be immediate. Questions can be asked and answered about the topic, the actors or whatever. The viewers can be linked to other sites of interest on the topic. They decide which bits of the site they want to use according to their tastes. The producers can evaluate the viewers' reactions and decide what they might like in a follow-up programme perhaps. This is marketing in action.

Know the competition

Know your competition

The companies that are successful in terms of repeat custom and sales are offering goods and services that meet the needs of their particular market. By studying what is on offer and comparing it with what others offer, they understand their competitors, and they can begin to define what constitutes competitive edge in their market. In interactive markets your competition is harder to identify because things can change so quickly. Traditionally the competition has originated from several sources – direct, close, similar products, substitute products and indirect competition.

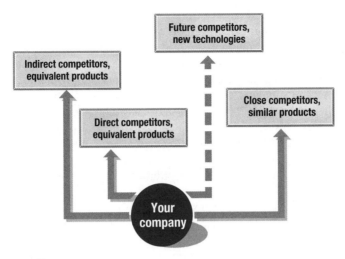

Identify your competitors

Direct competitors would be similar companies with a similar product who could sell this to your clients. Close competitors are companies that offer products that have similar benefits for a similar customer base. So let's say that your client is a soft fizzy drinks company. Their direct competitors would be other companies offering soft fizzy drinks. Close competitors might be companies offering non-fizzy soft drinks. Substitute products are ones that might be bought instead of your client's offering. These might be pure fruit or vegetable juices, varieties of water or even mixer bases like hi-juice squash or concentrates.

It is wrong to become complacent about the competition, because the worst threat might come from an indirect competitor. A company that had previously only made fizzy mixer drinks for alcohol, such as tonic water, soda water and ginger ale, might suddenly extend their brand to fizzy drinks not associated with alcohol. More unexpectedly, a previously indirect competitor that had never sold drinks might start promoting and selling them. In terms of our example of the fizzy drinks, the indirect competitor might be a company that specialized in producing themed children's party ware. They may have identified a lucrative niche market for fizzy drinks linked to children's party themes to complement their themed party fare.

Competition can come from anywhere; hence the span from direct competitor to indirect competitor. This applies more to online competition since the market changes and responds faster than traditional channels. The online market is now mature enough for it to act as the catalyst of change for traditional business, and the changes driven by the online environment can lead and affect the more traditional side of the market. It wasn't long ago that online business was seen as the poor relation to the traditional businesses. So, your online competitors may exert more influence than imagined and need to be watched carefully.

Amazon, for example, built its online branding by selling books, but it has diversified into many areas of sales. It would have been considered an indirect competitor for many of the traditional companies, but it is now big enough to act as the sales broker for what used to be considered large companies. The global market of the Internet drives new definitions of sizes of companies, it appears.

We predicted in an earlier edition of this book that broadcasters would experiment with interactive TV and might offer schools an interactive package. This is now happening. Traditional school publishers stand to lose out since the schools might receive many more materials across the whole curriculum for the cost of a year's online TV subscription or licence than they might get from the total supply of educational online packages from several suppliers. Local authorities have found that they can negotiate on behalf of their schools as a broker so that each school gets a better deal about access to online materials than if each had negotiated alone. The whole schools market for interactive educational materials has changed as a result, and this has had an impact on the sales of printed materials as well.

The Internet can be unpredictable in highlighting a neglected market or demonstrating a new market. The amazingly successful Crazy Frog jingle, initiated by a 17-year-old guy from Sweden who put his vocal attempt to mimic a motor bike on his website, was spread virally by natural online email distribution among the teenage population. Through recognition and revamping, this ended up as a number one recording. It is an example of this type of online success in uncharted water.

The Internet's success came relatively quickly and was a surprise to many businesses. It was an indirect competitor to traditional businesses but suddenly, because of its popularity and the computer literacy of its users, it offered a realistic market platform and possible distribution channel for information and products. Despite initial limitations on bandwidth, speed, restricted use of media and, more recently, the problems with spam, viruses and security, the Internet is rivalling other media channels and threatens to overtake them.

To return to the concept of knowing the competition on behalf of your clients, it is often valuable to get your client's reaction to some of their competitors' websites. With your wider understanding of their competitors – including immediate, close and distant – you may arrive at a more rounded view together. Your client's perception of their competition can affect your design of their site.

Alternatively, some marketing companies are offering the same market analysis of online competitors as they offered for offline. This can include their use of online advertising, its impact, customer reaction to the competitor website and so on. They use online tools to conduct surveys and the data is immediately processed into competitor reports. Your client may hand you reports like these to take into account as part of their brief to you. Unless you know the principles, you will not necessarily appreciate their significance. Your client, on the other hand, may not be aware that such services exist for online market intelligence. You might recommend they use them to get a better idea of what they want as part of the analysis stage prior to production. You might contract-in that service on their behalf since online market survey companies often design websites too, and you wouldn't want to lose your client to them.

Know your strengths

It is probably easier to get clients to define their own strengths in relation to those of their competitors and close competitors. They ought to know where their competitors are succeeding better than they are in a particular market segment and why they are better. This applies to both online and offline markets and online and offline competitors. Your client's website may need to capitalize on their strengths and help to

Know your strengths

redress the balance. However, their online customers' profiles may be so different from their offline ones that the site might need to have a different emphasis while retaining enough of the recognized brand image.

A well-known method to help clients with this type of analysis is known as SWOT. This asks a company to consider its strengths, weaknesses, opportunities and threats. Your client may already have a SWOT analysis, and this can help you make decisions about content and look and feel.

Your clients' strengths give them their competitive edge, and you need to consider whether you are representing their entire online potential in relation to the online market opportunities. You can also consider whether the strengths can be enhanced or focused because of online opportunities to give better results. At the same time, once your client recognizes their weaknesses and can explain them to you, you are in a position to use the site to start counteracting them. The same is true of any threats the client identifies.

If you are in a position of matching the analysis of the clients' strengths to the profile of their online market, you should be able to assess which areas of their online business can serve the market best. As a market matures and segments, then companies that have gathered intelligence within the market begin to specialize and line up with particular needs. Their website/mobile/iTV offerings would also need to conform with these needs. You are in a position to understand where the technology can form a good match with the client's strengths.

One of the most important strengths of a company is its branding. Branding builds loyalty and trust – two of the key attributes that businesses want from their customers. So traditional companies want to hold on to their branding if it is one of their strengths while reinforcing it or adding to it in their online business. All the aspects of design, online look and feel and subjective user reaction that have been discussed throughout the book come together when a client wants to make the most of their brand online. The analysis by the designers and the gathering of feedback about the users' reaction to the visual elements can make all the difference in creating a really successful online product.

On the other hand, if a dated brand image results in the company being seen as old-fashioned rather than current or modern, then it may be seen as a weakness. The developer and client may want to address this through an integrated campaign to change the company image, and the more 'modern' appeal of online and mobile may well fit with the tenor of the campaign. So knowing your weaknesses may be as important as knowing your strengths since the one indicates the other and directs the way to what is wanted.

A product might have built up a following or a trend that needs to be reinforced in any developments. It could be that a product has appealed to the 16–24 age range, and they might expect communication about it to follow the trend or even set a new trend. The product's strength in this case is its cachet, so any online reinforcement would need to capitalize on that. This is where the new and trendy, in terms of use of technology, might be just what is needed. The use of innovative techniques to present information about an already 'cool' product would fit its style and be more acceptable than a straightforward campaign. Here, you can see that the combination of knowing the market segment and knowing the strength of the product could combine to affect its presentation online. An interesting example of this is Coca-Cola. They capitalize on the known preferences of 11–24 year olds with suitably eye-catching advertising on music sites such as Apple iTunes, which are favoured by this market segment.

Again, it is important that you recognize that these principles can and should be applied to your own company and your own site. Often, clients will use your own website, and those of your previous clients, to get an impression of your approach. You need to be aware of your own strengths and weaknesses and begin to address these to keep up with your own competitors.

In terms of knowing your own strengths, it is important that you have confidence in your ability to recognize emerging trends in online marketing that have potential and which your client may not have picked up on. You work in the field, you know the technology, you use the technology. So what may be everyday to you will not yet be part of everyday for other people. Also, you know the boundaries of the technologies and where they can or cannot be shaped. This gives you an advantage in so far as you can quickly distinguish between what is possible and what is not yet possible or is too onerous. If you have conducted user research for site testing as part of your offering to your client, you will have gained a vast amount of tacit understanding of what users prefer, and even what users from particular market segments prefer. This can cut across design, navigation, look and feel and functional operation of a website or other online technology. There is a lot of good market intelligence here, so use it with your new client with confidence.

Know the market

Larger companies pay for market research and use the information to their competitive advantage. They have been the only ones who have the capability to do such large-scale

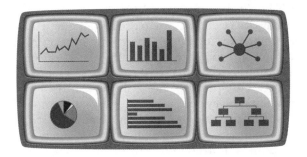

Know your market

research in new and emerging markets ... until now. However, tools for analysing online surveys and web traffic provide any company with its own research relatively cheaply. You need to realize though that formulating questionnaires to give clear and relevant information needs specialist skills. Also, different web analysis tools process the data in different ways. So you'll need to understand which ones are better for particular purposes or market sectors to be able to advise your clients on the best for their business.

Once a new market becomes big enough, marketing research companies start to do their own research because they know there will be enough people interested in buying the reports based on their data. Gradually, as online market segments mature, the research companies follow the trends and write more targeted reports to sell. These can be a useful source of information about your client's market sector so, even if they have not tapped into them, you may find the information invaluable. It is important that the information is current and that it is reputable if your client is to take notice. (See the references for some general marketing research companies that cover online and technology sectors.)

Increasingly, because the tools are integrated into the systems and sites of the companies conducting the business, marketing data is being collated directly rather than through an intermediary. Clients can have far more intelligence about online consumers and collect it more quickly than ever before. What data is collected and how it is presented and interpreted is vital since this drives business decisions. There can be too much data and it can be misinterpreted with disastrous consequences. Interpretation of data also remains an area where expertise is needed.

Research companies will employ their own research techniques, but less formal sources can also be invaluable. Articles in e-zines or the trade press can indicate when a client's competitors are putting effort into a new initiative. Attending exhibitions and monitoring competitor trends/products/pricing is also fruitful. Online forums and discussion groups can indicate attitudes and opinions. The rise of 'blogs' – web logs – by individuals who post their observations and opinions daily, weekly or monthly in their blog has surprised all those involved in the Internet. Some blogs have become so popular and influential that companies want to advertise on them and/or get their products mentioned positively by the blogger because so many people read the articles.

Some companies have even started their own 'blogs' on their own sites where one of their employees writes informally about aspects of the company and life in general. It is this informality and belief in what a person says that has made some blogs so popular. When people like something they've found on the web, they tell others. The news is spread from email to email. This was recognized as a potentially powerful tool by advertisers and has spawned the 'viral marketing' approach to adverts where small, exciting, often media-rich, web links are passed from one person to another, like gossip. These may embed an 'incidental' advertising message about a product; but usually they are designed to appeal to a particular type of person, an age range or a lifestyle. Blogs then capitalized on the 'viral' approach to messaging used by people online and allowed access to a personal, informal, opinion-based message. This personalization of information is being recognized as growing in importance across media and markets, but its full significance has not been tapped. There may be parallels with the current popularity of reality television and celebrities, and blogs may be the equivalent for the web. More information sites are asking for consumers to send in their own photos, text messages, articles and so on, in a move that is being called citizen journalism. This is an extension of the personalization process and also of the so-called Web 2.0, where content comes from visitors to your website as well as, or even instead of, from your own organization.

These trends form part of a micro picture about a market that you cap tap into if necessary to help understand your client's business. More rigorous and formal methods need to be applied to gain a macro picture of what is happening and where key players are heading, so if your client has bought or subscribed to market research about their sector, this can help you form decisions.

If your client has a marketing section but they are not directly concerned with the task you have been commissioned to do, you may consider interviewing them to get salient information about the market issues as they understand them. This might help you formulate decisions about the content, functionality and look and feel for the site.

Your clients themselves may gather information continuously about total sales in relation to products and geographic variance, for example. This will allow them to see whether their general marketing strategies are working and help to identify trends. This type of data is called continuous marketing research. Research companies also employ this method of continuous research to build up macro marketing trends. They may decide to gather data on an emerging market every year, for example. They will cover the same ground to monitor shifts and so identify emerging trends, scale of operation, increased investment and so on. With established market segments, they may produce more regular reports: monthly breakdown of interactive sales by sector and country, for example. The opposite of continuous research is *ad hoc* research that is carried out on demand for a specific reason. This might be to help a company make a particular decision: to find out why a popular series has dropped sales, or why hits on a highly popular website have declined and are therefore putting the advertising revenue it gets at risk, for example. The feedback can help the company decide what to do about the problem.

If you are revamping a client's website, it is important to understand their dissatisfaction with the old site and what they want to achieve with the new one. Often, there are marketing issues driving the make-over that need to be understood so that you can take the best direction. The information must be current. Markets can shift quickly offline, but online can shift even faster.

Know how to reach your customers with information and products

It seems common sense that if you are in business to produce products and services, your customers will buy more of these if they are easily available, the price is right and they compare favourably with competing products and services. The key has been dis-

Know how to reach your customers

tribution of or access to the goods and services. With the World Wide Web, it might appear that these are provided at a stroke, but the situation is not as simple as that.

The concept of search has evolved because of the difficulties people have had in accessing the right information. Personalized search has emerged so that people who have had enough of messy or unproductive searches can decide what works best for them and organize it into a home page that they configure for themselves with the information and links that work for what they want. So, for example, they may like news feeds about a particular topic sent through daily, they may want travel or weather news for their locality constantly available and so on. Alternatively, people may decide to pay a subscription to a trusted 'broker' who will filter much of the dross out of the mass of irrelevant information and serve the person with a more tailored and personalized result based on information that the person has shared with them. In this way, new services will evolve to suit people once it is clear what they like and what they don't like.

As a web developer, you need to understand the customer search and the search engine matching process that is done through the content of the web page and the use of metatags to describe content and list key words in the headers of your pages. These tags are not shown on the screen but are used to classify the information. Search engine optimization techniques can help your prospective clients get better access to your site. They are straightforward to apply and make sense. There are a range of strategies: from selecting an easily remembered domain name – preferably the same or based on the company's name unless it has already been taken, embedding the best key words in the metatags to match words customers might search on, paying a premium to be processed by the search engines faster than normal to get into the system and even paying to ensure that your company either comes within the first few returns on a search on a given key word, or is featured as a sponsored link along the side of the page.

Standards have emerged about how information should be 'tagged' or identified so that searches, and subsequent groupings of similar material, can be made more efficient. This is known as metadata – data about data – and it is becoming increasingly important to all kinds of users of information. The IEEE is active in developing standards of classification across several sectors. For example, they defined metatags for learning technology so that similar types of content can be identified and classified together. (See the references for their website.) MPEG 7, a strand of the Motion Picture Expert Group, developed an ISO standard for metadata describing audio-visual material to assist with indexing for libraries and media archives – a Multimedia Content Description Interface.

The recognition that online community groups are self-selecting, have common interests and share similar needs for certain information, goods and services has emerged as the equivalent of a megastore of attraction. The news and information relevant to the common interest underpin the community and attract people back to the same place regularly. Trust is built up in the community and it acts as an umbrella for the spin-off goods and services that are promoted through directories, adverts, news items, etc. that all have instant links through to their websites. The community itself becomes a brand and instils loyalty through the information passed freely between the participants. Specialized services can then be offered at a premium both for members of the community and for the sellers of goods and services.

Communities build up members while accumulating email addresses and often more formal registration profiling. Direct marketing using emails to communities that share similar interests has provided rich returns for companies. The communities are geographically diverse but have similar needs. This makes it easier to target specific groups that are more disposed to want your information and products. Unfortunately, since emails have been over-used for marketing information, and often contain spam and viruses, many companies and people now filter their emails and prefer to operate only through trusted brokers. Direct marketing emails are still useful, but it is increasingly harder to ensure that you reach the people you want.

The concept of brand in the traditional sense remains important in attracting customers to a site so, if your client has a strong well-recognized brand, their website should be integrated into their complete marketing strategy across all the communication channels. A strong brand means that people will know what to expect and have trust in the company. However, the site should still offer some extras for the customers that suit the functionality of the web over and above their usual relationship with their retailer or service provider.

But what if the client doesn't have a strong branding? How will you attract customers to their site? Affiliations may be an idea worth considering. This is a group of sites that can serve the same customer base but have complementary information, products and services. Often smaller information-led sites will affiliate to retailers such as Amazon and will encourage their visitors to click onwards to make relevant (and even not-so-relevant) purchases. Sometimes a group of sites will link to and promote each other's sites so that awareness and traffic increase for all. Affiliate marketing works on agreed percentage payments for sales that occur as a result of click-throughs from others, or similar types of deals. Strong brands use the affiliate strategy because of increased sales and spin-offs. Alternatively a prominent brand may host the equivalent of a shopping mall where websites compete with any others in the mall including competitors. The rationale is that they will get more traffic than if their site were alone.

Adverts can also play their part in leading people to a site. It is important that a website presence is integrated with a company's whole strategy because, if people become interested in the company through offline adverts, it is easier for them to check up on offers via a website than by phone. Site names can be easier to remember. Phones are often only manned at certain times whereas websites are accessible 24 hours. It is still surprising that companies often forget to put their web address on all communications that are linked to the company, such as press releases, company brochures, compliment slips, headed note paper, sides of vehicles and so on.

Banner adverts have to be placed and timed carefully if they are to have impact because many users ignore them when they are focused on obtaining specific information from the web page. Reading habits change on the web because of the environment, and so strategies that have worked offline are not guaranteed to work in the same way. It is this refining of marketing strategies to suit the new context and user behaviour that is desirable and has ultimately produced results over the last few years. Other online forms of advertising such as buttons, skyscrapers, pop-up, pop-under, interstitials, MPU (message plus unit), viral and so on have their place. They work best when there is a match between who views them and an existing interest in the content or products. There is also evidence that visitors are more receptive to advertisements once they have achieved the task they came to do. Here, an advert can be seen as an option for where to go next, rather than an irritating distraction. Just as with offline adverts, clients need to know what is working where and who is taking notice. Online advertising can actually offer better and clearer information if there is good tracking of the advertising data.

Online advertising has expanded quickly over the last few years and continues to do so. It is a subject in its own right with many facets, but advertising is only one part of a marketing strategy and will be touched on here only because this chapter needs to cover the complete marketing strategy outline. There is a lot of controversy about online advertising; how it is capturing data, how it is viewed by the users and how some people are abusing the technologies in a hidden competitive war with false data. To fully understand the issues, you should explore this in more depth with resources dedicated to online advertising.

Ad servers are companies that offer to place your adverts in front of the right viewer to ensure that more of them click on the adverts, leading to sales. They gather information about demographics and use on sites and can match the profile of users with adverts that suit them by tracking the users as they move between sites that carry ads from the server. Ad formats – meaning their design and use of media for attraction – can increase the click-through rate 10 fold if rich media is used, for example. (See the Ad Format reference.)

With data from a company's advertising campaigns and web analytics as well as relevant market research now available, it is easier to recognize main markets and niche markets. Your client can become more flexible in matching the needs of their niche markets and offering them the information or goods they want faster and cheaper than they ever could offline. This can diversify services and encourage and satisfy new customers. All this is part of knowing how to reach the customers with information and products. This is relevant knowledge for your own company within its own sector as well as for your present and future clients.

Know how to keep your customers

Traditional marketing has recognized the true value of retaining customers and the sense in developing loyalty and trust. A satisfied customer will spread the good news and will be as beneficial in attracting new clients/customers as other marketing techniques. We have seen the rise of loyalty programmes with loyalty cards and reward schemes. Companies have recognized that profiling data on information access and buying habits helps them respond to market forces faster. It also helps to actively target them and plan new products and services.

Know how to keep your customers

Now there is increasing emphasis on customer relation management (CRM), particularly from the service sector. Treating this as a relationship means being in tune with a customer's attitude, lifestyle and aspirations. To achieve this, the company needs precise information on its customers so that it can tailor information and products for them. The information may come from any communication source – phone, fax, email, website interaction and mail – and is integrated into a customer profile. This amount of information will only be given freely if and when the customer trusts the company in every respect from the quality of its service and how it deals with people to the quality of its products and the security of its transactions. Companies are increasingly asking the person's permission to send specific information to them, partly so that they do not injure the relationship through unsolicited mail and partly to comply with increasingly stringent regulations. As indicated before, this also raises aspects of data protection that need to be adhered to, and these are covered in Chapter 10 on Legal issues.

Building a relationship involves time, effort and interaction. Online technology provides more and cheaper interaction opportunities with a client. So utilizing the interaction points is important for building the relationship. These happen within a context that is equally important. Companies that buy into this marketing perspective want their websites to reflect their integrated strategy. They will look for a strategic process implicit in aspects of a website that will satisfy both new and old customers; a process that will lead new customers through the stages leading to loyalty and ensure that old customers continue to be satisfied and rewarded for their custom.

Interactive media companies that work with marketing clients may well need to talk in terms of strategic customer phases being covered, such as awareness, attraction, interaction, community and loyalty. These phases can be linked to specific techniques that will be part of a web presence, like online advertising, affiliate programs, targeted email or permission-based mail, newsletters, online competitions and rewards programmes.

Satisfaction with your service and products will lead to loyal customers and return business. Online satisfaction begins with the ease of use of your website, if it provides what the customer wants, if you give good service, if your products are of expected quality or better and if you offer more or better value than your competitors.

Online products can be much cheaper than offline if transport, display and storage as well as traditional shop rents, employees' wages, fixtures and fittings and so on are taken into consideration. In fact, price differentiation is a key driver for web purchases.

Interactivity through the technology allows exchange of information or placing orders 24/7. This is an enormously increased service potential for many businesses. It can handle certain enquiries automatically, broaden existing services, provide additional service and give standardized services globally. All these can be important to customers whose lives have changed because working hours have changed, expectations about shopping have changed – especially opening hours and access to the shops, and now their expectations about access to information have altered too because of the Internet.

Companies that listen to their customers and provide the range of services they want online will build loyalty and return business. This was true of offline as well. Building on niche markets as well as main markets allows expansion of services and offers the potential of loyal new customers. The global nature of the web particularly offers instant export opportunities as well, so that loyal customers may be acquired world-wide.

Summary

Marketing summary (from a client's point of view)	
Know your customers *Online considerations*	Personalization of offerings is easier online. You can easily serve small niche markets as well as target larger markets.
	Cookies can match content to users in real time as they look at a site.
	Web logs and web analytics give the site owners various snapshots of use through segmenting the type of use, time on site, popular pages, best selling products and so on.
	Encouraging people to register before giving them information provides important marketing data about who is using your site and why. Not always liked though.
Know your competition *Online considerations*	Online competition is global and can come from many sources.
	Online competitors can be direct, close, offer similar products, offer substitute products and originate as indirect competitors – just as in traditional markets. However, online companies react faster and change faster so you need to keep a closer eye on all these types of competitor in terms of your own business.

▶

Know your strengths *Online considerations*	Capitalize on your traditional strengths, but be more flexible online. Branding, product strengths (market segment, positioning) are still important and can be used online. Keep abreast of competition online by regular analysis and revision of your offerings. Know your weaknesses too and counter these online.
Know the market *Online considerations*	Learn from your logs, learn from the marketing research companies, learn from your developers who can be closer than you to the technological behaviour of users. Most of all listen and learn from your users. (See Chapter 8 on usability.)
Know how to reach your customers with information and products *Online considerations*	Technology and its features – how they can work for you to this end? Search engine optimization – helps you get noticed by people searching for sites like yours. Email marketing is effective when directed at communities of users that have shown a pre-disposition to your particular products and services. Consider gathering profiles on your users through registration to target their needs better. Ad servers – get your online advertising (banners, buttons, skyscrapers, MPU (message plus unit), viral, pop-ups, pop-under, interstitials and so on) placed where they are most likely to be noted and acted on. Ad formats can make it more likely that adverts will be clicked on (i.e. rich media apparently helps increase this 10 fold – see the reference for online ad formats). Analyse your web logs to see where people are referred from to your site. This will help you decide how best to reach the majority. Also see which products are most popular online buys and analyse why. Affiliate marketing – drive more potential customers to your site by paying percentages to affiliates who link people through to you for sales.
Know how to keep your customers *Online considerations*	The values of engendering loyalty and trust are still valid. Your website and technology channels need to keep the existing customers satisfied and loyal as well as build new customers and move them to loyalty through satisfaction with products and service. The Internet is a new competitive market so price differentiation and competitive offers are just as important – if not more so. Listen to the online customers and respond quickly in the fast-changing marketplace where access at all hours is expected.

Top Tips

Strategy	Potential pay-off
Exactly how do you ensure that you are providing what customers want? What analysis are you recommending to clients? Using what tools?	Better sites that serve the users and build the clients' business.
What market research serves you and your clients best? Know what is available and learn from it.	Be on top of the latest market trends and user feedback. Use it to influence your design and build and serve your clients. It will make business sense to them and increase customer satisfaction.
Do you have a competitive edge in a market segment because of your client set? Recognize it and grow it.	Become a leader in a market segment because of your knowledge and expertise. Win new clients in the area.
What are your own strengths as a company? How can you market yourself more effectively?	Apply the marketing insights from this chapter to yourselves. Build on your core services/brand and respond to new service possibilities online.
Why not try out some of the marketing techniques and trends on your own site to get your own data to feed your intelligence and skills.	Confidence in what you know and promise. Re-work your own site to serve users better.
How do you analyse your client's competition online? Do you have a set approach to looking at and evaluating the worth of competitor sites?	Using a consistent approach to evaluate your client's competitor sites will allow you to determine which features are working well for the sector and which are not. They will drive redesign decisions that make business sense to your clients.

Application Task

Applying marketing insights means getting to know your market, customers and competitors well enough to inform your business decisions. You may be able to help your clients by performing this service for them. It may already be part of your service through your SEO team. If you have no history of doing online competitor analysis you may learn a lot by starting the process. The results can drive your design and build decisions, and they are immediately important to your clients because they make business sense to them. You can also apply these to your own website and competitors.

Use the following table and adapt it if necessary to suit your company. It provides some basics that can be applied to all websites as a bench mark. Use it against what you consider your top three online competitors as well as your own site. The competitors need to be as

▶

near to offering the same type and range of services as you or the near comparison will be difficult and less meaningful.

What does it tell you about your own site? How can you improve? Would this type of analysis serve your clients? Would it affect the way you approach design and build?

	Weak				Good
Competitor analysis tool (websites)	1	2	3	4	5
Search engine ranking					
Metatag use					
Initial impression of site					
Target market					
Content structure					
Navigation/usability					
Product/service features					
Offers/promotions					
Innovations					
Overall score:					
General comments/profile:					

References/Resources

General

New Media Age – weekly magazine (UK) with supplements
www.nma.co.uk

Chaffey, D., Smith, P.R. (2005), *Emarketing Excellence (Emarketing Essentials)*, Butterworth-Heinemann, Oxford, UK and Burlington, MA, USA: Elsevier.

Damani, R., Damani, C., Farbo, D., Linton, J. (2005), *Online Marketing: Online Media Planning, Pay Per Click Search Marketing, Organic Search Engine Optimization, Email Marketing, Affiliate Marketing, Rich Media and Banner Advertising, Viral Marketing, Social Networks and Analytics*, London, UK: Imano PLC.

Eisenberg, B., Eisenberg, J. (2005), *Call to Action: Secret Formulas to Improve Online Results*. Austin, TX, USA: Wizard Academy Press.

Market research

Clikz Network – solutions for marketers
http://www.clikz.com/stats/

Emarketer
http://www.emarketer.com

Forrester – helping business thrive on technology change
http://www.forrester.com/my/1,,1-0,FF.html

Internet World Stats – global marketing
http://www.internetworldstats.com/links5.htm

O'Reilly Research
http://research.oreilly.com

OVUM Ltd
http://www.ovum.com

Gartner
http://www.gartner.com

References

Crazy Frog ring tone history
http://en.wikipedia.org/wiki/Crazy_Frog

Online ad formats, Sean Hargrave, NMA magazine (explains online advertising), pages 6–8, 24 April 2006

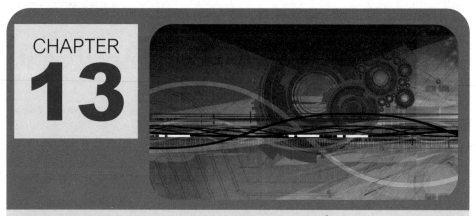

CHAPTER 13

Team management and interactive projects

Industry Insight

Many challenges face managers in charge of leading multi-function teams... perhaps the least known and understood is the power of widely different paradigms governing decisions and behavior inside various work units. Since paradigms are invisible to insiders by their very nature, the savviest managers of the future will learn how to identify, communicate and bridge across them. Otherwise much time and money, not to mention work relationships, could be lost.

When world's collide: managing a cross-functional team, Jagoda Perich-Anderson, Futurist News, Nov 2000
http://www.futurist.com/portal/creating_your_future/crf_cross_functional_team.htm

Overview

The communication role of the project manager has not always been appreciated. It is a leadership role as well as a management role since the project achieves success through managing the people as well as the processes. The interactive media project team offers many challenges because it is most likely a cross-functional, virtual team. These conditions add complexities to the communication process and to the team's successful management.

Definition of interactive media team

A group of people with a variety of interactive and business skill sets that work together towards a common goal and share accountability for the results.

Interactive media teams – who?

Since the roles for interactive media or digital media have not stopped evolving, it's actually difficult to determine the number and role titles of the people involved. Each interactive sector has its own specialists – instructional designers for e-learning, producers of various types and names for iTV and games, account manager in the ad and marketing agency sector (mostly) and so on. The titles are diverse so it's no good getting hung up on them as the way to describe the make-up of interactive teams.

A generic team might comprise several of the following hands-on roles or equivalent:

- a team leader/project manager/producer;
- the account manager, marketing manager or equivalent – sometimes a director;
- graphics designers/creatives;
- programmers with various skill sets;
- content specialists – information architect, instructional designer, copy editor, usability expert, accessibility expert;
- Quality Assurance (QA) – testing specialist;
- media specialists – film, animation, audio;
- subcontractors to fill any gaps.

Extra roles that might be involved in a less hands-on way might be:

- functional management – various;
- top management – nominated representative;
- client's representative(s) or project sponsors.

Interactive media teams – are they different?

The diverse specialist mix and the need to create projects through the use of technology – technology that is innovative, unstable and evolving – does make a difference to interactive media teams and therefore to their management. Some of the general principles apply up to a point, but after that the new business environment, the creative culture associated with the interactive media sectors and the combined attitudes of young 'alternative' talented people all contribute to a different team management experience.

Management styles and leadership

A good deal of research has been conducted into management and management styles. Personality, the structure of a company/organization, its culture and the industry sector may all have affected management styles. The more autocratic and directive styles are readily recognizable in the military, for example. The collaborative and supportive styles are more readily recognizable, perhaps, in the charity and social work sectors, for example. On the other hand, the fluid work environment and the innovative challenges of interactive media projects demand a mix of appropriate styles according to each situation that confronts the team.

In terms of the interactive media industry and the type of management styles deemed appropriate for its sectors, there are no clear-cut conclusions. It would be easy to say that the autocratic approach was wrong and the democratic, consensual approach was right but, in reality, this would not represent the truth about interactive media and team management. Sometimes you'll have to be directive. If, for example, too much time has been wasted trying to reach a consensus because the team's perspectives are pulling in different directions, you may have to drive the decision. On many occasions, however, you'll take the time to ask everyone's opinion, get the rounded view and move forward in general if not absolute agreement. In between there will be all shades of styles needed and a lot will come down to the personalities, the knowledge and the experience involved. Because each interactive media project – by its nature – will have aspects of 'newness' for the team, some decisions will be innovative and have elements of risk attached to them. The decision will have to be the best possible under the circumstances. Knowledge and experience of these aspects may come later and will feed into the next project. In an evolving fast-changing industry, life's like that.

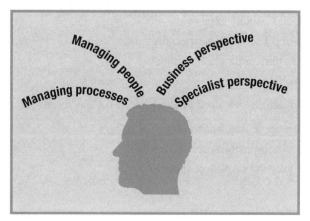

Management of different aspects

The emphasis has shifted gradually from management concepts towards leadership and its analysis. Leaders are considered visionary, strategic, communicative, motivational and able to influence others by their qualities – perhaps even charisma. Management is equated with planning, budgeting, control, risk avoidance and rationality. So, just from this straw poll of the differences between them, we can see that this book has lined up with both sets. The management aspects are well represented by the project management principles; the leadership elements look to the strategy and influence, such as from the stakeholders, the customers, the marketplace and, here, your relationship with the team. Management involves the processes to achieve results: leadership drives the communication process to influence people to achieve results. However, management can be about managing people through the processes, and this is where the overlap with leadership occurs and causes confusion. It might be best to consider that leadership is more about your personality and its effect on others while management is the focus on using processes to achieve the required results and is less personality-driven.

It is hard to move from being a team member to being a team leader because the joint responsibilities of managing processes and managing people come together. At the same time, you have to adjust your specialist perspective to embrace the business perspective. This means giving up your edge in your specialism to others in the team and building your business focus. This strong shift in a role is problematic, and many interactive specialists do not want to compromise their knowledge and experience in this way. It can result in internal personal conflict. Some people opt out of the management move and return to their specialisms. You need to recognize what the transition means and decide if you want to pursue the management career line.

Team roles

The approach to defining and analysing team roles has changed in the last few years because the work environment has changed. The strong move away from traditional, hierarchical, functional job types to more team-based activities – such as project-based work that cuts across functions – has prompted this. How a person operates in a team and contributes to team results has grown in importance as a skill set. This team value has proved difficult to appraise and reward because traditional appraisal systems in education and companies have rewarded individual achievement for individual tasks. So, if the definition of a role changes, many other aspects of how an individual's performance is judged are called into question.

What has happened? The definition of a role has evolved to include generic skill sets and generic tasks that have more value in today's team-oriented companies. A manager and an individual can then assess how performance relates to these generic sets. These sets include team disposition and individual performance. There is still a need for people to recognize and accept their pre-dispositions and personality attributes, but these are further analysed to understand the contribution that they can make within a team and within a company.

Meredith Belbin has led the field in analysis of people and teams for many years. His pioneering work in the 1980s has continued to evolve. He isolated and explained nine core role types that people take in team tasks – plant, co-ordinator, monitor evaluator, implementer, completer finisher, resource investigator, shaper, team-worker and specialist. These have been devised from extensive psychometric testing and a diverse range of team types across many industries. If a team is balanced then these roles will be in balance. This does not mean that there should be nine people in each team. One person may be able to fulfil a few roles even if one predominates. The role types show a disposition towards how a task is achieved through behaviour. Some members of the balanced team will work more to a team goal, such as the co-ordinator, the monitor evaluator, the team-worker, resource investigator, shaper, and completer finisher. Others will work towards individual contribution, such as the plant, specialist and implementer. These are generalizations to set these role types in the wider context here and you are referred to Belbin's books and website to get a clearer idea of the analysis of the roles.

Belbin has gone on to give a context to these specific team roles in terms of work roles. He defines the relationship between manager and individual in terms of compliance with work directives (work standards), use of personal discretion and judgement (individual development), support and help to others and joint responsibility to achieve set objectives (teamwork). The individual can add to this appraisal by demonstrating any extra work taken on, showing initiative and suggesting improvements to work processes. All these general sets are given an associated colour and can be plotted in a matrix where individual achievement and team achievement are matched against the level of responsibility taken. Colour coding has been found to help people relate to the general sets.

This work role demonstrates how a person can now be appraised according to work directives, individual development and team performance. These insights may help interactive media team managers take an overview of defining performance in a project-based environment. It might also encourage them to adapt the concepts to suit their purposes.

In terms of individual characteristics and roles in teams, Belbin now offers an online assessment tool to determine your characteristics. (See his website www.belbin.com.) You can use this to analyse your own team and yourself.

Cross-functional team

Cross-functional teams

In this context, cross-functional is synonymous with cross-department, or cross-specialism. A cross-functional team is made up of people who come from a variety of backgrounds and experience. This is true of interactive media teams, and research into how cross-functional teams operate successfully appears to have stronger relevance for interactive media because of this. The typical interactive team brings together several strands of expertise to fulfil the project's needs. Cross-functional teams offer flexibility, responsiveness and a variety of skills, knowledge and experience.

Implicit in the cross-functional team is a willingness to agree to team rather than individual criteria of success and failure. This also implies shared responsibility for the outcomes of effort. This can be hard for specialists who are happy to accept responsibility for their own contribution but feel that the team's success may compromise their individual standards. Interactive media teams have many specialists, so this can give the team leader/project manager a lot to contend with – as indicated in the Industry Insight.

You can emphasize the benefits of cross-functional teams to help in this case. These types of team offer speed and responsiveness to the task. Often parts of the project will be developed in parallel rather than sequentially – saving time. The multi-skilled team can solve more complex tasks faster than traditional functional teams. They also take more notice of the customer's needs since these unite their focus. Creativity occurs naturally in cross-functional teams because they bring together different perspectives, cultural values and backgrounds. In terms of learning, the mix of the team allows a strong development for each member since there is transfer of skills and knowledge from diverse areas, collective problem-solving, observation of others in action and framing of new insights. This learning represents value for the company in three ways, individual development, learning about the organization and appreciation of competencies in other people.

However, it is precisely the diversity of the team members that can make for difficult interpersonal relations, conflicts of perspectives and personalities as well as lack of trust. The team leader will need to set a clear vision of what the project means, set clear goals for each member to attain and make sure that each realizes their collective responsibility for the complete success of the whole task. It is often the case that the supposed leader of the team is unclear of his/her authority within the project. If this is so, the leader needs to make the limits of delegated authority clear with their management so that decisions can be made quickly and efficiently without question, and the team understands their collective limits too.

Virtual teams

A virtual team works across geographic boundaries, organizational location, time and space. They are also known as geographically dispersed teams or dispersed teams. Otherwise, virtual teams follow the characteristics of cross-functional teams in so far as they are made up of people with diverse skill sets to suit a particular task/project. The team collectively holds responsibility for the successful completion of the task. They tend to work with communicative technologies – such as web and mobile – to keep each other abreast of what they are doing. Methods of communication may involve emails, posting electronic files including timesheets, work in progress, etc., video or phone conferencing. Increasingly, in interactive media particularly, virtual teams have a common project web space where communication and progress on pieces of the project as well as spend, time spent and decisions will be shared. These enterprise-wide project systems allow such virtual teams to trap and monitor progress. This progress can be made available to management and clients as and when necessary. (See the references to integrated project management systems and enterprise-wide project systems in Chapter 5.)

As the team is dispersed, meetings occur infrequently if at all. This does make a project manager's job harder since misunderstandings can occur more easily because of lack of non-verbal communication signals and cross-cultural differences. Note that body language is extremely important in establishing meaning in communication and that this can cover facial expression, gestures, posture, eye contact, tone, and so on. It is said that only 7% of a message is communicated verbally with 93% coming from non-verbal means. Facial expression accounts for 55%, while 38% is absorbed through the tones used.

Deficiencies in non-verbal cues because of distance add to the already difficult management role of having a team of diverse specialists each with their own perspective. It is recommended that, if at all possible and where the team does not know each other, they should try to meet up early in the project to establish a working relationship.

The negative aspects of a dispersed team are gradually becoming tempered with the increased experience of people working this way. Team managers can anticipate some difficulties and try to work around them. So if the team cannot physically meet, video conferencing can go part way to the team seeing each other and forming impressions about personality, communication pre-disposition, sense of humour, gestures and language implications, together with a sense of non-verbal language.

It is notoriously easy to misread the tone of an email message, and distressingly easy to press the 'send' button without reading a message carefully. Emails are not the same as letters since they are written less formally, have no commonly accepted format and can be part of several sub-cultures according to the person's familiarity with using them and the medium. Text messaging is even more cryptic and prone to misunderstandings, of course. It is best to clear things up with a phone call to check if you have correctly interpreted an email or text message that might appear to be causing some confusion. Then the tonal information can add to your understanding.

Experience in the use of web-based project management systems and virtual teams can help a project manager with a dispersed team. Making each team member report in a common way also helps standardize communication practices so that all can quickly understand the import of others. (See Chapter 5 for references on integrated project systems.)

Because virtual teams are becoming more common, the added difficulties of managing this kind of team need to be understood and controlled by the team leader as far as

Effective team leaders and successful teams: is there a formula?

possible. This can take extra time and effort and so project managers should allow more time for managing teams of this type. This extra time might well be balanced by the less frequent meetings of the team and the faster electronic posting of work in progress.

● Characteristics of successful teams

It is difficult enough to bring together the right mix of technical and creative skills for each project without extra problems being caused by the mix of personalities. Personality attributes and behavioural characteristics can account for the success or failure of projects. Interaction skills within the project team can make or break it. To help with these, the project manager can benefit from understanding the research into team dynamics and may be able to use the knowledge wisely to help in difficult situations.

Belbin has researched the qualities of a variety of successful teams, and the research he carried out into IT teams is the closest to interactive media teams. They are inherently difficult to manage. It appears that critical debate is a characteristic of these high-ability teams and that there are difficulties for them in reaching coherent decisions. Teams of high mental ability tend towards analysis rather than synthesis: they will debate endlessly but not reach a consensus. This would appear to show that the individuals are vocal about their specialist perspectives. These insights ring true for interactive media teams who are high-ability and cross-functional. The findings pose a dilemma for a project manager because in teamwork for a purpose – i.e. project development – analysis needs to be synthesized to move ideas through to tangible development and progress.

Critical debate is necessary in a creative, high-tech field, and specialists thrive on it. It forms part of their drive and motivation, both of which you need in the project. But if you recognize that the avenues explored lack cohesion, and no one else in the team provides a unifying stance, it becomes your responsibility. There will be a balance between allowing constructive debate and letting it run away with itself.

High-tech teams, according to Belbin, also fail to have a rounded approach to viewing problems. This is a weakness associated with teams that have a concentration of specialists. Specialists were often found to have anxious-introverted personalities too. If the specialists had risen to management levels, they continued to display specialist tendencies. These insights may prompt you to think about yourself and your own tendencies in relation to leading a team, as well as help you understand some of the negative aspects associated with groups of specialists as found in interactive media teams.

There is a further dilemma because the literature has also shown that every project needs to be personally challenging for the team if there are specialists involved. They want to give their best, otherwise they become bored or indifferent. They aim higher than others would. Again, you have to find the balance between personal challenges for your team members and achieving the project within time and budget. The business principles will help give the rounded perspective needed, or you might opt to invite a business specialist into some of the initial team meetings to add balance.

The other option might be to share the criticisms of high-tech teams with your team as part of the critical debate. People can learn. They can begin to recognize when the team displays these tendencies and can move towards accepting the need to balance them. They may come up with some surprising strategies to compensate for them. It is important that your own specialist views, as well as those of the other specialists, are considered within the business context of the application so that the criticism of narrowness in the team vision is avoided.

There are some points in favour of the project manager being a specialist where other specialists are present in the team. Specialists are difficult to manage, but they are more pre-disposed to respect people who are achievers within a related specialism. It will not necessarily make the role easier, but it will be easier to voice your opinion with confidence.

Belbin also noted that if teams were composed around creatives, there appeared to be weakness of follow-through. There was an abundance of ideas, but they were not utilized effectively. A team needs a creative source, but also needs the backup of people who create the opportunity for the ideas to move into action. There are, by definition, many creative people as part of the interactive media team, and so this might present possible difficulties.

In looking at the qualities of successful team leaders, Belbin's research found that the team leaders who were most effective with computer application development teams were selected not for their experience and seniority in the field but for their 'chairmanship' qualities. These were defined as the ability to recognize the strengths of the others in the team, to explore options that were raised, to back the right person at the right time and to obtain good results. This does not, and could not, define how the leaders knew who to back or when. The data seems to support the premise that the leader should not be the cleverest person in the team but should appreciate the strengths in others, help them communicate in ways appropriate for the whole group to understand and keep them focused on the objectives. However, the tasks that the team need to perform can also define the type of leader that is needed. If the team has been in a rut, someone who is extrovert can galvanize it into action and drive it forward, and so might be more appropriate than a 'chairman' character.

Christopher M. Barlow confirms and extends Belbin's insights into successful creative teams. He reminds us that younger people may well know more than their managers in fast-changing fields such as interactive media. The combination of conflicting perspectives in a cross-functional team adds complexity and makes it difficult for the team members to trust one another. Barlow suggests that the team leader harnesses the diverse perspectives in the members of the team and makes them specific and accepted. One of the insights that could prove invaluable for interactive team managers is that the team can continue to work in relative disagreement. This will take some pressure off the individuals if they realize that they do not always have to reach consensus and that this is acceptable. Remember though that in these circumstances you, as project leader, have to drive the decision forward and take responsibility for the direction even if it later proves to be wrong the project needs to progress, not stagnate because of lack of consensus from the business point of view.

The appreciation of the differences that the team embodies is a recurring theme for project managers of cross-functional and virtual teams. The Industry Insight at the start of the chapter forewarned that the manager who appreciated the mix of perspectives and could draw out the strengths of each team member while providing the bridge between them would be more likely to get the results needed for business. Recognizing the importance of the management of people in the project team will be critical for the project manager. The project can only be successful if the people pull together rather than pull apart, no matter how well the processes are defined and controlled. The communication aspects of project management are under-estimated at the peril of the business. More training is needed in this area for the leaders of teams and for the consequences of team failure. If a team gets into difficulties because of interpersonal issues, conflict resolution techniques might be needed. Conflict resolution is becoming more important in relation to teamwork. It is a substantial area in its own right and you should consider expanding your knowledge about it as part of your self development.

Team management is a skill that businesses are giving more attention to, because more and more businesses are operating in a project or team structure. The abilities to be a good team member and a capable leader are increasingly valued in job descriptions for interactive media, as well as in other professions. Companies and recruitment agencies will become more adept at explaining the communication and team skills they want in a project manager and the behaviour they expect from a competent leader of people as well as the processes they need in managing projects.

Summary

Managing an interactive media team is not straightforward. It asks you to leave behind any specialism and work to bridge the diverse skill sets of the multi-talented team. You have to blend managing the project management processes with managing the people. These require different skills. Lack of clear communication within the team can impede the success of the project. But getting clear, non-confrontational communication between a diverse set of people who may operate cross-culturally at a distance is a challenge. There are some insights from the management of successful IT teams and successful creative teams that can help the interactive media project manager.

Top Tips

Strategy	Potential pay-off
Are you comfortable in the role of project manager? Are you happy leaving behind your specialism for more of a business focus?	This is a dilemma for many, so decide your stance and be true to yourself. This will be better for you and the company in the end.
Define yourself in terms of your management style and your leadership style.	Do you need training in either to help you manage your team better? Look up a couple of training courses and discuss them with your management. Better management of processes and people can only add business value.
Does your company use web-based multi-project management systems, enterprise-wide project systems, etc.? If not, look at several of these to understand the functionalities of each. Decide which functions would suit your teams best.	Consolidating similar management information within and across projects helps you control the project and gives a discipline to the team members in reporting on projects. This frees time for you to deal with the softer issues.

▶

Consider if your company demonstrates the value of teams in their appraisal or reward systems. If not, what might be appropriate and help motivate your team without causing competition with other teams?	People respond if they feel valued and their effort is appreciated. You need this in your team – so what could incentivize this?
Does the company realize it uses cross-functional and/or virtual teams? Do they know what this means and what extra strains it places on their successful management?	If you see the need, offer to do a briefing session for the company on managing interactive media teams. Introduce them to these concepts. Ask for feedback. Ask for suggestions of how to improve team management for all. Get commitment to the top two suggestions and plan to implement them.
Tap into the opinions of your present and past team members. Ask them to comment confidentially on the highs and lows of being in a project team – from the 'people' point of view.	You may get invaluable insight into the perspectives of the team and any underlying gripes. This might give you a heads-up to potential problems that you can counter to help your projects run more successfully.

Application Task

Have a meeting with other project managers/team leaders and those who have had experience managing project teams. Draw up a list of pointers to help manage successful teams from your own experience. Ask your colleagues to add to the list. Also draw up a list of problems/conflicts that people have experienced in managing the teams and the effects on the projects. Could some of the pointers have helped? Could they help in future? Are there any other suggestions of how the problems could have been avoided?

Update the lists and repeat the meeting a couple of times a year. Post the list and any discussion as an electronic support for team managers within your company.

● References/resources

General on teams

Teamwork Links – selected reviews of teamwork websites
http://reviewing.co.uk/toolkit/teams-and-teamwork.htm

Harvard Business School (2004), *Creating Teams with an Edge (Harvard Business Essentials)*, Boston, MA, USA: Harvard Business School Press.

Belbin, R.M. – his site – tools available on team role analysis and more
www.belbin.com

Belbin, R.M. (2004), *Management Teams – why they succeed or fail*, 2nd edn, Oxford, UK and Burlingon, MA, USA: Elsevier Butterworth-Heinemann.

Belbin, R.M. (2000), *Beyond the Team*, Oxford, UK and Woburn, MA, USA: Butterworth-Heinemann.

Belbin, R.M. (1997), *Changing the Way we Work*, Oxford, UK and Woburn, MA, USA: Butterworth-Heinemann.

General on creativity and innovation

Harvard Business school (2003) *Managing Creativity and Innovation* (Harvard Business Essentials), Boston, MA, USA: Harvard Business School Press.

Cross-functional teams

Cross-functional collaboration, Glenn M. Parker, Oct. 1994
http://deming.eng.clemson.edu/pub/tqmbbs/tools-techs/crossfun.txt

Kettley, P., Hirsh, W. (2000), *Learning From Cross-Functional Teamwork*, IES Report 356
http://www.employment-studies.co.uk/summary/summary.php?id=356

Building and managing cross-functional teams, Patrick Mosher, Workforce Performance Solutions, June 2005
http://www.wpsmag.com/content/templates/wps_article.asp?articleid=221&zoneid=15

Creativity and complexity in cross functional teams, Christopher M. Barlow (The Co-Creativity Institute, Nov 2000)
http://www.cocreativity.com/papers/iproconfpaper.pdf

Virtual teams

Gibson, C.B., Cohen S.B. (2003), *Virtual Teams that Work: Creating Conditions for Virtual Team Effectiveness*, San Francisco, CA, USA: Jossey-Bass.

Leading Dispersed Product Development Teams, Preston G. Smith, in KNOWvations, Aug. 2002
http://www.sopheon.com/inknowvations.asp?id=8-1-2002

From experience: leading dispersed teams, Preston G, Smith, Emily L. Blancks, *The Journal of Product Innovation Management*, Vol. 19, pp 294–304, 2002
http://www.newproductdynamics.com/JPIM7-02/JPIM7-02.pdf

Non-verbal communication

Non-verbal Communication, Zero Million.com, Management and Personal Skills section, 2005
http://www.zeromillion.com/business/management/non-verbal-communication.html

Non-verbal communication, Dilek Eryilmaz, Steve Darn, BBC and British Council, 6 Sept. 2005
http://www.teachingenglish.org.uk/think/methodology/nonverbal.shtml

Select, Assess & Train, Non-verbal Communication, Management Files, no date given
http://www.selectassesstrain.com/hint6.asp

Glossary

Note: This glossary builds on the glossaries published in previous editions of the book. As a result there are terms, mainly technical ones, that are not covered in the current edition. However, we still think they will be useful.

16 by 9 Aspect ratio (width to height) of widescreen television (conventional TV has an aspect ratio of 4 by 3).

2G Second generation mobile phone systems. The first generation were analogue; **2G** systems are digital but designed for speech and small messages (SMS). So-called **2.5G** systems added data capability such as GPRS and HSCSD while **3G** systems add higher-bandwidth multimedia capability including photographs and movies.

2.5G Intermediate stage between current mobile telephones and **3G**. See also, **HSCSD, GPRS, EDGE**.

3-D Three-dimensional, appearing to have depth.

3-DO Obsolete consumer multimedia player.

3G Third generation mobile telephone systems, another name for **UMTS**.

8-, 16-, 24- or 48-bit image The more **bits** a colour image has, the more colours can be shown in it. An 8-bit image can have 256 colours because eight bits can be used for numbers from zero (00000000 in binary arithmetic) to 255 (11111111 in binary arithmetic). However, these colours can usually be chosen from a larger palette of perhaps millions of colours. If the 256 colours are all shades of grey then a photographic-quality monochrome image can be reproduced. A 16-bit image will have thousands of colours, and can look photographic in many circumstances. For a truly photographic colour image the millions of colours available in 24 bits are necessary (or even more). Note that on the Apple Macintosh an 8-bit **matte** or **alpha channel** can be added to the 24 bits, and the image can be referred to as being 32-bit. Also the **PNG** format can handle 48-bit colour images with an alpha channel.

- 1 bit gives you two colours (usually black and white).
- 2 bits give you four colours.
- 4 bits give you 16 colours.

- 8 bits give you 256 colours.

- 16 bits give you 65 536 colours.

- 24 bits give you 16 777 216 colours.

- 48 bits give you 281 474 976 710 656 colours.

above-the-line cost A cost that you would not be paying as part of the overhead of running the company. Your in-house resources and/or staff are a below-the-line cost whereas a freelancer hired for a particular job is an above-the-line cost. These two kinds of cost are both real, since somebody has to pay them, but your attitudes to them are likely to be different.

acceptance testing This is testing that is applied according to pre-determined parameters agreed with the client at the end of the project to show that the project conforms to the standard expected and warrants payment.

Access Microsoft database software sold as part of the Office suite.

accessibility designing **websites** and other programs to give equal access to them by people with disabilities. In the case of web design, it includes such considerations as designing the page or a version of the page that makes sense when read by a speaking **web browser** (**screen reader**).

accessibility standards The World Wide Web Consortium have a web accessibility initiative (WAI) which gives guidance on making **websites** accessible. The Watchfire company in the US developed the Bobby as an aid to assessing the accessibility of **web pages**. Although these are more guidelines than formal standards, following them will make the **websites** more user friendly for everyone, not only users with disabilities.

ActiveX Microsoft technology for adding dynamic content to **web pages**.

adaptive palette A relatively limited palette of colours that is calculated so as to best reproduce a full colour image. Often 256 colours but sometimes less.

ad hoc research Relating to marketing, this is specific research defined and carried out for a particular purpose.

ADPCM Adaptive Delta (or Difference) Pulse Code Modulation, delta PCM is a sound-encoding method that reduces the data rate by storing only changes in the size of samples rather than the absolute value of the sample. The adaptive part is where the encoding of the difference values adapts so as to more accurately follow large changes between samples.

ad server A **web server** which holds advertisments and supplies them for inclusion, on the fly, in **web pages**. By centralizing the ad serving and using **cookies** it is possible to determine the browsing habits of users and target ads accordingly.

ADSL Asymmetric subscriber line (or loop), a means of carrying very high speed data down a conventional copper telephone cable over distances of a few kilometres.

affiliate marketing Where a company will pay a commission on any sales or registrations that are generated from another company promoting their products for them.

agent A piece of **software** that is empowered to act on the user's behalf, to carry out tasks like network maintenance or booking a holiday. A mobile agent is an agent which is able to move around a network from computer to computer in order to do its job.

Agile Relating to **software** production where small discrete units are coded every few days to allow speed of reaction from customers and faster development paths.

aliasing Occurs when the way something is recorded produces errors that look or sound as if they should be parts of the real thing. The wheels of racing covered wagons in a Western movie, which often seem to be going backwards, do so because of aliasing. In this case the 24 per second frame rate of the film is not fast enough to accurately record the motion of the wheel. In digital audio it is possible to produce false sounds if the rate at which the sound is sampled is not fast enough to accurately represent the **waveform**. See also **anti-aliasing**.

alpha channel Besides the red, green and blue channels of an image that determine the colour of each **pixel**, there can be another channel that sets how transparent the pixel is. This is known as the alpha channel. The effect is similar to a **matte** except that a matte is usually only 1 **bit** deep so that the transparency is either full (so the background shows through) or opaque. In television this is known as *keying*.

alpha test The first test of a complete or near-complete application, usually by internal users. The term originates from computing, and is not always used by web agencies and multimedia companies originating from other disciplines.

always on A mobile phone system where data connections are charged by data transferred rather than by duration of connection. Also used to describe an **Internet** connection using, for example, **ADSL** where users do not have to dial in to connect.

ambient noise or **ambience** Extraneous sounds intruding on a sound recording due to such things as traffic, distant voices, bird song and the like, possibly including the **echo** and/or **reverberation** of the room.

analogue Strictly speaking an analogue is any kind of representation or similarity. However, analogue is used in interactive media (and in audio and video and electronics in general) to differentiate from **digital**. In digital, a signal is turned into a series of numbers, and the numbers are stored or transmitted. In analogue the signal itself is either stored or transmitted directly as a **waveform**, or is converted into another medium that can follow its variations and itself be stored or transmitted. Whereas analogue systems are prone to distortion and noise, digital systems are much less susceptible.

animatic An application that demonstrates and prototypes the final application.

animation Simulated movement of objects using computer or video effects. A simulation of a building rising from its outline foundations to completion is an example of an animation.

anti-aliasing In graphics it is possible for edges of objects to look jagged because the resolution screen display is unable to accurately represent the object itself. To alleviate this problem the colours of the **pixels** around the edge of the object are mixed gradually between the object and its background. In this way the colour resolution compensates for the lack of spatial resolution that causes the jagged edges. By definition, this technique cannot be used where only pure black-and-white pixels are available. Some computer displays will now automatically anti-alias text to make it look cleaner on the screen.

applet A very small computer application (usually in the **Java** language) downloaded from a **website** to run on the user's computer as part of a **web page**.

application A general term for an interactive media (or any kind of **software**) title or project.

application-based program A program that is either self-contained or which runs entirely within one environment, such as an authoring package.

artefacts Disturbances and defects to an image or sound that are not supposed to be there, but which are the results of errors in digitization or display.

ASCII The main standard for representing letters and numbers in computing.

ASP Active Server Pages, a **server side** web technology from Microsoft that allows the production of dynamic **web pages**. Similar to **PHP** in that special tags and code in the web page are interpreted by the **server** as the page is generated in order to insert the dynamic content.

assets The media components of an application or **web page** – audio, video, graphics, animations, text – that combine to form the content.

authoring tool A computer program designed to be simple to use when building an application. Supposedly no programming knowledge is needed, but usually common sense and an understanding of basic logic are necessary.

B2B Business to business, trading between two businesses carried out electronically. See also **B2C** and **C2C**.

B2C Business to consumer, trading between a business and consumers carried out electronically. See also **B2B** and **C2C**.

back end A computer program whose operation is not apparent to the user, such as a supporting programming on the **server** which provides information that the **web server** can send to the user over the **Internet**.

bandwidth The amount of data passed along a cable or communications channel of any kind. Sometimes the data channel, or pipe, is described as *fat* if it has a high bandwidth and can carry a lot of data quickly, or *thin* if it cannot. Bandwidth is usually expressed in **bits** per second or **bytes** per second. Because of this confusion you should be clear whether bandwidth is being expressed in bits or bytes to understand how fast the data can be transmitted.

banner An elongated narrow advertisement placed on a **web page**. There is a 'standard' size for banners of 468 by 60 **pixels**. Usually, clicking on a banner takes the browser to the advertiser's **website**.

bearer A protocol that transparently carries another protocol.

beta If your application or **website** has 'gone beta' then it should be finished, but it needs **testing**. This testing may be carried out by people outside the production team and even outside the production company.

bi-directional language Enabling a computer to cope with a language that reads and writes from right to left – like Arabic or Hebrew – as well as left to right as in English. The individual languages would of course be uni-directional. This goes hand-in-hand with being able to handle many more characters than the standard European-centred **ASCII** text. See also **double byte**.

bit The smallest unit in binary numbers. A bit can have a value of either 0 or 1. The number of bits used to represent a binary number limits the maximum value it can have. For example a 4-bit number can have values from 0000 to 1111 (0 to 15 in decimal).

bit depth In graphics, the more **bits** a colour image has, the more colours can be used in it. An 8-bit image can have 256 colours, but you can usually choose those colours from a larger palette of perhaps millions of colours. If your 256 colours are all shades of grey then a photographic-quality monochrome image can be reproduced. A 16-bit image will have thousands of colours and can look photographic in many circumstances. However, for a truly photographic colour image the millions of colours available in 24 bits are necessary (or even more). Note that on the Apple Macintosh an 8-bit **matte** or **alpha channel** can be associated with the 24 bits, making 32 bits. See also **8-, 16-, 24- or 48-bit image.**

bitmap A graphic image that represents the image by a matrix of every **pixel**, usually going from top to bottom, left to right. Bitmap images usually have a resolution in pixels per inch and a size in pixels.

bit rate reduction Audio and video engineers often use this term to mean compression of data, as the term compression has another meaning, especially in audio. See also **compression**.

blanking In **analogue** television, the time between the end of one TV line and the start of the next (horizontal blanking) or the end of one field and the start of the next (vertical blanking or vertical interval).

blog Short for weblog, this is a **website** that can be easily added to by the author to produce what is essentially a running multimedia diary. Often used to express points of view on current issues and to point readers onwards to other interesting blogs and pages.

Bluetooth A short-range high-speed wireless data standard especially promoted for consumer and mobile telephony use. Named after a Scandinavian king. See also **Wi-Fi**.

boiler plate A standard form of contract that is then modified or qualified to make up the contract for a particular agreement.

bookmark A function of an application, notably a **web browser**, whereby users can store their place so that they can quickly go back there later, even saving the bookmark for retrieval many days later. The electronic equivalent of a piece of paper between pages of a book.

brand The image that a company has built up from customer perceptions about its profile.

browser A piece of **software** that allows the user to look through a number of resources, usually held in a variety of formats. A **web browser** is designed for viewing **World Wide Web pages** on the **Internet**. Firefox, Internet Explorer and Opera are examples of web browsers.

buffer A place for temporary storage of data, often to smooth out differences in speed between a data input and output.

build The process of taking all the component parts of a multimedia application (or indeed any piece of **software**) and making the finished version.

bump mapping In computer graphics, a technique for giving a surface texture to objects by slightly distorting the shape.

business case The presentation of arguments to support the request for a budget to spend on the development of a project that will aid the business. Companies may have devised their own method determining the type of arguments and evidence that is needed for making a business case to the budget holders.

Button A graphic on a **web page** that links to a feature or page on a **website**. A button is also a form of advert on a web page, being relatively small.

buy-out Paying for all the necessary rights in one go rather than paying **royalties**.

byte In binary arithmetic, and hence in computing, a byte is an eight-bit number and can have a value between 0 and 255.

C, C++, C# Powerful computer languages, often used to write sophisticated code to carry out specialized or difficult tasks in multimedia applications. C++ and C# are more recent and are designed for **object-oriented programming**. **Java** is based on C.

C2C Consumer to consumer, trading carried out between consumers, like auctions or jumble/yard sales, carried out electronically. See also **B2B** and **B2C**.

cache Computer memory or disc space used for temporary storage of data in order to speed up a task. A web browser has a cache on disc to hold recently downloaded pages and graphics so that if a page is revisited and has not changed the information can be quickly loaded from the local disc rather than downloaded again over the network.

call centre A centralized enquiry centre that people phone for information relating to a business, its services and/or products.

carousel Model for **interactive TV** where a sequence of information is transmitted repeatedly.

cartogram A style of illustration in which a map shows statistical information in a diagrammatic way.

CD burner A machine that can write compact discs, including **CD-ROM**s. The discs were originally called **WORM**s (write once read many) and so the machines are sometimes called WORM burners. The term CD-R is more common now, and there is a re-recordable version called CD-RW, which has limited compatibility with standard CD-ROM drives. Similar devices exist for **DVD**s and these will also burn CDs.

CD-i Compact Disc-Interactive, an obsolete interactive multimedia platform that uses a television monitor with a CD-i player as the delivery system. Primarily developed by Philips for the consumer market, it allows use of all media on the system. It has its own set of authoring tools and conforms to the Green Book technical specification standards. With the decline of consumer **CD-ROM** CD-i remained in a niche market for training and other professional applications, primarily because of its inexpensive player cost and use of a television set rather than a computer monitor. As the Green Book was proprietary, there are no **emulators** available to play CD-i discs on PCs.

CD-ROM Compact Disc Read-Only Memory, has progressed from allowing only text and data onto the disc to now include audio, graphics, animations and video. It conforms to the Yellow Book and ISO 9660 technical specifications. Although CD-ROMs can now be made on home computers very cheaply, for many applications, especially video, they have been replaced by **DVD**s.

CD-TV A short-lived obsolete consumer multimedia system based on the Commodore Amiga.

cellular radio A system for radio communication that uses a large number of low-powered transmitters, each operating in a small area called a cell. Mobile telephones use this system – the telephones move their connections from one cell to another, hence cell-phone.

certificate An electronic document that authoritatively identifies a web server so that secure (HTTPS) transactions can take place. Without a valid certificate a **web browser** will not set up a secure link. See also **HTTP**.

CGI Common Gateway Interface, **Internet** standards for the passing of information between applications such as **web browsers** and pages and the **server**. Programs that make use of this, called CGI programs, allow sophisticated generation of **web pages** based on dynamic data, and mean that such things as forms and databases can be used on the web.

change management A system set up by developers to monitor and control the number and type of changes made during development, whether the changes originate in-house or from the client. Also known as *change control*.

change request form The document used to request a modification to an already agreed specification. Used in **change management**.

channel See **distribution channel**.

character generator A piece of software or hardware designed to make captions for video and superimpose them on the picture.

chat and chuck Name given to very cheap and disposable mobile telephones.

chrominance The colour part of a colour television signal, as distinct from the brightness part, which is **luminance**. Often abbreviated to chroma.

circuit switched data In mobile telephony, a dial-up call where users have continuous use of the circuit and pay by duration of call. See also **always on**.

Citizen journalism The ability to take photos on mobile phones and quickly describe events in a **blog** makes it possible for anyone to write up current events, often because they were involved. Sometimes this is even fed to traditional media, and such organizations now often encourage people to email photos or other information into newsrooms. The concept of the average person in the street as reporter is known as citizen journalism.

clearances The overall term for **copyright** and similar permissions.

click-through In advertising, a click-through is the result of a user clicking on a **banner** or other ad on a **web page** to reach the advertiser's site.

client side A process, such as display of a **web page**, which happens on the user's local computer rather than on the **server**.

clip art/media Illustrations, photographs or any other media items available, usually inexpensively or even free, for use in productions with no further payment. See also **royalty free**.

close competitor Companies that are in a similar line of business, competing for sales from similar people.

codec A piece of **software** that compresses and/or decompresses audio or video. Stands for coder-decoder. See also **compression**.

coincident needles A stereo meter for showing volume of sound where the two needles of the meter, representing left and right signals, revolve around the same point.

coloured In audio, the detrimental change in a sound due to the influence of the physical environment (such as the room) or distortions in the recording system.

competences The definition of skills evident from practices carried out in the workplace. This term has become prominent in training circles through the link to NVQs (National Vocational Qualifications). These are new-style qualifications concerned with accrediting people for the skills they employ naturally as they carry out their work.

compile To take the **source code** of a computer program and turn it into **machine code** using a compiler. The source code is written by the programmer. Extra code from programming libraries is incorporated at this time. The opposite is **interpreted**.

component A video image in which the colour information is kept separate from the **luminance** or brightness information. Usually two signals are used to represent the colour information. This is similar to **RGB**, and the RGB signals can be extracted from the three components. The components are also specified to take into account the eye's response to different colours.

composite A video image in which colour and brightness are encoded together in the same signal. **PAL**, **SECAM** and **NTSC** are composite television systems. Obsolete in digital systems, which are usually **component**.

composite image In video, an image in which colour and brightness are encoded together in the same signal; in graphics, an image made up of several other images, blended together.

compressed but lossless A compressed signal from which the original signal can be retrieved without any changes or errors.

compressed with loss A compressed signal from which it is impossible to retrieve the original signal, in which a version of the original is retrieved that is satisfactory for its intended purpose. Also known as **lossy**.

compression In computing, reducing the amount of data needed to carry something; also known as **bit rate reduction**. When the term **video compression** is used it will almost certainly have this meaning, and will refer to such systems as **MPEG** and Sorensen. In audio, reducing the **dynamic range** (range of loudness) of a sound recording.

computer-based training A method in which some or all of the training content of a course is turned into an interactive computer program. Often referred to as CBT.

concept map A visual representation to help show relationships between different items.

concept testing Testing of ideas on an audience chosen from a sample market. The aim is to check the feasibility of the ideas for the market before incurring expense implementing them. The method for implementation can, but may not, involve interactive methods. Concept testing originated with marketing, and may be called **focus groups**.

conflict resolution Techniques employed to identify and resolve conflict between people.

conforming In video editing, taking the edits noted from an **offline editing** session and using them to edit the real high-quality recording for final distribution. If done automatically based on the list of edits it is known as *auto-conforming*. Still used in digital editing if a low-resolution version of the video has been used for editing to minimize **bandwidth** requirements.

content management system A collection of tools that allow the creation, organization, modification, removal and archiving of content on a **website**.

contention ratio In an **ADSL** connection, a measure of the number of other users sharing your connection to the **Internet**. This will be a small number, typically less than 100, and it assumes that few users will be demanding **bandwidth** at any moment. Not all ADSL systems make the users share the connection.

contingency In **project management**, predicting the need and reserving funds, time and/or resources to cope with unforeseen circumstances that affect the project schedule. Interactive media project management needs more contingency than many other forms of project because it is a volatile environment. Sometimes referred to as **tolerance**.

continuous marketing research Long-term marketing research that captures the same information over time to note the effects and changes in the market.

contouring An artefact in graphics reproduction whereby smooth changes of brightness or colour become changed so that discrete steps are seen. Sometimes also called **posterization** (especially when used for artistic effect) or **quantization**.

convergence The gradual merging of computing, broadcast media and telecommunications technologies.

cookie A small amount of data stored by a **browser** on behalf of a **web server** to help track a visit to a **website**.

copyright The right of a creator of a work of art, literature, music and so on to have control over the reproduction, distribution and exploitation of the work.

credit The linking of people to the tasks they performed. This is normally done by listing the name and function performed, as in credits at the end of a television pro-gramme. The crediting of personnel in media is very important and is often governed by agreements between production companies and unions.

critical path The identification of the optimum sequence to carry out tasks to achieve a project on time and within budget. See also **task analysis** and **network analysis**.

CRM Customer Relationship Management, a system based on collecting information on each customer from many sources within an organization into a central electronic file and using this to tailor information on goods and services to their needs.

cross-functional team A team that is formed of people from different sections of the company so that they have complementary skill sets and in which all are needed to achieve a result for the joint project.

cross-platform Describes the development of applications that will run on more than one **delivery platform**.

CSS Cascading Style Sheets, a set of definitions which control how a document (such as a **web page**) will look, as distinct from its content and how it is structured. For exam-ple, an **HTML** file will define structure using tags to denote headers of different levels and the associated stylesheet will define how each level of header should be displayed.

CUI Concept User Interface, tools that help a group of people debate, define and rank their most common and important concepts. These tools can be helpful in the analysis of requirements for a project.

custom palette A palette of colours chosen specifically to represent an image.

DAT Digital Audio Tape, an obsolescent format using 4 mm tape in cassettes origin-ally designed for digital audio (48 kHz sampling 16 **bit**) but also used to store data when it operates as a streamer tape format, when it is called **DDS**. Being replaced by hard disc and memory-card recorders.

data protection The concept in European law whereby personal information is pro-tected and the organizations who use this data and the use they can make of the data are registered and regulated. See also **safe harbour**.

DCT Discrete Cosine Transform, a mathematical technique for transforming a **bit map** of an image, which contains individual dots of the image from left-to-right and top-to-bottom. The DCT analyses the image block by block to find the large areas of colour and the fine detail in them. The resulting file can then be analysed to determine what can be removed without seriously affecting the look of the image. This is the basis of **JPEG** and the first stage of **MPEG** compression.

DDS Digital Data Storage, data format that uses **DAT** tapes.

debug To study an application with the intention of removing any errors found.

deck The equivalent of a **website** in **WAP**. The analogy is a deck of cards.

decompile To take the **machine code** version of a program and change it back into something a human can understand.

decryption To remove the **encryption** from something so that the original is produced.

delivery medium The system used to distribute an application. The **World Wide Web** can be considered to be a delivery medium.

delivery platform The multimedia system or systems that people will use to interact with the application. The total specification of the platform is important so that the application is developed within the capabilities. A **web browser** can be considered to be a delivery platform.

design brief Usually a document – but may be oral instructions – produced by clients for developers to describe the outcomes they expect from a project.

development platform The multimedia system that is used to develop the application. This may not be the same as the **delivery platform**. It is important that the final application is tested on the delivery system to check that it will perform on the specified platform.

development testing This is iterative testing applied naturally during the development of a project to ensure that all the pieces work.

diaphragm In a microphone, the membrane that is vibrated by sound and so causes the production of an electrical signal that represents the sound.

digital In a digital system, the signal (including such things as sounds and pictures) is turned into a series of numbers, and it is these numbers that are stored or transmitted. In an **analogue** system the signal itself is either stored or transmitted directly, or is converted into another medium that can follow its variations and itself be stored or transmitted. Whereas analogue systems are prone to distortion and noise, digital systems are much less susceptible, although such degradation is likely to lead to total failure.

direct competitors Companies that are in the same line of business, competing for sales from the same people.

direct marketing email Emails sent to lists of addresses informing people about products or services. These may be solicited or unsolicited emails. See also **spam**.

discovery learning A learning situation that is structured to allow the learner to explore and find answers rather than simply being given the information.

distance learning A learning situation in which the student studies a course away from the institution using any medium that is provided. This may include interactive programs. See also **open learning centres**.

distribution channel A well-defined and sustained system for moving goods from production out to the people who will buy the products.

dither Small, seemingly random perturbations to a signal or image designed to fool the eye or ear into thinking that it has greater quality than it really does. In graphics a dither is a seemingly random pattern of dots of a limited range of colours that, when viewed from a distance, appears to have a greater range of colours. When digitizing a signal a dither is used to reduce the effect of digitizing errors because our eyes and ears are less distressed by noise (which dither looks like) than by the sharp changes in a signal that the dither disguises.

DLT Digital Linear Tape, a streaming tape format used for data backup and also used to send **DVD** masters to replication facilities. Replaced **exabyte** and **DAT** for these purposes where large quantities of data are involved.

document-based programming Programming in which the format of the document is standardized and one or more applications can be used in concert to read or display it. The **World Wide Web** is an example of this.

Dolby The company (and inventor) famous for a system for reducing noise in an audio recording and for systems providing multichannel (surround) sound in cinemas and the home. The name is often used ambiguously for either. Dolby is a trade mark.

domain name The **Internet** equivalent of a street address, showing the route to a particular computer. The name will end with the top-level domain name (TLD), which designates a user sector, primarily in the USA, such as .com for commercial, .gov for government or .edu for education. There are also internationally agreed country names used as TLDs such as .us, .uk, .fr and .dk, and a machine will usually be situated in that country. New TLDs are occasionally added. The US sector top-level domains are often used by organizations wishing to show an international presence even if they are based outside the USA. In an email address the domain name appears after the @ symbol. An individual computer can have a fully qualified domain name (FQDN), which uniquely identifies it. Every FQDN must have a corresponding **IP address** but the reverse is not true.

domain name registrar A company authorized to sell domain names and arrange for them to be made available on the **Internet**.

domain name system Usually just called DNS, this is a distributed database on the **Internet** that maps **domain names** to **IP addresses** and vice versa.

dot com company Usually used to refer to a company that exists and trades solely in cyberspace. The name comes from the top-level domain where many businesses have their **domain names**.

dot pitch The distance between dots of phosphor on a colour television or monitor tube. Figures of .23–.28 mm are common, and a smaller dot pitch means a higher resolution is possible.

double byte The use of 16 **bits** (2 **bytes**) that allows all the characters needed for all world languages to be represented in **software**. This includes Hindi, Thai, Chinese and Japanese, for example, and the standard for this is called Unicode. Most Western European languages can be represented in 8 bits using the standard called **ASCII**. See also **bi-directional**.

downtime The period of time when the development team are waiting for a response or assets from the client and cannot continue with productive work until they receive these.

dpi The density of dots in an image or on a computer screen.

draw object In graphics, an image that is defined in terms of simple graphics 'primitives' such as lines, arcs and fills. It has no actual size, only a shape, and can be scaled cleanly.

drop frame In **NTSC** television time code, a time code format which adjusts to compensate for NTSC not having a whole number of frames per second by dropping some time code numbers to keep in step.

dub To copy something, usually an audio or videotape recording. A dub is the copy itself. In **digital** terminology a direct digital copy is often called a *clone* since it will be indistinguishable from the original.

dumb terminal A computer terminal with a keyboard and screen that does nothing other than show a display generated at a distant computer and send back your typed input.

DVB Digital Video Broadcasting, the system used in most of the world apart from the USA. Also a mark used on European **digital** televisions to show that they will receive digital TV programmes.

DVD Digital Versatile Disc, originally called digital video disc, this is the successor to **CD-ROM** and has many incarnations. The capacity of a DVD disc is much greater than that of a CD-ROM because the system packs the information more tightly on the disc, has the possibility of two information layers per side and can have information on both sides of the disc. As with CD, recordable, re-writeable, audio, and ROM versions are possible. DVD Audio is one of two new formats designed to supersede compact disc audio; the other is **SACD**.

DVD-ROM Use of **DVD** to hold a large amount of data (up to almost 18 **gigabytes**), which can then be accessed by a computer. Basically the equivalent of a big **CD-ROM**.

dynamic range In audio, the range of loudness or volume of a sound.

dynamic web page A **web page** that is composed by a program running on the **web server** computer based on factors such as the kind of request from the **browser** and what information is currently available. To the browser it looks exactly like a static page.

e-business or e-commerce Business involving goods and services carried out electronically, usually via the **World Wide Web**.

e-learning Relating to learning systems and content delivered, monitored, recorded and perhaps examined electronically.

e-marketing Promotion or gathering of marketing data electronically. See also **web access logs** and **web analytics**.

echo In audio, delayed and distinct individual repeats of the original sound, either due to sound bouncing off the walls of the room or deliberately added electronically. Famously used on the vocal of Elvis Presley's 'Heartbreak Hotel'. See also **reverberation**.

EDGE Enhanced Data Rate for GSM Evolution, a **2.5G** mobile technology.

educational technology The study of the ways in which the use of media and structured approaches to organizing material can aid teaching and learning.

edutainment A term derived from the words *education* and *entertainment* coined to describe a category of interactive titles. These are designed to be used in the home to inform and motivate through the use of media.

electronic certificate An encrypted identification that can be exchanged between computers, or between a computer and a **web server**, to verify the identity as each party to the transaction.

electronic programme guide A guide to what is available on the channels of a **digital** television system, shown on the system itself and enabling viewers to actually call up programmes. More usually called EPG. In a multichannel world, if a channel is not listed in the EPG it is virtually invisible to viewers.

electrostatic Describes a system for microphones and, less commonly, loudspeakers and headphones, whereby electrostatic charge is used to detect or cause the movement of the **diaphragm**.

emulator A system that pretends to be something it is not, such as a **software** system that pretends to be a piece of **hardware** or another software system.

encryption Changing a data file so that it is unrecognizable but can be turned back into its original form on receipt, if the receiver has the key to decode it.

enhanced TV Use of interactive technology, either **iTV** or a **website**, to add value to a television programme.

environment map In computer graphics, a method of reproducing reflections on the surface of an object by determining an image of what the object 'sees' from its position and wrapping the object in this image.

environment variable Information passed to a **web server** when a distant **browser** requests a 'page'. It includes information on the computer making the request and what **web page** included the link being followed (if any).

EPG See **electronic programme guide**.

evaluation Often confused with the term 'testing' and used interchangeably, but when used in a strict technical sense, there are differences. Evaluation of an application is the broad appraisal of any factors that influence the development, delivery and reaction to it. See also **testing**.

exabyte A type of computer streamer tape using 8 mm cassette tape in the same format as Video-8 but now replaced for professional applications by more recent formats. The Exabyte Corporation still exists and still produces data storage solutions. Also used to denote 2 to the power 16 **bytes** of data.

exclusively assigned rights **Copyright** passed on to someone else so that the original copyright owner no longer has rights in the material.

external clients People who are not part of your organization who commission you to carry out a piece of work. They define the brief and specifications. Budgets are agreed and negotiated between you.

extranet A private network whereby the main company allows some other companies to share some or all data on their **intranet** with strict controls on access.

eXtreme see XP.

ezine An electronic equivalent of a magazine.

fair dealing or fair use In **copyright** law, an exception to infringement under certain limited circumstances because your usage of the material is very slight and/or under circumstances where free usage is seen as reasonable. Examples of this include use of extracts from books in a review and limited use in education. What constitutes fair use differs from country to country and is often misunderstood.

feature creep A gradual and insidious increase in the capability of a piece of **software** as it is developed, usually without any overall plan of implementation.

field trials The use of the product *in situ* with the intended users prior to release to identify problems for correction.

file path The combination of disc or volume name, directory names and file name that uniquely identifies a file on a computer.

firewall In networks, a computer which monitors traffic flowing between the **Internet** and an internal network so as to prevent unwanted connections.

fixed-term contract A contract that cannot be extended beyond its original duration without positive action being taken by both parties. To extend the term either a new contract would be written or a new clause added to the original contract.

Flash A vector-based animation technology developed by Macromedia (now part of Adobe). Allows sophisticated interaction in a **web page** with minimal data and can be used to produce entire self-contained sites. Can also include video and audio.

flow chart A diagram that shows step-by-step progression through the content blocks of the proposed **website** or program.

focus groups See **concept testing**.

force majeure A condition in a contract where neither party has control over the circumstances. This might include war, loss of electrical power and acts of God.

formative A term used to describe evaluation processes carried out during the development cycle. These are contrasted with summative evaluation processes, which occur at the end of development. In this context, team review meetings that occur during the project could be called a formative evaluation process. See also **summative**.

FQDN Fully Qualified Domain Name. See **domain name**.

frame-grabbing Synonymous with digitization of video but dating back to the days when computers had to digitize frames individually.

frames In video a complete single image, which forms part of a moving sequence of images. On the web, a technique that allows several distinct parts of a **web page** to be defined, and which can be operated separately by the viewer. Usually used to allow an index to be shown alongside the different items referred to in it.

front-end A computer program that provides **interface** and set-up procedures for a less user-friendly, but probably more powerful, **back-end** program. On a **web server** this might be the program that formats **web pages** having drawn information from a back-end database.

FTP File Transfer Protocol, protocol for transferring files between computers over the **Internet**.

functional specification The document that says how an application works. The application will be written by referring to this document.

gallows arm A kind of microphone stand with a vertical part to which is connected a horizontal extension. This is like the arm of a gallows, and it is used to extend across a table (for example). The mic is fixed to the end of the arm.

gamma The relationship between the brightness of an original (such as a **digital** image) and the way that signal is displayed by a monitor or on a printed page.

Gantt chart This is a chart that shows progress in relation to a timescale, often used in planning and tracking a project. It was named after Henry Lawrence Gantt, an American engineer.

gateway A computer which connects one system to another, for example a local network to the **Internet**. In **WAP** a gateway translates and mediates between **web pages** using **HTML** and WAP phones which use **WML**.

GIF Graphics Interchange Format, a standard for 8-**bit** graphics, widely used on the **World Wide Web**. One version of the standard allows part of the image to be defined as transparent.

gigabyte 1024 megabytes.

global culture An international group of people who share similar needs for communication based on profession, business sector, hobby, interests or whatever.

golden master The final version of an **offline** application; the one that will be distributed.

GPRS General Packet Radio Service a system added to 2G mobile phone systems to allow continuous data connections, usually to the **Internet**. Whereas switched data calls, such as **HSCSD**, are charged by duration, GPRS usage is charged by the amount of data transferred.

GPS Global Positioning System, a satellite-based system provided by the US Government (mainly military) which allows a GPS receiver to pinpoint its location and altitude on Earth. Precision of the system was initially limited to protect military interests, but this has been improved. It is also possible to use a local fixed beacon to augment the satellites and give very high accuracy. Now incorporated into mobile telephones and motor vehicles.

graduated mask In graphics, a mask that determines how much of a second image shows through the first. It is graduated because it has values such that a mix of the two images is seen.

graphical structure editor In programming, a programming environment whereby the author can lay out the relationship between sections of the application in a graphical way, like a **flow chart**.

GSM Global System for Mobile Communications, the most popular standard for mobile phones in the world. GSM is a digital system and besides speech the network also carries messages (**SMS**) and both switched (**HSCSD**) and 'always-on' (**GPRS**) data channels. It is considered a **2G** mobile phone system.

GUI Graphical User Interface, a method of interacting with a computer through direct manipulation of graphical images rather than typing in commands. Most GUIs use what is sometimes referred to as WIMP: Windows, Icons, Mouse, Pointer.

hacker A person who uses considerable computing skill in deviant ways, including introducing computer **viruses** into a computing community. The term is also used, less often and informally, to denote a skilled computer programmer with no malicious intent. Similarly **hacking**.

half-toning In graphics, a method for reproducing shades of grey by using black dots of varying sizes. See also **dither**.

hardware A piece of equipment; as distinct from **software**.

HCI Human–Computer Interaction, the analysis of interaction between people (users) and computers. This originated with stand-alone computer systems but is increasingly important for integrated public systems such as the **Internet**. The analysis of successful use for a segment of the public market can drive the design and makeovers of **websites** and similar systems. See also **interface**.

header The invisible part of a **web page** in which formatting information for the page and meta tags are placed. See also **metatag**.

high-level design The first attempt to define the interactive structure and content of a program. The term comes from **software** engineering. See also **outline design**.

hits, hit rate Either the number of individual requests for data that a **web page** receives or the number of different visitors who have called that page up. This latter is now more usually called *page impressions*.

host machine The computer on which a program runs.

hot-spot A section of an image on the screen that instigates an action when the pointer enters or clicks in it.

HSCSD High Speed Circuit Switched Data, a higher speed version of **GSM** and a **2.5G** mobile technology. Unlike **GPRS**, an HSCSD connection is made like a call and charged by time, rather than being 'always on' and charged by data transported.

HTML Hypertext mark-up language: the system used in **web pages** to describe a **web page** and its contents. Eventually a combination of **XML** and **Style Sheets** (CSS) will together describe the contents and define how they should be displayed. XHTML is an XML-based version of HTML.

HTTP HyperText Transfer Protocol, the **Internet** communications protocol used in the **World Wide Web**. Basically, a **browser** calls up a **web page** by sending an **HTTP** request to the **server**. HTTPS is the encrypted and secure version of HTTP.

hybrid web, web/CD or web/DVD A multimedia application that needs both a web connection and a CD or DVD to function fully. This could be a disc that updates itself from a **website** or a website that uses a disc to hold large multimedia assets such as movies.

hypertext Non-linear text that is read by following jumps and links in the text itself.

icon A pictorial symbol or representation used on the screen to denote an active area. It will allow access to further data or trigger an interactive reaction of some type. It has become common for a text explanation to appear when the user positions the cursor over the icon to help the user understand its significance. See also **picon** and **micon**.

ICT Information and Communication Technologies, term used as short-hand in describing aspects of convergent technologies.

image map A graphical menu of a **website** usually put on the front page. This has fallen out of favour as it often took so long to download.

IMAP Internet Message Access Protocol, a recent alternative to **POP** for email.

i-mode Web service originally provided by NTT DoCoMo in Japan for mobile telephones and now used elsewhere in the world.

implied licence In the context of a **website** it is usually assumed that the **web pages** are published so that they can be viewed across the **Internet**. Any other use of the pages, such as extracting images from them or displaying them out of context, would breach this implied licence to view. Many **websites** now have an explicit set of terms and conditions under which the site is viewed.

in-bound communication Communication that needs to be understood by the person receiving it only sufficiently to fulfil a specific need. The need can be linked to various levels of understanding – gist, relevance, decision, action, etc. Here the context is understanding a level of another language enough to understand the message without actually seeing a correct translation.

indemnity A guarantee that if any cost is incurred as a result of your action, you will cover it.

indirect competitors Companies that are in related lines of business to you who may win sales from your potential customers with their products.

information architect Helps users find and manage information successfully by designing organizational and navigational systems (also called information analyst or information strategist).

inlining Linking to someone else's image so that it appears to be part of your **web page** even though it does not reside on your **server**. Potentially a breach of **copyright** because of a breach of the **implied licence** under which web pages are published on the **Internet**.

instructional design The study of methods of teaching and learning with particular reference to the selection and use of media to aid instruction. The term is widely used in the USA. Europe tends to use the term **educational technology**.

instructional designer A person who applies the principles of instructional design to convey information using a variety of media and methods.

insubstantial portion A qualitatively small proportion of a literary work that can be reproduced without infringing **copyright**.

integrity (of moral rights) The author's right for the work not to be changed.

intellectual property A general term for rights such as those protected by **copyright** and **patents**.

interactive design The definition of how to structure the content and interactive paths through the material for an interactive application.

interactive TV Interactivity applied to broadcast television and including multimedia electronic programme guides, information systems and adjuncts to the transmitted programmes allowing viewers more involvement. This last application is also known as **enhanced TV**.

interactive video An interactive system that uses an interactive **videodisk** to deliver sound and pictures and combines them with text, sound and graphics from a computer source. Prevalent in the 1980s and used by large corporations for training, it is now obsolete. Also denoted by IV.

interface The way an application is designed for people to use. This includes the screen designs, the use of **icons** or menus, the way interactivity is set up and the overall structure of the application.

interlaced Describes a television picture that is made of two halves, which interlace with each other like the lines of a comb and the spaces between.

internal clients People – part of your own organization – who define a piece of work for you to do. Budgeting for the work might be affected by company practices.

internationalization Producing **software** in a way that facilitates adaptation to suit other languages and cultures without the need for reprogramming.

Internet A world-wide interconnection of computer networks, originally set up between the American military, its suppliers and research base to make a network that, by virtue of its multiple interconnections, would be safe from destruction. Up to the 1990s the Internet was largely the preserve of the academic and research communities, but the invention of **HTTP**, **HTML** and the **World Wide Web** has made the **Internet** into a mass communications medium.

interpreted In computing, a computer program where each individual command is translated into **machine code** instructions for the computer before moving on to the next one. The opposite is **compiled**.

interstitial An advertisement which appears between the user clicking on a web link and reaching their destination.

intranet A local area network, such as in a company, which operates using **Internet** protocols and systems. This will now usually include a local implementation of the **World Wide Web** with **web pages** read by **browsers**. Intranets have changed the way most large companies communicate with their staff.

ionizing The process of electrically charging something by removing or adding electrons.

IP address A number, in the form 123.123.123.123, which uniquely identifies a computer on the **Internet**. See also **domain name**.

iPod Trade mark of Apple Computer. A family of tiny music players.

IPTV Internet Protocol Television, broadcasting by using broadband telephone lines and Internet technologies and protocols.

IRC Internet Relay Chat, a protocol for typing messages between computers in real time.

IrDA Infrared communications standard used in mobile telephones, **PDAs** and laptop computers for interconnections and connection to fixed devices such as printers.

ISDN Integrated Services Digital Network, a digital phone line which provides a link of either 64 kilobits per second (European standard) or 56 (US standard) per channel with a minimum of two channels.

ISO The International Standards Organization.

ISP Internet Service Provider, the organization that connects you to the **Internet**, usually by means of a dial-up telephone connection with a **modem**. Some ISPs operate nationally and internationally (such as AOL, MSN and Demon), while others operate locally.

iTV See **interactive TV**.

jaggies See **staircasing**.

Java A computer language based on **C** and devised by engineers at Sun originally for use in cable television **set top boxes**. It allows efficient sending of small applications (**applets**) across the **Internet**, which are then executed on the user's computer.

JavaScript A scripting language that runs in recent **browsers** and allows more sophisticated control of pages and interaction than **HTML**. No relation to **Java**.

JPEG Joint Photographic Experts Group, a standardized method for compressing still photographic images so that little is lost from the image with high rates of compression. Almost always **lossy**.

kilobyte 1024 bytes of data (not 1000).

layer (of graphics) Several layers of images can be combined together in graphics to make a new single image. The relationship between the layers is controlled by their **alpha channels**.

leadership The employment of appropriate management styles to ensure and maintain progress of a team towards common goals.

lean back Like watching television, at a distance, as distinct from **lean forward** and sometimes known as *couch potato*.

lean forward Like using a computer, close to the screen, as distinct from **lean back**.

learning styles Part of the theory of learning, which indicates that people develop preferred ways of learning. This has implications for designing learning materials so that people can process the information in ways appropriate for their preferred style.

letters patent Formal term for the document that defines a **patent**.

library music Recorded music produced especially for use in film television and other audio-visual productions. Usually available for licence based on a standard rate card. Also known as **production music**.

limiter In audio, an electronic circuit that automatically controls volume to stop short peaks of volume exceeding a certain amount.

link On the web a word, phrase or graphic on a **web page** that, when clicked by the user, sends an **HTTP** request to the **server**, usually calling up another **web page**. Sometimes referred to as a *hot link*.

load balancing Sharing the traffic on a **website** between a number of **server** computers in order to handle very high numbers of hits. See also **scalability**.

localization Using translation and cultural adaptation to produce **software** and support materials ready for use in particular languages and cultures.

location-aware or location-based services Services provided to a mobile telephone which take account of where the phone is located, to offer lists of nearby restaurants for example.

log Record kept by a **web server** of every **HTTP** request it receives, with details including the time and date, who asked for the page and how much data was transferred. Strictly speaking, these logs should be referred to as access logs to distinguish them from others such as error logs.

log analysis Analysis of the log records of a **website** into meaningful data that help the site owners make decisions about the further design of the site based on knowledge of present use.

look and feel Common name for the interface of an application. See also **interface**.

lossy In **compression** this means that the original data cannot exactly be retrieved from the compressed version. This does not necessarily mean that the effects of the compression are visible or audible.

luminance The black-and-white or monochrome part of a colour television signal or other image.

machine code Zeros and ones in a program that a computer can execute directly.

magneto-optical disc A type of disc used for data storage for which both a laser and a magnetic field are required to write data.

mainframe A very large computer – in capability if not in size. Probably run by a dedicated team of people and able to handle many tasks simultaneously.

market research Information about the changing behaviour of people and their habits, gathered by a variety of methods and organized into statistical or analytical representations.

mark-up language A system of marking text so that it can be understood or displayed correctly using a computer. See also **HTML**.

master tape The definitive and original recording of something.

matte A technique, used particularly in movies and television, to enable two or more images to be combined into a single scene. Traditionally the matte is a masking inage that defines which portions of another image are foreground (and should be shown) and background (and should be replaced by another image). Sometimes the matte consists of a false section of background, painted onto glass, so that when the scene is shot though the matte the false and real backgrounds are seamlessly combined. Sometimes the matte is automatically generated from portions of the scene that are a particular colour, when the technique is also known as colour-separation overlay, chromakey and green- or blue-screen. In modern use the foreground, and the matte that blends it into the scene, are often computer generated.

mechanical right The right to record a piece of music.

megabyte 1 048 576 **bytes** of data – 1024 kilobytes.

memory leak A bug in a computer program which causes it to gradually fill up its available memory and finally crash.

merchant services Service to facilitate trading, primarily used to mean accepting payment using credit cards. The merchant service is usually provided by a bank and ultimately has to link to a bank. May include **online** validation of the credit card transaction so that the merchant (i.e the online shop) can safely dispatch the goods.

metadata Data about data: would include information on things like the format of the data. Examples include library catalogues. **e-learning** also has metadata standards for defining the learning elements in its content.

metatag A tag which is placed in the header of a **web page** to pass control or similar information to the **web browser** or indexing program that reads the page.

menu A set of options listed or otherwise available on screen for the user to select. A main decision point in an application might be called a *menu screen* even if it does not contain a conventional menu list.

MHEG Multimedia and Hypermedia Experts Group, ISO standard to facilitate use and interchange of objects in interactive systems.

micon An icon that has moving images. Few make the distinction between icon and micon and generally icon is used to cover all selection images. See also **icon** and **picon**.

middleware **Software** that manages interaction between different programs, especially in a network. It might link a **web server** and a database.

MIDI Musical Instrument Digital Interface, a standardized way of describing music and how it is played so that a MIDI-compatible instrument can then provide the sound.

milestone Defined key points of the project's development. Milestones are often linked to the end of a phase of development, and can be linked to phased payment stages of the project as well.

MIME Multipurpose Internet Mail Extension, a standard way of identifying what a file is so that it is handled correctly by **web servers** and other computers.

mirror site A **website** that contains the same content as another website. This is usually done so that access speeds can be optimized depending on where in the world the user is. Mirroring a website requires permission, otherwise it is infringement of **copyright**.

mobile Pertaining to a small and transportable device, such as a hand-held computer or telephone.

mobile agent See **agent**.

modelling In **3-D** graphics, building a scene by defining objects in the scene and arranging them and their environment.

modem Stands for modulate–demodulate and usually refers to a device that takes **digital** data and converts it into an **analogue** audio signal so it can pass through the telephone system. The signal is converted back using another modem at the other end. The term is also used for any similar translation and so an **ADSL** system would include ADSL modems.

montage A single graphic made from several sources.

moral rights Rights, related to **copyright**, which protect a work from unauthorized changes or misattribution. This is currently a mainly European concept but is applied to works of art in US law.

morph To change one shape into another in a smooth transitional movement.

MoSCoW This is an example of an approach to eliciting client needs in a project where you define the items the client Must have, Should have, Could have and Would like to have. This approach derives from **RAD** programming techniques.

MP3 MPEG Audio Layer 3, one of the ways of compressing audio in the **MPEG** family of standards, widely used on the **Internet**. A limitation of MP3 is that it does not contain any form of rights management to control copying and so has been seen by some rights owners as a vehicle for piracy.

MPEG Motion Picture Experts Group, a group of ISO standards for **compression** of video and definitions of multimedia objects.

MPEG-1 The version of **MPEG** that compresses video to a data rate of around one megabit per second. The quality is similar to that of S-VHS.

MPEG-2 The version of **MPEG** for broadcast quality video at bit rates of the order of 8 megabits per second. **Digital** television, **DVD** and Sony's Betacam-SX use

MPEG-2. (MPEG-3 was to have dealt with high definition but it was eventually included in MPEG-2.)

MPEG-4 An extension to **MPEG** introducing object-oriented structures to audio and video and **compression** for low bit rates. Increasingly used as compression for high-definition TV.

MPEG-7 An extension to **MPEG** to provide a standard framework for indexing audio-visual material. (There is no MPEG-5 or 6 and the number 7 is the sum of 1, 2 and 4. The next MPEG is MPEG-21 which is a multimedia framework allowing an overview of all aspects of content delivery covered by the other MPEGs.)

MPEG audio The **MPEG** standard includes three levels of audio. Level 1 is used for DCC (digital compact cassette), Level 2 is used in **DVD** and **digital** broadcasting and Level 3 (better known as MP3) gives the best **compression** and is widely used to compress audio on the **Internet**.

MPU Message Plus Unit, a large advertisement placed within the body of a **web page**.

multicultural Communication that needs to be produced specifically for different languages and cultures.

multimedia narrative The structure underpinning forms of interactive communication. Interactive narrative allows the user to take control of the sequencing of information, and this is what differentiates multimedia narrative from more traditional forms of narrative.

multiscan Referring to a computer monitor that can work with a range of display resolutions and scan rates. Most computer monitors are now multiscan to some extent, although with a flat-screen monitor only one resolution will be the native resolution and so give the best results.

multi-session disc A **CD-ROM** that can be/is written to more than once with each new set of data being added onto the end of the rest until the disc is full.

multitasking Able to do more than one task at once.

MySQL An open source relational database management system widely used on the **Internet**. Often used on **websites** in conjunction with **PHP**.

NAT Network Address Translation, a way of 'hiding' the **IP addresses** of the computers on a network from the **Internet** at large. This might be done for security or to avoid unnecessarily using up Internet IP addresses.

needs analysis The primary stage of a training project where the definition of the criteria for success takes place. The competence level of the target audience and the gap between this and the proficiency needed is analysed.

network analysis Also referred to as *critical path analysis*; this is the definition of the core tasks and the dependent tasks needed to complete the project. These are mapped out in a network diagram to show their relationship to each other. See **critical path**.

news groups See **UseNet groups**.

non-disclosure agreement A contract, usually brief, whereby one party agrees not to disclose information given to it by the other party. Usually known as an NDA.

non-exclusive rights A licensing of rights that still allows licensing to other people.

non-linear In audio-visual production, the use of a computer to edit digitized sound and/or vision. Synonymous with *random-access.*

normalizing In audio, adjusting the volume of a digital audio file so that the loudest parts have a predetermined value, often 100%.

NTSC National Television System(s) Committee, the **analogue** television standard used in North America and Japan, with 525 lines in a frame (of which 480 are visible) and approximately 30 frames per second. See also **PAL/SECAM**.

objective A precise definition of a result that is wanted, in terms that will allow the result to be measured. Objectives are used particularly in education and training applications where the results of learning need to be stated, and ultimately measured, to demonstrate the effectiveness of the materials. Objectives are often confused with aims. Aims are more general statements of direction rather than measurable statements.

objective evaluation Evaluation carried out with pre-set criteria that give a measurable indication of the results. See also **subjective evaluation**, **qualitative evaluation** and **quantitative evaluation**.

object-oriented programming Programming as interaction between self-contained mini-programs or objects.

offline A multimedia application that works in isolation on a computer and does not need a network connection. A **CD-ROM** application is an example of offline.

offline editing Video editing with working copies of the 'real' videotapes and low-quality equipment in order to prepare for **online editing**.

off the shelf Used to refer to **software** that is bought as a pre-existing package. Sometimes also called 'shrinkwrap'.

on-demand services A method of providing entertainment and other audio-visual material to consumers (and others) whereby they can demand a particular item, such as a film, and it will be sent to them immediately down a communications link. Some early video-on-demand systems even sent **MPEG-1** video to consumers down their telephone lines.

online Applications that operate over a network, particularly the **World Wide Web**.

online editing Video editing with the 'real' videotapes on high-quality equipment or using a computerized system but with high-quality digitized audio and video.

open learning centres Centres usually set up in the workplace where a variety of learning and training materials are gathered for people to use. They can have access to the materials as and when they want. Many use interactive materials as well as videos and books. This approach to learning reflects the need for quick access to training in organizations that are changing faster than ever before.

open plan An office arrangement that assigns space according to changing need. There are no or few permanent partitions between desks, so that the space can be reorganized efficiently when needed. An extension of this principle allocates desks and even computers to workers as they are needed, and is known as *hot desking*.

operating system The lowest level of computer **software** in a computer. It manages the operation of the **hardware** and provides the programmer with ways of controlling the machine. Often the term *operating system* is taken to include the GUI as well.

option bars Part of a graphic on the screen that provides **hot-spots**, **buttons** or **icons** grouped together for the user to make a choice. Also known as *menu bars*.

OS See operating system.

out-bound communication Information that is distributed to numerous people who are likely to have specific uses for it. Therefore its accuracy is important. Also, in this context, the accuracy of any information translated from another language is essential if its integrity is to be retained.

outline design The first attempt to define the interactive structure and content of a program. The term comes from interactive training design. The later stage from this discipline is called the *detailed design*. See also **high-level design**.

PAL, SECAM The **analogue** colour television systems used in Europe and most of the world outside North America and Japan, with 625 lines in a frame (of which 576 are visible) and 25 frames per second. See also **NTSC**. SECAM encodes the colour information differently to PAL and is used mostly in France, the Middle East and eastern Europe.

palette The colours available for use in a graphic.

pan Moving the viewpoint of a camera from side to side by swivelling it and not actually moving the camera.

Pareto method An analytical representation of data in graphical form; used to help identify the products that can make the best contribution to the company.

PAS78 Standards document: 'Guide to Good Practice in Commissioning Accessible Websites'.

patent The right to exclusive implementation of a process as defined in the patent document.

patent agent A lawyer who drafts letters patent.

paternity The moral right whereby you have a right to be identified as author. Also known as *attribution*.

PDA Personal Digital Assistant, very small hand-held computer also known as *palm top*.

peer review Appraisal by colleagues or people performing similar jobs, where the sharing of experience and insights is used to adjust, in this case, the design and functionality of the application.

penalty clause Clause in a contract specifying what should happen if either party defaults on the agreement.

perceptual map Analytical representation of the results of a survey; used to understand the relative positions of two variables plotted in a matrix.

perceptual matrix See **perceptual map**.

performance monitoring A management process in which people agree criteria of acceptable achievements for a period and review performance according to the criteria at the end of the time. The performance agreement might be linked to bonus payments. Any shortfall of performance accredited to lack of skill might prompt training initiatives.

performing right The right to perform a piece of music to an audience.

Perl A computer language widely used on **web servers** to produce dynamic **web pages** based on data received from users. It has powerful string manipulation capabilities, which make it well suited to generating **HTML** on the fly.

personal construct Term originating with George Kelly, a psychologist from the 1950s, who devised techniques for people to define and prioritize concepts that were important to them. A personal construct is the construction and interpretation of meaning by an individual.

PHP A **server side** programming language which allows dynamic content to be inserted in **web pages**. Code in a web page is interpreted by the **server** when the page is displayed. See also **ASP**.

picon An icon that shows a realistic image or picture rather than a representation or symbolic image. Few make the distinction between picon and icon, and generally icon is used to denote all selection images. See also **icon** and **micon**.

PID Project Initiation Document, a preliminary stage from **Prince2** project management methodology that outlines the information that should be collected and presented in this document.

pilot projects Experimental projects designed as a run-up to a full-blown development.

pitch The process of a few companies presenting their ideas to a prospective client in a competition to win a **tender** for a project. Can be used as a noun or verb.

pitch protection policy A legally drafted document designed to protect the **intellectual property** of the developer pitching for work so that the potential client does not discuss the ideas presented with rivals. Has similarities with **non-disclosure agreement**.

pixels Picture elements, the basic building blocks of a picture: sometimes used to be called *pels*, which was short for picture elements.

placeholders A temporary use of images, audio and/or text that are representational of the navigational feel of the final version but not part of the real content.

platform The combination of **hardware** and **software** on which a computer program will run. In web terms this is usually taken to mean the combination of **operating system** and **browser**.

plug-ins Small extensions to the functionality of a piece of **software** such as a **web browser**. The use of the term *plug-in* refers to the ease with which they can be added, usually involving simply copying the plug-in into a particular computer directory.

PNG Portable Network Graphics, a graphics standard devised to replace **GIF** but giving much higher quality and more versatility. PNG can be used as an archive format.

podcast POD is derived either from the iPOD or from Personal On Demand and refers to downloaded audio files that are intended to be listened to using portable music players like the **iPod**.

POP Post Office Protocol, one system used to handle mail boxes for email users. An alternative is IMAP.

pop-up, pop-under A **browser** window that is opened using **JavaScript,** when a link is clicked. Usually, but not always, used for advertising. A pop-up appears in front of the current browser window and a pop-under appears behind it.

port (number) A **software** identifier saying how a computer should treat an **Internet** request. **Web pages** are usually requested from port 80.

port (to and a) Move a computer program from one machine/platform to another.

portable document format A standard for encoding documents in a file so that the look of the document, including its fonts and graphics, is retained no matter which computer it is shown on. Devised by Adobe.

posterization Reduction of the smooth variation in colours in an image to a series of discrete steps. Also known as **quantization** and **contouring**. Although this effect is usually seen as an error, posterization is sometimes used for artistic effect.

POTS and PANS Light-hearted terms used to describe changes in telecommunications. POTS are Plain Old Telephone System and PANS are Positively Amazing New Stuff (or similar).

pre-alpha A very incomplete version of an **offline** program.

pricing policy The decisions made on the price of goods based on the understanding of the market, competitors' prices and what people are prepared to pay.

primary colours The smallest set of colours which can be combined to produce virtually all other colours. For light these are red, green and blue and, when combined, they produce white. For pigments they are red, yellow and blue and, when combined, these colours produce black.

primitives Basic building blocks of a computer system.

Prince2 An approach to **project management** devised by the UK government in the late 1980s now growing in use as a standard methodology for many large projects. It has several considerations if applied in interactive project management. See www.atsf.co.uk/mim for more about this approach.

prior art In patents, a **patent** can be invalidated or refused if the idea has been publicized before or already existed (uses *art* in the same way as the term *state-of-the-art*).

production music Recorded music produced especially for use in film television and other audio-visual productions. Usually available for license based on a standard rate card. Also known as **library music**.

programming language Since computers can work only with zeros and ones it is rather difficult for mere mortals to program them. To alleviate this problem, programming languages have been developed that understand almost real English.

programme manager The title of a person who has responsibility over a group of projects and/or project managers.

progressive scan A television picture that scans each line in order, as distinct from **interlaced**.

project champion A person nominated to represent the project inside an organization to protect its development and completion from undue influences, both internal and external.

project management The specification, planning and control of time, cost, quality and resource issues to complete a project on time and within budget.

project manager A person who carries out **project management**. Used here to describe the leader of an interactive media team.

proposal The document in which the developers outline the application content, development schedule and cost for the commissioners of a project.

prototype A limited working version of the application; used early in the project to get reaction to the general design and interface so that adjustments can be made.

proxy server A computer that sits between a computer and the **Internet** and helps to handle transactions such as **web page** accesses. A proxy is commonly used to locally store distant web pages that are frequently called up so as to speed up the apparent web access and reduce network traffic.

psycho-acoustics The science of hearing, taking into account the psychological aspects of the way the brain interprets sounds as well as the pure acoustics and physics.

psychometric tests Psychological tests that use measurable factors to attribute a score for the person being tested. The tests are used in recruitment and career management decisions, particularly in large organizations.

public domain Used to mean out of **copyright** and so freely available for use. This is not strictly true since copyright material can be placed in the public domain by the owner with the intention of it being freely available, but while still retaining the **copyright**.

pushing the envelope Trying something new, usually without sufficient experience and with an element of risk.

PVR Personal Video Recorder, a set top box television receiver which also contains hard disc storage and can record programmes for time shifting just as a VCR does. But a PVR can do more than this; the two main features being the ability to pause live programming and for the box to learn your viewing habits and record programmes speculatively to offer you later.

qualitative data Information collected by less structured means than **quantitative data**, e.g. free response questions, and relating more to impressions and feelings.

qualitative evaluation Evaluation that takes into account a wide variety of factors that might influence the results being analysed. The attitudes of the users, the culture of the institution or country and the general environment would be examples of qualitative factors. See also **quantitative evaluation**.

quantitative data Information collected by methods that can then be processed and represented numerically or statistically.

quantitative evaluation Evaluation that is concerned with measuring the results against pre-determined criteria to assess whether they have been achieved. The number of times that help is used might be an indicator of how effective the **interface** of an application is, and the percentage of correct responses after taking help might be used to indicate the effectiveness of the help messages. These would be examples of quantitative measures of evaluation for interactive media packages. See also **qualitative evaluation**.

quantization An artefact in graphics reproduction whereby smooth changes of brightness or colour become changed so that discrete steps are seen. Sometimes also called **posterization** (especially when used for artistic effect) or **contouring**.

quantizing Inaccuracies in the digitizing of a signal caused by the integer distance between levels of sampling.

RACI chart or matrix A diagram showing the people involved with a work initiative, their accountability for the work and the communication they have been given about the work. RACI stands for responsible, accountable, consulted and informed.

RAD Rapid Application Development, an approach to **software** production that splits development into small functions that are programmed quickly.

RAM Random access memory, basically the memory in a computer.

Rationalized Unified Process An iterative **software** development approach that provides a framework of best practices based on an assessment of project failures and how to avoid them.

ray tracing A technique used in computer graphics to produce realistic images by following the path of light as it travels from the light source, via the objects in the scene, to the observer.

refractive index The amount by which light changes velocity when it passes between media, usually between air and glass or water. The refractive index is different at different frequencies and therefore colours; hence a prism is able to break white light into its constituent colours.

relational database A database with a complex structure allowing the data items to relate to each other in many ways. If the relationship is simple the database is often called a *flat-file* since its structure resembles that of a card index.

render In computer graphics, to build an image.

requirements agreement A document explaining what the client wants from the program that indicates the range and scope of the work you will produce according to the time and cost you define.

residuals Extra rights in a licence that are not involved in the primary use but which may be applied later, usually at extra cost. Also called secondary rights.

responsibility matrix A chart used in some business circles to denote who has responsibility for an initiative and which type of responsibility – prime, responsible, secondary responsibility and support responsibility are examples of the types commonly used.

return path In an interactive system, the way a user can send data back to the interactive system in order to control it.

reverberation In audio, delayed repeats of the original sound, either due to sound bouncing off the walls of the room or deliberately added electronically, which are so close together as to be indistinguishable. See also **echo**.

RGB Red, Green, Blue, the three primary colours of light from which virtually all colours can be built. Also refers to an image that stores the three primary colour components separately.

rights Permission to reproduce and/or sell something.

RISC Reduced Instruction Set Computer, a microprocessor with relatively few built-in operations but which can execute what it has extremely quickly.

ROI Return On Investment, a measure of the effectiveness of capital invested in a project, calculated by expressing average profits from the project as a percentage of average capital invested in it.

role play A technique used in teaching and psychology, in which a person acts out a situation, perhaps from different perspectives, to get insight into decision-making and reactions.

royalties Payments based on the number of copies sold or distributed.

royalty free A **copyright** licence which allows the licensee to use the material without any further payment. A similar term is *buy-out*. See also **clip art/media** and **royalties**.

RSS Really Simple Syndication, provides a simple way of asking a **website** to tell you what significant or new items have been added and to provide you with a link to them. The so-called RSS feed is essentially a **web page** that is designed to be read by the computer and is written in **XML** rather than **HTML**. With news sites, the RSS feed will tell you what the latest stories are, and on someone's blog it will be the latest entries. RSS is becoming more sophisticated, with audio, pictures and video being listed and linked. An RSS listing is the way in which a **podcast** is publicized and disseminated.

run-length encoding A form of **compression** that stores the colour of a **pixel** followed by how many subsequent pixels are of the same colour. This works best with images made up of large areas of flat colour, such as a cartoon.

run-time The execution, or running, of a program.

SACD Super Audio CD, one of two super-quality **digital** audio formats designed to supersede compact disc audio (the other is **DVD** audio).

safe harbor A principle whereby individual US companies agree to comply with the principles of European data protection so that they can be legitimate recipients of data. See also **data protection**.

sample rate The frequency with which an **analogue** signal is sampled on digitization. For accurate representation the sample rate must be at least twice the highest frequency in the signal.

scalability The ability of a **website** (or any other system) to function under very high load.

scan To convert a flat image such as a photographic print into a **digital** form by measuring the relevant parameters of sections of the image in an ordered fashion, usually left to right, top to bottom.

scanner A device that converts a flat image such as a photographic print into a **digital** form by scanning across it.

screen reader An accessibility tool that translates computer screen text into speech for visually impaired people.

screen resolution The number of **pixels** on a screen.

scripting languages Computer languages that are designed to be used without detailed knowledge of programming. They are specialized to particular tasks.

script writer A person who writes TV, radio or film scripts for entertainment or documentary programmes.

seamless branching in **DVD**, a technique to allow users to choose different paths through moving video without there being any discontinuity.

search engine A **website** designed to help find information available on the **World Wide Web**. The search engine allows users to ask for content meeting specfic criteria (typically those containing a given word or phrase) and retrieves a list of **web pages** that match those criteria.

segment An identifiable part of a market that has enough common needs to influence products being designed for it.

SEO Search Engine Optimization, a process of promoting **websites** to the top of online searches through various methods including **metatag** optimization and payment to search engine companies.

server In a local area network, a **server** is effectively the hard disk that is not on your own computer but elsewhere. You can use it to store your files or you can look to it to supply material available to the whole network. In a **wide area network** or **video-on-demand** system the server is the centralized repository for data.

server side A program or programs running on the **server** to dynamically produce, find and/or format information to be sent to the **browser**. **ASP** and **PHP** are kinds of server side programming.

session fee A payment for performing in a music recording as a session musician or recording a voice-over. A principal performer would probably take royalties on sales, not a session fee.

set-top box A computer-based system that is designed to be like a piece of home entertainment **hardware** (for example, a VCR or CD player), and may actually sit on top of the television set. Satellite receivers and decoders for video-on-demand and **digital** TV are usually referred to in this way.

severance In employment, the terms under which the employment is ended.

sibilance Exaggeration of 's' sounds in a voice, sometimes natural but sometimes caused by poor acoustics or microphone placing.

sign-off The signature of a person given the authority to agree that a phase of work has been completed satisfactorily. Sign-offs are often linked to **milestones** in the project, which can coincide with staged payments. See also **staged sign-offs**.

simulation A technique used to reproduce a situation as realistically as possible to allow people to develop the skills needed to handle it. This is often used in management training. The easiest computer-based example to quote is that of a flight simulator used to train pilots, and in many ways this kind of simulation is better known as **virtual reality**.

site map Graphical or topographical representation of the structure of a **website**. See also **image map**.

skyscraper A form of **web page** advertising in the form of a tall, thin image.

slippage The amount of time that has been lost according to the agreed schedule and the present project position.

SMS Small Message System, a method for sending short text messages, usually between mobile telephones.

software A computer program or computer programs in general. Usually used to differentiate from the equipment or **hardware**.

source code The human-readable version of a computer program before it is compiled into object or machine code.

spam Unwanted and unsolicited emails: junk mail. Named after a song in a Monty Python sketch.

speech recognition The identification of spoken words by a **software** tool. The words are identified by being digitized and matched against coded dictionaries.

spider The agent of a web **search engine** that automatically surfs the web, following **links** and indexing pages.

spiral approach An iterative approach to developing and testing **software**.

SQL A standard for database queries. Several database management systems conform to the SQL standard, one of which is **MySQL**.

stakeholder A person that can exert power, authority or influence over a project's development.

staircasing Appearance of lines on a screen that are almost, but not quite, horizontal and under some circumstances will appear jaggy. Also referred to as **jaggies**.

staged sign-off Points across a project that have been planned as a phase completion point where the client needs to agree that the stage is complete and they will approve it by signing it off. These are often linked to payment points as well.

standards conversion In television, conversion of a video signal between the **PAL**, **SECAM** and **NTSC** standards or vice versa. Changing from PAL to/from SECAM and between high and standard definition is usually referred to as transcoding.

standing waves In sound, self-reinforcement of a sound wave when it is reflected back on itself by a wall or the end of a tube. Between two walls this will reinforce certain frequencies and so colour the sound.

star A configuration of a cable television network where there is a distinct path from the cable centre to an individual subscriber.

start-up The preliminary stage in project development according to the **Prince2** project management methodology that provides the basis for project initiation. Often referred to as SU.

static web page A **web page** that is fixed and stored on the **server** as a simple text file.

storyboards A scripting convention that includes mock-up visuals; used in video production originally, and now sometimes used in interactive media projects.

streamer tape Magnetic tape, usually in cartridges or cassettes, onto which computer data is recorded or streamed for archiving and backup purposes.

streaming On the web, playing of an audio or video file over the network so that it is heard or seen as soon as it arrives. The audio or video file does not usually remain on the user's computer, and it is possible to stream a live event, rather like a radio or TV broadcast.

style sheet A document that defines how the parts of a **web page** are to be displayed based on markup tags in the text. These could be a simple redefinition of the standard **HTML** tags or they could be completely unique to the page, possibly working in conjunction with **XML**.

stylus In computer graphics, a special pen without ink that is moved across a special tablet in order to draw a line or shape on the computer screen. In audio, the tip, usually diamond, on a gramophone pick-up that actually makes contact with the disc groove.

subcarrier A secondary frequency added to a signal in order to carry extra information, such as colour in a TV signal.

subjective evaluation Evaluation that is based on observation and analysis of non-quantifiable factors, and is affected by the experience and bias of the evaluator. See also **objective evaluation**.

summative Term used to describe evaluation processes used at the end of development. This can include **testing** but could also include such practices as the end of project review or debriefing procedures. See also **formative** and **evaluation**.

SWOT A method of analysing a company's position against competitors by defining its Strengths, Weaknesses, Opportunities and Threats.

synchronization licence A licence to take music and juxtapose it with pictures in a film or video.

synchronization pulse Part of a video or **digital** signal that identifies a position in the signal, such as where a frame of video starts.

take In a take, or a recording, an attempt to record something. If you have to try again, then you do another take.

talking head In film or video, a sequence which only shows a single person speaking, possibly direct at the camera.

task analysis Identification of all the processes and sub-processes needed to complete a project.

TCO Total Cost of Ownership, the estimation of costs throughout the life cycle of a product through development, deployment, training, use, maintenance and repair.

TCP/IP Transmission Control Protocol/Internet Protocol, the protocol used to pass messages around the **Internet** and which in many ways defines the Internet.

technical specification Document describing a task to be undertaken in terms of the equipment and techniques required.

telco Shorthand term used generally for telecommunications company.

telecine In television and **DVD** production, the machine that scans the film and produces a television signal from it. Now usually working digitally and in high definition.

telemedicine Remote access to medical facilities using audio and, especially, video connections. The implementations can range from diagnosis assistance to remote participation in surgical procedures.

telephony Ordinary telephone traffic, in which people talk to each other.

teletype A teleprinter or telex machine, used to communicate with computers before monitors, or VDUs, were available.

TelNet System for remotely controlling a computer as if you were sitting at its own keyboard.

tender A document developed by a client about their needs for a project for potential developers to use to formulate their ideas for a **pitch**. Also referred to as the brief and can be a verb, to tender.

testing The use of methods and procedures to check the performance of an application according to pre-defined criteria. Testing is often confused with evaluation. It can form part of evaluation, which has a wider remit. See also **evaluation**.

texture mapping In computer graphics, adding a texture to the 'surface' of an object drawn in **3-D**.

time and materials contract A contract for work in which the cost is directly related to the time spent and the materials used. It is the opposite of a fixed-price contract where the fee for the job can only be changed by renegotiation.

time-based media Media that change over time, such as audio and video.

time code Information added to video and to audio for video, to uniquely identify the individual frames. This is a great help when editing. Time code can be displayed or even recorded on top of the picture in which case it is referred to as *time code in vision* or *burned-in time code*.

time, cost and quality equation A method used in **project management** to define the relationship of these three components in relation to what the client wants from the project.

time-lapse photography Photographic technique in which a camera remains fixed in position and records events in detail by taking pictures at intervals over a period of time. The film is then speeded up when shown, to allow people to see the changes take place in seconds rather than days. An example would be the change of a flower from bud to bloom to death.

timesheet a record of time spent on each task for a project for all involved in its development. These are often electronic records that are amalgamated across the team to show the total spend across the project at any one point.

TLD Top-level domain, see **domain name**.

tolerance A term used in **Prince2** project management methodology for the monetary allowance added to a phase of development that caters for the unknown or unexpected. It is equivalent to such terms as contingency money.

transcribe To make a written copy of a document or communication.

tree and branch A configuration for cable TV networks where there is no individual path between the cable centre (head end) and a subscriber.

trimedia Media production where content is produced for radio, television and the **Internet** simultaneously.

UDF Universal Disc Format, a standard for computer storage directory structure (etc.) defining the dataspace on a **DVD** disc but which can also be used with other media. Optimized for large files.

UMTS Universal Mobile Telecommunications Services, a plan for mobile telephony that includes high data rates and the use of multimedia. Better known as **3G**.

uncompressed Describes the original form of an image, sound or other data.

UNIX A computer **operating system** used extensively in tertiary education, industry and for **web servers**. Linux and Mac OS X are versions of Unix.

URL Uniform Resource Locator, the full string that both defines the path to a remote service on the **Internet** and also says which kind of transaction is requested. The most common is to start the URL with http:// which means that the user wants a **web page**, but there are alternatives. A URL is a special case of the more general Uniform Resource Identifier (URI).

usability The measuring of the facility for using **online** products according to recognized criteria including ease of use, layout considerations, readability, accessibility, consistency and integrity among others.

usability laboratories Specially constructed rooms where people are observed using applications and their actions are recorded on video, through the computer and on paper by the observers. The information is analysed to indicate the effectiveness of the program and to make recommendations for improvements.

usability testing The recording and subsequent interpretation of people's usage of a computer-based system through a combination of methods that can include observation, electronic records and video taping. See also **usability laboratories**.

use stories The documentation and interpretation of projected use scenarios of a project that form the basis of capturing requirements of a system.

UseNet groups A long established system of bulletin boards distributed around the **Internet**. Sometimes called *news groups*.

user profile Information about the way a typical user would interact with the program.

user requirements The needs of the users; studied to determine how the application should be structured and how it should operate. Similarly *user specification*.

user trials Try-outs of a system by the users to test certain features and record the results so that the system can be refined according to its use.

validation An appraisal of the methods that have been used to check that they are consistent with the results. It is sometimes used with the sense of evaluation, but strictly it is part of an evaluation process. Also sometimes used with the meaning of field trial as a validation exercise. See also **field trials**.

VBI Vertical Blanking Interval, the part of an **analogue** television signal between the bottom of one picture and the top of the next. Used for teletext, closed captioning, time code and test signals. In computing the VBI is useful because it provides time to change a displayed image.

version control or tracking In **software** development, keeping track of changes to the software so that development is co-ordinated. This is especially important where more than one person is writing code.

video CD A compact disc, actually a Mode 2 **CD-ROM**, which contains **MPEG-1** video and audio, and can be played on a television or PC screen like a videocassette. Although this early **digital** video disk has not been widely accepted by consumers in the West, it is very popular in the Far East.

video compression Reduction of the amount of data needed to carry something; also known as **bit rate reduction** to avoid confusion with **dynamic range** reduction in audio which is also known as **compression**.

video conferencing Basically the combination of a telephone conference call and television or a video telephone. Recent video-conferencing systems operate using personal computers, allowing both ends of the conference to work together on documents that each can see.

videodisk See **interactive video**.

video on demand A system whereby a home subscriber can access television material stored remotely on a **server**. Some systems use high-bandwidth cable and others use ordinary telephone wires for the link between the **server** and the consumer's television. See also **set-top box**.

viral marketing Marketing or advertising of a product that relies on people spreading the information via email for others to look at a particular **online** feature or **web page**. The feature may be embedded as attachments in the emails sent from one person to another.

virtual machine A layer of **software** between a computer program and the computer such that the **interface** between the program and this software is standard no matter what actual machine is used. The new software exists in different versions for different machines.

virtual reality or **VR** A **3-D** visual environment which reacts to a user's presence and input so as to give the impression of actually being there. Non-immersive VR uses a screen whereas immersive VR is shown using goggles to give a pseudo-realistic stereoscopic view.

virtual team A team that operates across time and distance often through electronic communications. They are not co-located.

viruses Tiny pieces of code that can inadvertently be run on a computer and can cause damage or other mischief.

voice-over An audio commentary that accompanies video or graphics. Hence *voice-over artist*, a person who reads the commentary.

walled garden A self-contained mini version of the **Internet** which a service provider produces in order to provide a 'safe' web experience to its customers. This might be to avoid certain kinds of content (a school might do this to limit pupils' web access) or to make sure available material is in the right format for cable TV or **WAP**.

WAP Wireless Application Protocol, web-like system for use on mobile phones. Uses a mark-up language called **WML** which is based on **XML**.

waterfall approach A traditional **software** development approach where one stage sequentially follows another. This has received criticism because it is slow, methodical, heavy on administration and relies on strong documentation.

waveform A visual representation of a signal, usually electronic in nature, that changes over time, such as recorded sound.

WBS Work Breakdown Structure, a stage in classic **project management** methodology where the development of a project is split into phases of development showing the time and resources needed. Each main stage may be linked to a **milestone**.

web access logs Continually growing list of all the **web pages** and other files accessed from a **web server**. Will usually include information on what computer made the request and which page contained the **link** that was followed to get to the site.

web analytics The analysis of data gathered online about the use of a **website** including time spent on site, most viewed pages, success of promotions and sales figures among others.

web browser A piece of **software** that takes as its input a **web page** – with all its text, images, links and even sounds and moving images – and formats and displays it on the user's computer.

web editor Either a person who is responsible for the content of a **web page** or a piece of **software** used to lay out web pages.

web pages The individual documents, based around **HTML**, that make up a **website**. Analogous to the pages of a magazine.

web safe palette A set of 216 colours which will always reproduce correctly in a **web page**. It is not 256 colours because some places in the computer's palette are reserved for the windowing environment.

web server A computer that accepts **HTTP** requests from client, which are known as **web browsers**, and returns **web pages**, which are usually **HTML** documents and linked objects (images, etc.), or runs programs that generate web pages. Also, a program that provides that functionality.

website A group of **web pages** and possibly other networked resources that are designed to be viewed as a distinct entity in the same way a magazine is made up of pages and separate articles.

web surfer Person who accesses the **World Wide Web** and looks at **websites**.

web-television Display of **web pages** on a television set rather than a computer screen.

white balance A setting of a camera to make sure that what is white in a scene is recorded as white by adjusting the relative proportions of the primary colours and so compensating for the inherent colour of the light source. Also known as colour balancing if carried out after recording.

WHOIS A part of the **DNS** which allows you to look up who owns a particular domain name. See also **domain name system**.

wide area network Computer network that extends beyond the home or office building or complex. Often consisting of linked local area networks, as in the **Internet**.

wide latitude Of film, able to record a wide range of brightness levels in a scene, or cope with under- and/or over-exposure.

Wi-Fi trade mark name used to denote IEEE 802.11 standard wireless network as used by companies including Apple and Lucent. Has 11 megabits speed over a medium range sufficient for use in buildings or a close neighbourhood.

WML Wireless Markup Language, based on **XML** and similar to **HTML**. Used to mark up web pages for **WAP**.

WMLScript Extension scripting language for **WML**. See also **JavaScript**.

World Wide Web (WWW) The multiplicity of **HTML** documents on **websites** spread around the **Internet**. On a technical level the web uses Hypertext Transfer Protocol (**HTTP**) for communication between **web browsers** and **web servers**, although other Internet protocols such as **FTP** (File Transfer Protocol) are also used in tandem.

WORM In data storage, Write Once Read Many, a type of computer disc that can be written to but not changed. Often used to denote a **CD-ROM** that has been written rather than pressed or replicated. The process is known as burning a WORM or burning a CD.

WYSIWYG Describes an application that shows you the end result of your work exactly as it will be seen by the end-users: What You See Is What You Get.

XML eXtensible Markup Language, a very versatile mechanism for defining ways of marking up documents which can be used for **web pages** and many other media.

XP eXtreme Programming, a programming management methodology that assumes continual change and is based on a number of very short 'sprints' producing elements of the full program.

zoom To increase the focal length of a lens in video or photography. It magnifies the scene and looks similar to, but not exactly the same as, moving closer to the subject.

Index

Note: Page references in **bold** refer to entries in the Glossary

3G phones 47, **240**

access logs 55
accessibility 64, 185, 150–1, **241**
account director 17
account managers 12, 81, 86
accountability 67
accreditation 22–3
ActiveX 54, **241**
ad formats 221
ad hoc research 218, **241**
ad servers 221, **241**
administrative project manager 13
advertising
   context-sensitive 196–7
   interactivity 50
   online 220–1, 222
affiliate marketing 208, 220, **241**
affiliate programs 222
Agile 4, 13, 28, 51, 57, 67, 108, 161–3, **242**
Amazon 98, 196, 213, 220
archiving 157
   budget information 167–8
   chaotic 166
   closing the project 168
   definition 163
   maintenance 168–9
   material for 166–7
ASCAP 198
ASP (Active Server Pages) 160, **243**
assets 180, 181–2, **243**
attribution 192
authority 82, 85

B2B 7, 95, **243**
B2C 7, 95, **243**
back-end programming 62, 159, 160, **243**

ball-park estimate 162
banner adverts 221, **243**
blogs (web logs) 185, 208, 211, 217–18, **244**
BMI 198
Bobby 64, 185
body language 233–4
boilerplate clauses 175, **244**
Boo.com 146
brainstorming 83–4
brand 220, **244**
brand image 216
brand loyalty 18, 50
brand recognition 18
branding 60, 215–16
bread and butter projects 8
broadband 50, 60
broker company 23
browser incompatibility 118–19
budget 176–7
   information, archiving 167–8
   see also costs
budget holder 82
bugs fixes 180
business benefits 97, 99, 100–1, 102
business case 95–8, **245**
business manager 17
business needs 108
business terms 98–102
buttons 221, **245**
buy-outs 180, **245**

C2C 95, **245**
cable TV 47
cache 195, **245**
carousel 47, **245**
change management 38, 85, 105, 162, 178, **246**

Chinese walls 184
cinematograph films, copyright of 200
citizen journalism 218
clearances 179, 180–1, **247**
clearing the rights 179
client projects 7–8
clip art 201
clip media 200–2
close competition 212, 213
code, ownership of 181–2
commissioner perspective 129–37
Committee of Advertising Practice (CAP)
        Code 184
Common Gateway Interface (CGI) 160
communication 18, 96
    failure 135
    form of 88–90
    lines of 178
    muddled client 121–3
communication chart 88–90
communication paths 38
community 222
compliance levels of 185
conflict resolution 237, **248**
consideration 175
content management 46
content management system 55, **248**
content/resources, delayed 118
context-sensitive advertising 196–7
contingency 103, **248**
    planning, lack of 132–3
continuous marketing research 218, **248**
contract 167, 175–6
    budget 176–7
    change management 178
    contractor 182
    freelancer 182
    incentives and penalties 178
    lines of communication and sign-off
        responsibilities 178
    on-going support and clearances 180
    project description 176
    promotion and credits 180
    provision of content and clearances 179
    timescale and milestones 177–8
contractor contracts 182
conventions, tacit 144
cookies 184–5, 211, **241**
copyright 179, 180, 189, **249**
    code 181
    duration 200–1
    exemption 193–4
    infringement 179, 192, 201, 202
    music 198–200
    obtaining 191–2
    origins 190–1

ownership 192
    WWW 194–7
Copyright Act (US) (2001) 201
cost of doing nothing 97–8, 99
cost/benefit analysis 96
costs 3, 4, 37, 38, 162
Crazy Frog jingle 214
credit card handling 49
CRM (customer relation management)
        183, 222, **249**
CSS (cascading style sheet) 176, **249**
customer attraction 222
customer awareness 222
customer knowledge 210–12
customer loyalty 215, 221, 222, 223
customer satisfaction 96, 223
customer trust 216, 221

daily rate 103
data protection 183–4, **249**
databases 197
DDS 169, **249**
deadlines
    impossible 136–7
    missed 129–30
delivery environments 119–20
development process controls 102–10
digital media testing 158–60
direct competition 212, 213, **250**
direct marketing emails 220, **250**
directors 81
disabilities, users with 150–1
Disability Discrimination Act (1995) 185
Disability Rights Act (UK) 150
disability rights legislation 185
distance selling 49, 182
distribution channel 207, **250**
documents
    final proposal document 167
    formal 167
domain name 46, 196, 219, **251**
dot com company 95, **251**
Dreamweaver 160
droit d'auteur 190
DVD 46, 61, **252**
    archiving and 169

e-commerce 49, **252**
e-learning 1, 95, 102, **252**
electronic certificates 49–50, **253**
electronic programme guide (EPG) 48, **253**
electronically delivered services 182, 183
emails 234
    direct marketing 220, **250**
    marketing 208
    targeted 222

e-marketing 1
end dates 66
enhanced TV 28, 212, **253**
escrow arrangements 179
European Commission *see* European Union
European Union (EU) 20
  copyright 190
  Distance Selling Directive 183
  Privacy and Electronic Communications
     Regulations (2003) 184
  Procurement Directives 20
  taxation 182
exabyte 169, **253**
exclusivity 180
external pressures 4
extranet 45, **254**
e-zines 217, **254**

fair use (fair dealing) 193, **254**
false deadlines 136
Feist decision 197
firewalls 50, **254**
fitness for business purpose 157
Flash 131–2, 146, 151, 160, 179, 185, **254**
free fix time 117, 180
free trade 20
freelancer contracts 182
front-end programming 159, 160, **255**
functional testing 157

G3 44
Gantt chart 40, **255**
good will projects 10–11
Google 56, 145
Google Ads 197
graphics 40, 61

hard benefits 99
Harry Fox Agency 198, 199
heads of agreement 176
high-level project manager 13
hijacking 196
hours of development work 66
HTML 176, 185, 196, **256**
hybrid 46, **257**

IEEE 219
image 60
image libraries 61
i-mode 47, **257**
IMP (Interactive Media Project) 1–14
implied licence 195, **257**
incentives 178
indirect competition 212, 213, **257**
information architecture 66, **257**
initiation, project 18

initiative, lack of 134–5
inlining 196, **257**
integrity 192, 193, **258**
intellectual property 25, 174, 179, 180–1,
    189–204, **258**
interaction 222
interactive advertising 95
interactive context 3–6
interactive educational materials 214
interactive games 26–7
interactive media team
  composition 229
  cross-functional 232–3
  definition 228
  management styles and leadership 229–31
  roles 231–2
  successful 235–7
  virtual teams 233–5
interactive TV (iTV) 39, 44–5, 46, 111,
    207, **258**
  advertising 1, 28, 61
  project initiation 28
internal clients 8, **258**
internal pressures 4
internal stakeholder analysis 83
internationalization 63, **258**
Internet 7, 64, 182, **242**, **243**
  copyright 190, 194–7
  copyright infringement 202
Internet Archive (Way Back Machine) 169
Internet/DVD hybrid 46, **257**
interstitial 221, **258**
intranet 95, 152, **259**
investment projects 9
IPTV network 47, **259**
iPod 44, **259**
ISP (Internet Service Provider) 46, **259**
iTunes 199, 216
iTV *see* interactive TV

J shape project model 4–5
Java 54, 160, 179, **243**, **259**
JavaScript 54, 159, **259**
jurisdiction 186–7

letter of intent 176
libel 185–6, 187
library music 199, **260**
life cycle, project 2–3
links, web 196, **260**
localization 63, **260**
loyalty cards 221

mailing lists 184
maintenance projects 9
marketing channel 207

marketing, definition 206
marketing intelligence 208–9
marketing interactivity 50
marketing manager 17
marketing messages 184
marketing principles 209
    competition knowledge 212–14
    keeping customers 221–3
    know your customers 210–11
    market knowledge 216–18
    online customer knowledge 211–12
    own strengths 214–16
    reaching customers 218–21
marketing-driven project initiation 26
Master Right 198
matchmaker company 23
materials budgeting 57
Mechanical Copyright Protection Society
    (MCPS) 198, 199
mechanical right 198, **261**
medium, wrong use of 131–2
metadata 219, **261**
metatags 148, 196, 219, **261**
Microsoft X-Box 27
MIDI files 198
milestone 38, 105, 177–8, **262**
    missed 129–30
mirrors 195, **262**
mobile phones 1, 39, 207
mobile web browsing 47
mock-ups 161
montage, moral rights 193
moral rights 182, 189, 190, 192–3, **262**
MoSCoW 51, **262**
MPEG 7 219, **262**
MPU (message plus unit) 221, **263**
Multimedia Content Description Interface
    219
music
    copyright 198–200
    moral rights 193
MySQL 160, **263**

NASA 201
news services 219
newsletters 222
Non-Broadcast Audio-Visual Productions
    199
non-disclosure agreement (NDA) 204, **264**
non-verbal communication 233–4
notice and take-down 186

object-oriented coding 161
object-oriented programming 108, **264**
Office of Government Commerce 20
on-demand programming 47

on-going and return business 18–19
online advertising 220–1, 222
online charities 95
online community trust 220
online competitions 222
online discussion groups 217
online forums 217
online marketing, definition 206–7
online newspapers 211
online satisfaction 223
online surveys 212
out-of-copyright material 201, 202
out-of-scope input 50
overspending 133–4
ownership of rights 179

paid market assessment 26
parody 194
PAS78 151, **265**
passing off 196
patent agent 203, **265**
Patent Cooperation Treaty 203
patents 202–4, **265**
paternity 180, 192, **265**
PDA 1, 44, **265**
penalties 117, 178
penalty clauses 130
    downtime initiative 117
Performing Right 198, **266**
Performing Right Society (PRS) 198, 199
Perl 150, **266**
permission-based mail 222
permissions 179
personalized search 208, 219
photographs, copyright 193, 194
Photoshop 160
PHP 160, **243**, **266**
PID (Project Initiation Document) 27, **266**
Pitch Protection policies 24
pitches 11
    commissioner perspective 22–3
    developer perspective 23–5
place of supply 182
podcast 1, 39, **267**
pop-under advertising 221, **267**
pop-ups 221, **267**
power/interest grid 83, 84
preferred supplier list 21, 22
Prince2 methodology 13, 36, 41, 69, 103,
    152, **267**
    project initiation 27–8
prior art 202–3, **267**
production manager 86
production music 199, **268**
production project manager 14
programme manager 12, **268**

project brief, changes to 124–5
project content, changes to 120–2
project life cycle 2–3
project manager 86
  definition 12, **268**
  high-level or administrative 13
  production 14
project scoping 34, 35
  detail 39
  dilemma 35–9
  information required for 36–9
  project management and 35–6
  see also Project Scoping Questionnaire
Project Scoping Questionnaire 39, 72–80,
  119
  access and use 57–9
  accessibility factors 64
  benefits/achievements wanted 56–7
  browser/platform expectations 53–4
  budget 65–6
  client database 53
  emotional reaction considerations 59–60
  functionality requested 52
  hybrid Web/CD/mobile/iTV 46
  importance ranking 50–1
  Internet/intranet/website make-over
    45–6
  iTV 47–8
  market sector of client 48
  media mix 60–1
  mobile 47
  previous interactive media experience
    42–3
  project contacts 41
  project content bias 48–50
  project management tools 40–1
  project type 44–5
  security issues 64–5
  site maintenance 54–6
  size of section 51
  special considerations 62
  statement of client wants 43–5
  testing and localization 63
  time for development 61–2
projects
  bread and butter 8
  client 7–8
  definition 6
  good will 10–11
  investment 9
  maintenance 9
  pitches/tender/winning 11
  quick fix projects 9–10
  R&D 10
prototyping 161, **268**
public domain 200–2, **268**

public sector tenders 20–1
pushed programming 47–8

quality 105–6
  in integrated media 60–1
  project 37, 38
quality assurance 163
quasi-streaming 199
quick fix projects 3, 9–10

R&D projects 10
RACI responsibility chart/matrix 86–8,
  269
RAD (Rapid Application Development) 4,
  51, 161, **269**
Rationalized Unified Process 161, **269**
red-button programming 47
Rehabilitation Act (USA) 150, 185
responsibility 67, 85
responsibility matrix 67–9
reward schemes 221, 222
rights 179, **270**
  clearances 65
  duration of 180
  see also copyright
risk exposition
  commissioner perspective 129–37
  developers' perspective 115–25
ROI (return on investment) 96, 149–50,
  157, **270**
Royal National Institute for the Blind 185
royalty-free licences 180, **270**
RSS (really simple syndication) 46, **270**

Safe Harbor principle 184, **271**
sales taxation 182
satellite broadcasting 48
scoping, project *see* project scoping
scoping questionnaire *see* Project Scoping
  Questionnaire
search capability 148
search engines 1, 50, 56, 148, **271**
sector search 208
SEM (search engine marketing) 208
SEO (search engine optimization) 1, 50,
  56, 148, 208, 219, **271**
SESAC 198
sign-off 104–5, **272**
  delays, staged 115–17
  hesitation over 117–18
  responsibilities 178
similar products 212, 213
skyscrapers 221, **272**
slippage 118, 123–4, **272**
slush fund 36
small and medium-sized companies 17, 36

small project management 66
SMS 7, 47, 184, 207, **272**
soft benefits 99
software 2, 4, **242, 243, 272**
software approach 161–2
Sony PlayStation 27
specialist self-development 131
specialists 235–6
spin-off problems 115–16
spiral approach 161, **283**
staffing costs 176–7
stakeholder analysis 81–2, 83–4, 88
stakeholders **273**
   interactive projects and 82–4
   key 84–5
subscription search 208
substitute products 212, 213
sui generis 197
sweat of the brow 191
SWOT analysis 215, **274**

tacit conventions 144
targeted email 222
TCO (total cost of ownership) 96
team leaders 236
technological information 118–20
technology
   changes in use of 121
   wrong use of 131–2
technology/functional testing 159–60
template design 108
template reporting 90
tenders 19–20, **274**
   private company 21–2
   public sector 20–1
test types 163, 164–5
testing 151–2, **244, 275**
text messaging 234
through-the-door business 25–6
time budgeting 57
time, cost, quality equation 102–3, 109, 120–1, 122, 123, **275**
time, cost, quality, customer satisfaction model 107–8
time, cost, scope model 107
time, resources/assets, quality model 106
time of project 37, 38
time-tracking systems 104
timescale 177–8
timesheets 3, 9, 104, 130, **275**
tolerances 36, 103, **275**
trade marks 180, 189, 196–7

trust 19
   customer 216, 221
   online community 220

U shape project model 4
URL 149, **276**
usability 96, **276**
   aspects covered in 145–7
   debate 144–5
   feel 146–7
   history and pre-disposition 143
   interactive 143–8
   look 145–6
   principles 59
usability tests 143, 144–5, 147, **276**
use cases 51, 147–8
use scenarios 51
use stories 162, **276**
use tax 183
useit.com 147
user scenarios 147–8
user testing 157

Value Added Tax (VAT) 182–3
video-conferencing 234, **277**
videodiscs 169, **277**
viral advertising 208, 221
viral marketing approach 218, **277**
virtual teams 233–5

WAI (Web Accessibility Initiative) 185
WAP 46, 47, **277**
waterfall approach 161, **277**
WBS (Work Breakdown Structure) 35, 66–9
   impact of design and software methods 67
   Prince2 and scoping 69
web 2.0 218
web access logs 211, **278**
web analytic tools 1, 211–12, 217, **278**
web development 1
web logs *see* blogs
web/DVD 46, **257**
website (access) logs 55, **278**
World Wide Web, copyright of 194–7, **279**
WYSIWYG 160, **279**

XP (eXteme Programming) 161, **279**

Z shape project model 5–6, 210